MERCIA

AND THE MAKING
OF ENGLAND

IAN W. WALKER

SUTTON PUBLISHING

First published in 2000 by
Sutton Publishing Limited · Phoenix Mill
Thrupp · Stroud · Gloucestershire · GL5 2BU

ISBN 0 7509 2131 5

Typeset in 11.5/15pt Garamond.
Typesetting and origination by
Sutton Publishing Limited.
Printed in Great Britain by
J.H. Haynes & Co. Ltd, Sparkford, England.

Contents

List of Illustrations

All credits are given with the illustration caption.

Acknowledgements

I would like to thank the following people for their assistance during the writing of this book. First and foremost Jane Crompton, Clare Bishop and the staff at Sutton Publishing: Jane for commissioning it on the basis of a brief outline of its proposed contents and for her constant enthusiasm and encouragement during the writing process; Clare for her help and guidance in steering it through the publication process with the minimum of fuss. The staffs of the National Library of Scotland, Edinburgh University Library and Glasgow University Library for their assistance in obtaining access to many of the books and articles necessary for my researches into this period. The various organisations and individuals who assisted in the process of collecting the illustrations and providing the necessary copyright permissions, in particular, Carolyn Heighway, who took time out from her own busy schedule to assist with the acquisition of photographs of St Oswald's, Gloucester. The various individuals who provided access to their computers, as I have yet to acquire one of my own. Professor James Campbell of Worcester College, Oxford, who was kind enough to read the original draft and offer a number of helpful suggestions for additional work and who saved me from making a number of errors. Last but not least, my father and mother, who helped with the index, the maps and many of the illustrations. I must, of course, accept the blame for any errors or omissions that remain in the finished work.

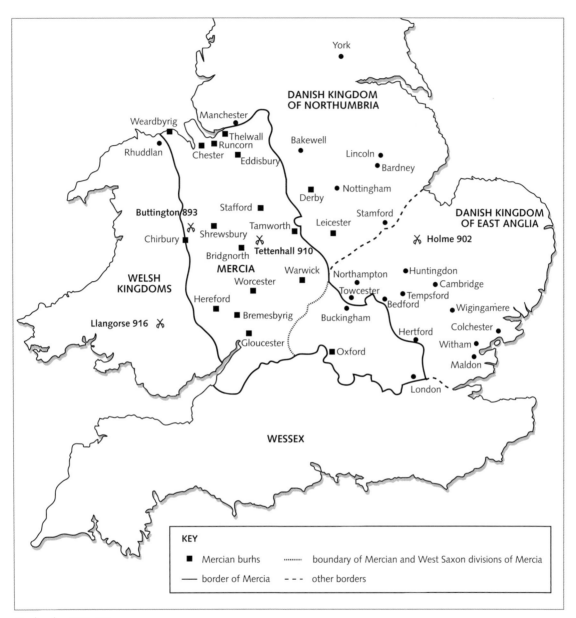

York

**DANISH KINGDOM
OF NORTHUMBRIA**

Weardbyrig

Manchester

Thelwall

Runcorn

Bakewell

Rhuddlan

Chester   Eddisbury

Lincoln

Bardney

Derby   Nottingham

Stafford

Buttington 893

Tamworth

Leicester

Stamford

**DANISH KINGDOM
OF EAST ANGLIA**

Chirbury   Shrewsbury

Tettenhall 910

Holme 902

Bridgnorth

**WELSH
KINGDOMS**

MERCIA

Warwick

Worcester

Northampton

Huntingdon

Cambridge

Towcester

Tempsford

Hereford

Bedford

Wigingamere

Llangorse 916

Bremesbyrig

Buckingham

Colchester

Gloucester

Hertford

Witham

Oxford

Maldon

London

WESSEX

KEY

■ Mercian burhs   ·········· boundary of Mercian and West Saxon divisions of Mercia

── border of Mercia   – – – other borders

England c. 900–20.

Author's Note

Various conventions of nomenclature have been adopted throughout this book.

English personal names are in the Old English form except where particular names have achieved general acceptance in modern English, i.e. Alfred, Edward, Edgar, etc.

Places in England are associated with their pre-1975 counties but those in Wales are associated with post-1975 local authority areas (the latter generally bear more relationship to the early Welsh kingdoms).

Place-names in italic relate to places that remain unidentified on modern maps.

I have attempted to describe as consistently as possible those Scandinavian raiders with no permanent settlement in England as 'Vikings', but to describe those subsequently settled in England as 'Danes' (reflecting the contemporary designation). The exception to this rule relates to the tenth-century Scandinavian kingdom of York under the Norse dynasty of rulers from Dublin. I have referred to its subjects as the 'men of York' to reflect their mix of Irish, Norwegian and Danish ancestry. If any anomalies remain, please accept my apologies.

Introduction

This book is not about how King Alfred of Wessex and his successors created the Kingdom of England from the confusion of the Viking invasions. That is the story that will be found in most accounts of this period of early medieval English history. It usually starts with the reign of King Offa of Mercia who dominated much of what later became England and briefly records the decline of Mercia after his death. Thereafter, the focus of attention quickly switches to the rise of Wessex and to King Alfred and his defeat of the Vikings and then moves on to recount the forging of England by his successors. In these accounts, Mercia simply ceases to exist in historical terms after the Viking invasions and little or no attention is paid to it thereafter. In this book the story will also begin with the succession of King Offa in 757. However, thereafter it will remain focussed on Mercia right through to the mid tenth century. It will discuss the decline of the kingdom of Mercia, the impact of the Viking invasion on the kingdom and the subsequent re-emergence of a reduced Mercia from this crisis. It will then consider the key political role played by this new Mercia in the making of England and the contribution of Mercian rulers, nobles, clergy, warriors and people to this process. It will end in 959 with the succession of King Edgar to rule over all England and what proved to be the final demise of an independent Mercia.[1]

THE KINGDOM OF MERCIA

The ancient Kingdom of Mercia, which once stretched from the river Thames to the borders of Yorkshire and Lancashire and from the coast of Lincolnshire and the borders of East Anglia to the Welsh border, is no longer shown on any modern maps of England and its name survives only in that of a regional police force. It is perhaps useful at the outset to provide some sort of context in terms both of time and space for this now vanished kingdom.

The origins of Mercia lie, along with those of the other early English kingdoms, with Germanic invaders from the northern coasts of Europe in modern Denmark, Germany and the Netherlands, who arrived in what was then post-Roman Britain in the late fourth or early fifth centuries of the Christian era. They exploited their control of the sea to assault the exposed coasts and invade the navigable river systems in the south and east of Britain. In this way these Germanic invaders, who later identified themselves as Angles, Saxons and Jutes, gradually took control of most of the eastern and southern areas of Britain and there imposed their rule, their language and their culture. It was this process which gradually transformed a Christian, Celtic-speaking post-Roman Britain into a series of small pagan, Germanic-speaking early English kingdoms.[2]

One section of Angles apparently entered the Humber Estuary and then moved inland using the various tributaries of that great river. It was a small group from this larger force that provided the foundation for the later kingdom of Mercia. They established themselves in the region of the upper valley of the river Trent around Lichfield, and Tamworth. The name of this group, in Old English *Mierce*, later Mercians, means 'frontier people' and probably originates from their situation as the most westerly group of English-speaking settlers on the edge of Celtic-speaking territory. In this exposed position and like many other medieval frontiersmen, they quickly gained experience of and developed skills in warfare and raiding which ensured their survival and expansion. This experience stood them in good stead in the intense struggle for resources and land that occurred during the fifth and sixth centuries.

Indeed, the Mercians proved so successful in the struggles of this period that, by the time they emerge into recorded history in the text of Bede, they were already a major power in Britain. In the early seventh century under the still pagan King Penda, they contested for the hegemony of much of Britain with their great rivals, the Northumbrians. They failed on this occasion, when Penda was killed at the Battle of *Winwaed*, but the struggle continued under Penda's successors, Wulfhere and Aethelred. It was a struggle in which the Mercians established their status as one of three great English-speaking powers in Britain alongside the Northumbrians and later the West Saxons. In addition, they subdued other smaller groups and gradually extended their control and influence south to the Thames, north to the Humber, west to the Welsh border and east to the Wash and East Anglia.

It was also during this period that Christianity was introduced into Mercia by the Irish monk Diuma and the English monk Cedd from Northumbria. The former, who became the first bishop of the Mercians, and his successors managed over a period of time to convert the population of this expanding Mercia to Christianity. This brought the kingdom into the mainstream of European development and provided a literate elite to act as administrators for the rapidly developing royal administration. It also provided the means for the Mercians to preserve records of their own history for the first time.[3]

The decline of the Northumbrian kingdom after 730 and the internal divisions of Wessex left Mercia to develop a supremacy over the other kingdoms of southern Britain largely unchallenged. According to Bede, King Aethelbald of Mercia had already succeeded in imposing this supremacy on every English kingdom, with the exception of Northumbria itself, by 731 when he completed his history. In a rare original diploma of 736, King Aethelbald could style himself *Rex Britanniae* with some exaggeration. He went on to reign for forty-one years until his murder in 757 and during much of this period he held the overlordship of most of the kingdoms of the southern half of Britain. This was the Mercian kingdom which would play such an important role in subsequent English history.[4]

THE SOURCES

The history of Mercia between the eighth and tenth centuries has remained largely unexplored due, in no small part, to a dearth of sources. The bulk of the surviving written sources for English history in this period relate to the rival West Saxon kingdom, which ultimately triumphed in the struggle for control of England. There are very few surviving sources that describe events in Mercia in this period and even fewer that reflect a Mercian view of these events. In addition, the few surviving sources that are of Mercian provenance are often extremely brief or very difficult to use for the purposes of historical enquiry. There are surviving material and monumental sources that reflect the cultural background of Mercia but these, by their nature, are often more difficult to interpret and to use.

The written sources, which will be used to explore the history of Mercia, fall into two broad categories; narrative and documentary. The first category consists of a number of contemporary chronicles and annals either compiled in Mercia itself or more frequently beyond its frontiers and a few later chronicles and narratives which may incorporate earlier material. The second category consists of a number of surviving administrative and legal documents which provide a fragmentary glimpse of contemporary government activities.

The main chronicle source for the period of Mercian history covered by this book is the Anglo-Saxon Chronicle, hereafter referred to simply as the Chronicle. This was first compiled in Wessex during the reign of King Alfred and consists of a collection of varied materials of very different value. The early sections dealing with the second half of the eighth and first half of the ninth centuries consist of information derived from earlier sets of annals. The origins of these are unknown but some may be of Mercian provenance. However, the tenor of these early entries is brevity and the information they provide is therefore of limited value. The sections from the second half of the ninth into the tenth century were composed almost contemporaneously during the reign of Alfred and his successors in Wessex. They present a considered account of events intended to support a strongly West Saxon view of the period. They highlight and, in some cases, enhance the actions of Alfred's dynasty and the West Saxons while largely ignoring or playing down the actions of others, including the Mercians.[5]

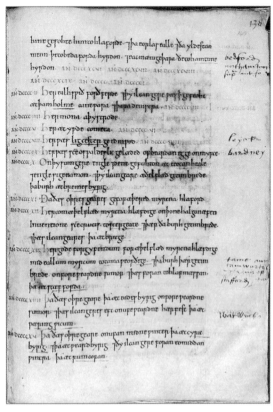

Opening of the text of the Mercian Register from the 'C' version of the Chronicle. (BL Cotton Tiberius B I, f. 140)

A key source composed in Mercia itself has survived as a result of its inclusion in two later copies of the Chronicle. This consists of a short set of originally independent annals, known as the Mercian Register, covering the years 902 to 924 but now found inserted into two surviving versions of the Chronicle. An apparently independent version of these same annals also survives incorporated in a later Latin translation of the Chronicle by the twelfth century historian Henry of Huntingdon. This Mercian Register provides a distinct Mercian viewpoint and has a particular focus on the activities of Lady Aethelflaed of Mercia. The text is very brief and difficult in places due to the inclusion of a number of as yet unidentified place-names. However, it records a great deal of information not found elsewhere and provides an important corrective to the information contained in the West Saxon inspired Chronicle. It will prove vital to the understanding of the final years of independent Mercia.[6]

The *Life of King Alfred* attributed to the Welshman Bishop Asser is a source which draws principally on the Chronicle itself. It has traditionally been viewed as a contemporary account of Alfred's reign compiled by someone who knew him, but recently this view has been vociferously disputed by Smyth. He considers that it was, in fact, written in the eleventh century and this would certainly undermine its value as an authority for the reign of Alfred. The balance of opinion is strongly against his suggestion. In relation to the study of Mercia, however, the dispute about the dating of this source presents much less difficulty than it would in relation to the study of Alfred. The information Asser's work contains about Mercia is relatively sparse and only the information on Offa's Dyke is crucial. In addition, the *Life* demonstrates a clear bias in favour of King Alfred and its evidence for Mercia must be considered in light of this fact.[7]

The later chronicle compiled by Ealdorman Aethelweard in the third quarter of the tenth century is also based in part on the text of the West Saxon inspired Chronicle.

It presents much the same account of events as the Chronicle until 892 but thereafter it seems to offer an independent account until 946. This independent section of Aethelweard's text offers additional information and a rather different perspective on events at a time when information on events in Mercia is particularly scarce. Thus he refers to Aethelred of Mercia using the title *rex* or king on two occasions where the Chronicle itself always uses the title *ealdorman*. Although Aethelweard compiled his account some time later, his close relationship to the West Saxon royal family and possible Mercian connections make it seem likely that he had access to reliable independent information.[8]

There also exist a number of contemporary annals compiled in Wales and Ireland which occasionally make reference to events in neighbouring England. These references, though infrequent, often focus on events in Mercia rather than Wessex, since the former was, of course, much closer to these Celtic areas. They can also therefore provide a useful contrast to the West Saxon centred views expressed by the Chronicle and some of the other surviving sources.[9]

A number of much later chronicles and narratives may provide fragments of additional information and need therefore to be accorded appropriate consideration. They include a number of accounts by twelfth- and thirteenth-century historians which, although very late, sometimes preserve information or traditions from earlier now lost sources. I have already referred to the inclusion of a text of the Mercian Register in the work of Henry of Huntingdon. William of Malmesbury preserves important details about the reign of King Athelstan which is poorly recorded in the main Chronicle. Similarly, Roger of Wendover and Simeon of Durham, preserve much information on events in northern England which otherwise receive little or no atttention in the Chronicle itself.[10]

The principle documentary sources for the history of Mercia at this time are the surviving diplomas or charters relating to the period. There are about 174 of these which relate to Mercia itself from a total of around 500 surviving texts dating from the period between 750 and 950. The great majority of these, some 148, are grants by kings or rulers, a smaller number, 18, are grants by various churchmen and only a few, about 8, are grants by other laymen. In terms of the individual kings more charters survive for those with longer reigns like Offa and Cenwulf and far fewer for those with shorter reigns. These figures are based on the statistics for surviving charters recorded by Sawyer. It is impossible to be certain how representative this surviving sample may be of what was originally issued but some of the difficulties in this area can be indicated.[11]

A significant proportion of these surviving Mercian diplomas or charters, around 54 from the 174, relate in some way to the diocese of Worcester and its lands. This appears to be the result of the higher rate of preservation from damage and loss of the records held at Worcester. It appears to have escaped destruction during the period of

Viking raids when many other archives must have been destroyed with the churches where they were kept. It lay beyond the range of the most dangerous early raids and apparently managed to escape, behind its new defences, the attentions of those later raiders who did reach the Severn Valley. It also, perhaps, reflects the strong tradition maintained at Worcester by St Wulfstan in the aftermath of the Norman Conquest. He actively sought to preserve and maintain the pre-Conquest records of his church through this difficult period.

In addition, the diplomas or charters that survive do so in a wide range of states of preservation. They can be found in a variety of conditions ranging from originals, through accurate early copies to later corrupt copies and even including some clear forgeries. The last category are often ignored because of their dubious origins but can sometimes contain fragments of original information and should therefore not be overlooked entirely. This wide range of conditions means that each individual diploma or charter and the historical evidence it presents must be judged on its own merits. Only then can it provide any useful historical information.

The difficulties with these particular sources do not end here, for even when we have made allowances for the overall rate of survival, the regional bias and the individual condition and reliability of these diplomas or charters the actual historical information that they offer can be of limited value. This is not because they tell us nothing but rather because the information they supply can seldom be compared with that from other sources. For example, many of the diplomas include lists of witnesses but all too often no further details about these people can be discovered. The general lack of Mercian sources means that there are few places in which to look for such information. Thus, we know the names and status of many of these witnesses but almost nothing about their family connections or the location of their activities.

In contrast to the position with regard to documentary sources, the material and monumental sources for this period in Mercia offer a much more balanced picture in comparison with those from neighbouring Northumbria and Wessex, though they undoubtedly represent mere fragments of what once existed. The range of these material and monumental remains is enormous and includes manuscripts, coins, sculpture, buildings and fortifications. It is true that these other sources, with the exception of the coinage, cannot provide us with much information about dates and political events but they provide an invaluable background for such events. The ability of Mercian rulers to command and direct thousands of men can surely not be doubted by anyone who has considered the immense scale of Offa's Dyke or the pattern of the new *burhs* built across Mercia under Aethelred and Aethelflaed. The vibrant state of learning and culture in Mercia shines out from the pages of manuscripts, the faces of sculptures and the facades of buildings. There may only be a few surviving examples in each of these categories but few of those who have seen them can be in any doubt about the skills of Mercian craftsmen and artists or the wealth of their patrons.

The Mercian coinage can tell us a great deal about the various individual Mercian rulers who issued them. So much is now known about the coinage of this period that historians are often tempted to fill in the gaps in documentary sources based solely on their interpretation of the coinage. However, historical interpretation of the coinage is not straightforward and the possibility of alternative views must always be kept in mind. The design of the individual coins can often tell us about the political activities and ambitions of a particular ruler either through the design itself or the accompanying inscription. However, they may be influenced by economic factors, in particular the need for their acceptance as units of exchange. The designs also provide practical examples of the work of contemporary artists, demonstrating their skills and achievements. The overall pattern of surviving coin finds is also important and can provide information about the uses to which money was put and its role in the economy.[12]

The great building works of the Mercian rulers demonstrate their ability to summon and direct large numbers of people to work on such projects. It clearly required an immense organisational effort to construct Offa's Dyke, which extends for some 149 miles along the entire Welsh border. In a similar vein, the construction of some twenty-two *burhs* in the short space of around twenty years must have called for considerable organisation of labour. On a smaller scale the sophistication of individual building projects could be equally impressive as witnessed by the royal palace complex and associated watermill excavated at Tamworth.[13]

When we move from such major projects to the architecture of individual buildings themselves, their decoration and associated monuments, we find many examples of great artistic and technical skill. The exquisite design of the surviving crypt at Repton in Derbyshire provides a flavour of much that has been lost. The surviving fragments of decorative sculpture from a number of contemporary Mercian churches, most notably that at Breedon in Leicestershire, bear witness to the splendour of many others that have now vanished. The few remaining examples of freestanding religious sculptures associated with churches also provide a glimpse of riches now long gone.[14]

The surviving remnants of the material that provided the contents of such buildings as palaces and churches also reveal considerable technical and artistic ability. The gospel texts and other religious manuscipts attributed to Mercian hands reveal the talents of its scribes and illuminators. The skill of these Mercian scholars and craftsmen, who produced such works as the Book of Cerne, the Hereford Gospels, the Book of Nunnaminster and others illustrated in this book or elsewhere is clear. The existence of many of these texts provides a fairly stark contrast to the bleak picture of contemporary English scholarship drawn by King Alfred.[15]

MERCIA AND ENGLAND

In view of the scarcity and difficulty of the sources and the fact that it was Wessex, rather than Mercia, which finally achieved the establishment of a unified kingdom of England, it might well be asked why attempt a history of Mercia in this period at all? The reason for doing so is to provide a more complete and more balanced view of the actual events which led to the making of England. This is often seen as the inevitable result of a process of gradual conquest of the rest of what is now England by the West Saxon kings. This is a rather simplistic view of events which does not address the issues of the survival of Mercia and the tensions arising from the old rivalry between Mercia and Wessex. In this context, the importance of Mercian co-operation in the process of unification remains largely unrecognised. In addition, the process which resulted in the unification of England was by no means inevitable and a number of other results were possible, including the continued survival of Mercia and Wessex as separate kingdoms. The reason for focussing on the history of Mercia at this time is therefore to explore these issues and the role of Mercia in the formation of England. Another reason is that it can offer a different perspective on the wider history of England.

The traditional view of English history in the period between the mid-eighth and the mid-tenth centuries has been one of the decline of Mercia and the rise of Wessex. This view starts with a focus on the pre-eminence of Mercia under Aethelbald and Offa and considers this as a precursor of the eventual unification of England. The suggestion is that a gradual process of absorption involving the smaller kingdoms would, almost inevitably, result in time in the formation of one large kingdom. The fact that this process did not occur under Mercian leadership is usually attributed to the intervention of the Vikings. The intrusion of these outsiders is seen as having disrupted the natural pattern of power in the region and brought an abrupt end to the Mercian kingdom. Thereafter, the rulers of the kingdom of Wessex assumed the mantle of power dropped by the Mercians and with it their role as the future unifiers of England. Thereafter, the process of unification was resumed under this new management but otherwise largely unchanged until the final formation of England in the tenth century.

There is certainly some value in the broad outline offered by this view but it falls far short of providing a complete picture of events in this period. There are many examples of other possible interpretations of these events and these can sometimes offer very different perspectives. For example, the Mercian overlordship secured by Offa involved an element of coercion which made many smaller kingdoms not only unwilling partners in his supremacy but all too eager to throw off his tutelage. The Mercian kingdom itself was already in decline and that of the West Saxons rising in the period before the Vikings arrived on the scene. The Mercian kingdom was reduced by Viking attack but it was not destroyed. It would continue to play an important role in the subsequent unification of England. The rulers of the kingdoms of Mercia and Wessex both sought to preserve and then extend their power against the Viking invaders rather than to unify England. The eventual unification of England was the fortuitous result of a series of unconnected policies by Mercian and West Saxon rulers and a number of dynastic accidents. It is these and other interpretations and perspectives that will be explored in this book.

There is not only sufficient reason to examine the history of the lost kingdom of Mercia in this period but also an urgent need to do so. This need comes from a desire to achieve a more balanced and satisfactory view of the process that led to the unification of England than can be found in many of the current accounts of this period. Almost inevitably, thanks to the ready availability and the bias of the surviving sources, these existing accounts show a common tendency to place King Alfred and Wessex at their centre. As a result, they almost universally either ignore or minimise the role of Mercia in these events. This book will attempt to redress some of this imbalance and suggest the essential importance of the part played by the Mercians and their rulers in this vital period.

The Hereford Gospels; decorated opening of St John's Gospel. (The Dean and Chapter of Hereford Cathedral and the Hereford Mappa Mundi Trust)

CHAPTER 1

A Mercian Empire?

In 757 Aethelbald, King of Mercia and overlord of the English, was murdered at Seckington by a member of his own bodyguard. This killing brought an end to his 41-year rule over a region equivalent to much of modern England. The strong element of treachery involved in this deed, whereby one of his own supposedly most loyal followers turned on him, probably reflects some deep-seated discontent with his rule. It would be a surprise if Aethelbald had not made many enemies during his long period in power. In 746 the English missionary St Boniface wrote to him from the relative safety of Germany to reproach him for his treatment of the Mercian Church. He had also found it necessary to grant lands to a Mercian abbess in recompense for having 'stabbed (or struck) her kinsman'. The many subordinate rulers under his control could not have welcomed his overlordship either. In this atmosphere there would have been many motives for an assassin, paid or otherwise. The great king was laid to rest in the monastery at Repton, the house where his kinsman St Guthlac, who was said to have prophesised his rise to power, had been tonsured.[1]

The death of this mighty ruler without a recognised heir rapidly brought about a struggle for the succession. Indeed, the swiftness of events may suggest that the murder of Aethelbald himself was part of a premeditated plan to seize the throne. A man named Beornred attempted to assume power immediately after Aethelbald's demise and may even have been successful for a time. However, within a year he was defeated in battle by a rival candidate named Offa. The latter was, or at least claimed to be, a distant cousin of King Aethelbald. He certainly had his genealogy recorded in order to justify his succession but whether it was entirely accurate or carried a claim any more legitimate than that of his rival we will probably never know. What was important was that Offa was successful and that he held onto power for the next thirty-nine years. In this long reign, King Offa would not only emulate the wide extent of Aethelbald's power but he would also wield an even greater control over his individual client kingdoms. He would create what amounted to a Mercian empire, wielding authority over all of the other English-speaking kingdoms and some Celtic-speaking lands as well.[2]

At this point, it is perhaps worth reviewing the extent and composition of the Kingdom of Mercia itself and the wider region of authority that surrounded it, which Offa had inherited. The ancient heartland of the kingdom, which remained the centre of King Offa's power, lay in the area around Tamworth, Lichfield and Repton in the valleys of the rivers Thame and Trent. However, it had grown considerably beyond this original core and now stretched out in all directions. In the north it ran from the Humber Estuary along the border with the Kingdom of Northumbria, that of the later Yorkshire, and then down the river Mersey to the Irish Sea at Runcorn in Cheshire. In the east it bordered the North Sea along the coast of the former Kingdom of Lindsey and thence ran along the borders of first the Kingdom of East Anglia, later Norfolk and Suffolk, and then that of the former Kingdom of Essex to the Thames just downstream from London. In the south it ran up along the Thames and then along the border with the Kingdom of Wessex, the later counties of Wiltshire and Somerset, and down the river Avon to the Bristol Channel. In the west it ran from Avonmouth north up the coast and the rivers Severn and Wye, including the later Worcestershire and Gloucestershire, and thence north along the line of Offa's Dyke and part of Wat's Dyke to the north coast of Wales at Basingwerk in later Cheshire.

Around this enlarged Kingdom of Mercia ranged a series of others; some were little more than satellites of Mercia, others fluctuated in status between independence and dependency and others still were largely independent of Mercian control. Northwards lay the usually independent Kingdom of Northumbria, which was undergoing a period of internal turbulence that effectively prevented it from playing a role on the wider English stage. Further north still the remainder of Britain was disputed between the various kingdoms of the Picts, Scots and Britons of Cumbria. The Kingdom of East Anglia, which alternated between the status of a sub-kingdom of Mercia and a temporary degree of independence, lay to the east with Essex, which was virtually a Mercian satellite, on its southern border. Southwards beyond the lower reaches of the river Thames lay the Kingdom of Kent which held a position similar to that of East Anglia, sometimes directly subject to Mercia but sometimes free of its control, along with Sussex which proved too small to resist direct Mercian control. Also southwards and beyond the Thames but further upstream stretched the normally independent Kingdom of Wessex, which suffered to a lesser extent from the sort of internal dissension that weakened Northumbria. In the west in the hills and mountains of Wales were the many smaller Welsh kingdoms, many of which were probably subject to some form of Mercian overlordship from time to time.[3]

In the south, across the Channel and at this time stretching from the Pyrenees to the coast of Frisia, was the great Kingdom of the Franks, which incorporated much of Western Europe. It was currently ruled by a new dynasty, that would subsequently be known as the Carolingians, under King Pepin. This immense kingdom and soon to be empire had a great influence on the smaller English kingdoms, providing them with a model to admire and emulate. It often provided an example of new innovations in government for its smaller neighbours. King Offa was almost certainly aware of the activities of Charlemagne, his great Continental counterpart, and may have sought to emulate them. However, the contacts between the Franks and the English were not all one way. In the fields of culture, education and religion the English had much to offer their neighbours. The activities of English scholars at the court of Charlemagne and the vital role of English missionaries in the conversion of Germany are examples of this. The essential point is that the English of this period were far from being an isolated island race but were instead closely related to their European neighbours.[4]

In 757 the evidence suggests that the outbreak of civil war following the death of King Aethelbald resulted in the temporary collapse of his control over many of the other English kingdoms. Unfortunately, there is little information in the chronicles or annals about the activities of King Offa between his succession and his defeat of the men of Hastings in 771. This is a great pity since this must have been a period of intense political and military activity. There were probably rebellions in Kent and East Anglia against Mercian rule which would have involved the overthrow of Mercian control and the restoration of a measure of independence for these ancient kingdoms. Initially King Offa could probably do little about this loss of control since he needed to focus his attention on securing his rule in Mercia itself and over its smaller component sub-kingdoms, like that of the *Hwicce*, located in later Worcestershire and Gloucestershire.

One of Offa's first recorded actions was a familiar one for any king of Mercia, namely dealing with Welsh raids on the borders. These ancient enemies of the Mercians had probably taken advantage of the opportunity presented by the outbreak of civil war after Aethelbald's death to resume raids against Mercian territory. However, they appear to have been careless and, according to the Welsh annals, a considerable Welsh force was caught in 760 and brought to battle near Hereford. King Offa was victorious in the fight that followed and it seems likely that Welsh raids ceased for some time thereafter.[5]

The swift elimination of this Welsh threat may indicate that King Offa had completed the process of securing political control of Mercia itself relatively quickly. This seems clear from the fact that he proved able, within the space of a few years, to commence the process of restoring Mercian influence over other English kingdoms. This could not have happened without a strong base of support in his own kingdom. There is no direct record of when or how Offa subdued each of the other English kingdoms. However, there are a number of scattered fragments of evidence that allow us to suggest how he may have achieved this in a number of individual cases. As we will see, it seems likely that he had secured the overlordship of most of these kingdoms before the end of the 760s.

The most important of these other kingdoms was Kent and it was one of the first to receive Offa's attention. In 764 he issued a charter concerning lands in Kent which was endorsed by a Kentish king named Heahberht. In the following year, 765, he confirmed a charter issued by two kings, Heahberht and Egbert, concerning lands in Kent. The latter appears thereafter to have been entirely under Mercian control as King Offa gradually extended the scope of his authority over Kent. In 774 Offa granted lands in Kent to the Archbishop of Canterbury without reference to King Egbert. A later confirmation charter of 799 reveals that he went further, revoking a grant made by King Egbert and reprimanding the latter, declaring that he had 'presumed to place land, which his lord had given him, under the authority of another without his lord's consent'. A later charter also records that Offa had declared that 'it was not lawful for Egbert to grant lands in perpetuity by a written instrument'. This sort of action served to curtail and undermine any remaining independent authority that King Egbert had and to place him on a very tight rein indeed.[6]

This vigorous enforcement of Mercian overlordship undoubtedly aroused resentment and opposition among those whose independence had been curtailed. Many powerful local lords must have had difficulty attempting to meet the heavy demands of their new overlord while still preserving their own power and status. In 770 King Offa had confirmed grants of land in Sussex by Osmund, King of Sussex. Simeon of Durham preserves a record, under the year 771, of the first signs of discontent with Offa's overlordship in this minor kingdom and his ruthless response. In that year he subdued the men of Hastings by force of arms. This was not simply an attack on the modern town of that name but an assault on a large area of East Sussex which had once been an independent unit. The former king of Sussex had already been reduced to client status but the men of the area clearly preserved traditions, leading them to resent outside interference in their affairs. It was probably this event that finally prompted Offa to deprive Sussex of its remaining independent status. In 772 a man named Oswald appears in a charter of Offa described as *dux* or *ealdorman* of the South Saxons alongside a man called *Ealdorman* Osmund, who may be the former king. This event highlights the sort of tensions and resentments which could exist within a powerful overlordship and Offa's impatience with such dissent.[7]

This same charter of 772 shows King Offa granting land in newly conquered Sussex at a court attended by his clients and allies including King Egbert of Kent, *Ealdorman* Oswald of Sussex and King Cynewulf of Wessex. In light of the charter evidence already noted, this charter strongly suggests that overlordship over Kent and Sussex had already been established by Offa by this date. On the other hand, the presence of King Cynewulf at Offa's court is more difficult to interpret. It may represent no more than a temporary submission, if it represents submission at all, by the West Saxon leader. The latter shows no sign of having sought King Offa's endorsement of his charters or any of the other traits of a client king. It seems more likely that he attended this court as an ally or guest of King Offa.

This restored Mercian overlordship under King Offa initially took very much the same form as that of his predecessors as kings of Mercia. This consisted of a number of principal elements; formal submission, the payment of tribute, a requirement to receive the overlord's endorsement of charters. A number of examples of the latter practice in operation have already been noted in charters issued by the rulers of Sussex and Kent. Similar evidence can be found in charters of the kings of the *Hwicce* dating from 767, 770 and 771. This indicates that the grant carries the endorsement of King Offa. In return, an overlord was expected to support his client kings against internal rivals and external enemies and to endorse their land grants.[8]

Panel showing St Mary, possibly originally from a sarcophagus, St Hardulph's Church, Breedon-on-the-Hill, Leicestershire. (Photograph by W. Walker)

The tensions which had been exposed in Sussex in 771 were also to burst forth in Kent only five years later in the form of a major rebellion against Mercian rule. In 776 the Chronicle records that the Mercians fought with the men of Kent at Otford in Kent. This battle appears to have been a defeat for Offa and the kingdom of Kent appears thereafter to have secured its independence from his rule. Thus, in 784, King Ealhmund of Kent was able to grant lands in Kent without reference to Offa, in stark contrast to the position of his predecessor, King Egbert.[9]

This setback in Kent could not be allowed to distract King Offa from maintaining his overlordship elsewhere. Indeed, it probably made it even more imperative that he enforce it more rigorously to avoid a domino effect with others slipping from his grasp. In 777 he therefore staged a major invasion of Wales during which he harried the kingdom of Deheubarth in South Wales. This may have represented a response to unrest within Wales itself, perhaps encouraged by the events in Kent. Alternatively, it may have represented an attempt, initiated by Offa himself, to restore Mercian prestige and fortunes, dented in Kent, by a success in Wales.[10]

In 779 the Chronicle records that King Offa fought with King Cynewulf of Wessex at Bensington in Oxfordshire and that Offa took control of this region. The reason for this battle is not revealed but it seems likely that it was part of a major power struggle between Mercia and Wessex. It may have represented an attempt by Offa to secure the submission of this previously independent kingdom. Alternatively, it could have been an attempt by Offa to restore a measure of control over this kingdom following a rebellion by Cynewulf like that in Kent three years earlier. Cynewulf had attended Offa's court in 772 although, as has been indicated above, whether as a subordinate or an ally is unknown. In either case the capture of Bensington on its own represented a poor return for what must have been a considerable military investment by Offa. Indeed, there is some evidence that he may have secured more than this. In 798 the record of a dispute involving the monastery of Cookham in Berkshire notes that Offa had seized this monastery 'and many other towns' from King Cynewulf of Wessex and brought them under Mercian rule. This may therefore represent the occasion when Berkshire first fell into Mercian hands. It was recorded as part of Mercia in 844 in a charter of King Beorhtwulf before being restored to West Saxon possession a few years later.[11]

This decade of the 770s had seen a series of blows to the Mercian supremacy over southern England. The traditional form of overlordship was clearly proving increasingly difficult to maintain. It may have been as a result of these experiences that Offa decided to move towards a much more intensive form of direct rule of client kingdoms. This was a process that was evident in the Frankish kingdom during this same period. There the Frankish kings sought to depose the native rulers of a number of client kingdoms and replace them with *duces* or dukes appointed by and loyal to the Franks. This permitted them to control these areas more effectively since their appointees had no local loyalties but only a loyalty to the Frankish king. This made them much less likely to rebel and instead gave them a vested interest in keeping their area under control. The contemporary conquest of the Lombard kingdom in 774 and the Bavarian duchy in 788 are cases in point. There Charlemagne deposed independent rulers, took direct control of the conquered territory and installed *duces* to wield his authority.[12]

It seems likely that King Offa was also able to consider employing this device as a result of the increasing sophistication of the administrative machinery of government during this period. The expansion of the Church and the consequent growth of a literary elite meant that kings could draw on an increasing supply of educated men to transmit instructions in writing to widely dispersed corners of their territory. This would have allowed them to command subordinates and servants at long range without any need for them to be present in person. It was probably in this context that King Offa moved to transform many formerly independent sub-kingdoms to regions ruled by an *ealdorman* directly responsible to him. We have already witnessed the reduction of Sussex in this way.

We are fortunate to have surviving record evidence which reveals some of this process taking place in the sub-kingdom of the *Hwicce* in the years between 778 and 790. This formerly independent kingdom had been ruled by a dynasty of local sub-kings under Mercian overlordship for many years. In 770 its sub-king Uhtred granted lands to his *minister* Aethelmund but only 'with the advice and permission of King Offa'. Only eight years later the last 'sub-king' of this region, Ealdred, the brother of Uhtred, appears in a Mercian charter where he is referred to as the *dux* or *ealdorman* of his people. Probably by 796, and certainly before 802, he had been entirely superseded by an *Ealdorman* Aethelmund. It has sometimes been suggested that this Aethelmund was related to the old royal dynasty of the *Hwicce* and this is certainly possible. He is probably to be identified with the Aethelmund, son of Ingeld, who first appears in the charter of Uhtred dated above to 770, where he was described as the latter's *minister*. Whatever his origins, he appears to have been fulfilling the role of Offa's local representative rather than serving the dynasty of local sub-kings. The record of his appearance in charters alongside the local kings makes it

Charter of Uhtred, sub-king of the *Hwicce* to Aethelmund, showing endorsement by King Offa, 770. (By permission of the Dean and Chapter of Worcester; photography by Christopher Guy)

likely that he had been intruded into the territory, initially as a political minder and later as a replacement for these kings. This is not to say that he might not have married into their line in order to cement an element of local support.[13]

It was in the light of his increasing administrative power that King Offa took more serious steps to control the Welsh. In 783 the Welsh annals record that King Offa once again harried the Welsh. However, on this occasion he mounted a great summer campaign, which appears to have been more significant than any previous such ventures. It was described in the annals as a 'devastation of Britain' and was apparently an attempt to cow the Welsh on a more permanent basis. This may have been a prelude to the construction of the great border earthwork that still carries his name, Offa's Dyke. This structure is one of the most impressive monuments surviving from the whole Anglo-Saxon period both in terms of its sheer scale and as a demonstration of the organisational ability of its builders. Unfortunately, in spite of a large number of excavations along its length there is still no firm dating evidence for this remarkable structure. However, there seems to be no good reason to doubt the statement of Asser in his *Life of King Alfred* that it, or a significant part thereof, was built by King Offa, 'who had a great dyke built between Wales and Mercia from sea to sea'.[14]

Offa's Dyke is the single most impressive monument to survive from the Anglo-Saxon period. It is longer than the Roman walls constructed by Hadrian and Antonine put together. It covers some 149 miles along the Welsh frontier, with fairly long gaps where it follows the line of the rivers Severn and Wye. It is probably to be associated with the nearby Wat's Dyke, which stretches for some 38 miles towards its northern end. These two great dykes, taken together, extend along the entire Welsh border from near Basingwerk in North Wales, southwards to the cliffs above the Severn Estuary, near Sedbury. The extant 80 miles of the earthwork itself originally consisted of an earth bank 30 feet high, fronted by a ditch 6 feet deep and 12 feet wide. The number of men required to construct this impressive earthwork and the administrative effort involved in directing and sustaining them in their work must have been considerable. It seems likely that the work was completed in stages but this cannot be established in the current state of our knowledge.[15]

The administrative basis on which this great work was undertaken is nowhere revealed. However, it was almost certainly based on the royal right to *burhbot* or the construction or repair of fortifications. This first appeared in a charter of King Aethelbald in 749, alongside military service and building and repairing bridges, as one of the three necessities that Mercian kings were entitled to demand from their subjects. The close association between these three services probably indicates a common basis for their implementation and delivery. As Chapter 7 will indicate, the organisation of military service was the summoning of men with their arms on the

A section cut through Offa's Dyke near Sedbury, Gloucestershire. (Photograph by W. Walker)

basis of so many from a particular number of hides of land. It seems likely that men and the tools required for building fortifications were drawn on a similar basis. In this way working parties could be summoned to attend a location on the line of the Dyke on a particular day and probably under the command of a local *ealdorman*. They would then work on a section of dyke which had already been marked out by a line of posts. The detailed surveys of the Dyke seem to confirm this method and it was one employed by the Franks on the Continent.[16]

In spite of more than a thousand years of erosion the Dyke remains impressive in places to this day and excavation has shown that many apparent gaps in the surviving Dyke were originally covered by sections that have not survived. Unfortunately, there is, as yet, no conclusive evidence as to the dyke's purpose. It is clearly sited to take full advantage of the lie of the ground and, wherever possible, to provide good observation into Welsh territory. However, it does not seem to have been permanently garrisoned since no evidence of any forts or of a palisade or walkway has been found along the Dyke itself. On the other hand, it is feasible that some use was made of ancient hillforts in connection with the related Wat's Dyke. It probably represented more than a boundary to identify Mercian territory and to preserve the memory of its royal builder. The construction of the rampart itself with its views into

Wales, some of which have revealed evidence of having been deliberately cleared by fire, suggests a military function. It was most probably intended to control the frontier by allowing peaceful traders to pass through at recognised crossing points while at the same time hindering Welsh raiding parties attempting to enter or leave Mercia.[17]

This great construction project offers another opportunity for comparison between Offa and Charlemagne. We have already seen that Offa's Dyke represents that king's greatest single achievement and that for which he is largely remembered to this day. In 793 Charlemagne had initiated a similar massive construction project by attempting to build a canal connecting the rivers Rhine and Danube. This project has been conservatively estimated to have required 6,000 workers over a period of fifty-five days to complete it. Although each of these great projects had individual practical aims and objectives, there is no doubt that they were also symbolic in physical terms of the power and prestige of their sponsors. The fact that Charlemagne failed in his project while Offa succeeded in his own, rather more ambitious one could only have brought the English ruler immense satisfaction.[18]

The Dyke was not the only construction project undertaken during this period and associated with King Offa. In Tamworth, at the centre of ancient Mercia, documentary evidence suggests the existence of a royal palace complex from the late eighth century onwards. Thereafter, it appears, on the evidence of charters issued there, to have been a favoured residence of the Mercian kings including Offa, Cenwulf and Beorhtwulf, who were to be found there at major Christian festivals. It is certainly the most common location for the issue of Mercian royal charters with no fewer than eleven issued there. The palace complex itself was probably situated around the present site of the church of St Editha. Indeed, recent archaeological work has provided some concrete evidence to support this suggestion. The remains of a sequence of watermills, which have been dated to the ninth century, were discovered on the old course of the river Anker. The second of these mills was an impressive vertical-axled watermill dated to the mid-ninth century. These mills would probably have provided the entire complex with regular supplies of flour.[19]

Other recent archaeological excavations have revealed the existence of what apppears to be a planned town at Hereford. The site follows a rectangular town plan with timber buildings aligned on a street. It has been dated to the eighth century and may perhaps be evidence for a trading settlement similar to those at London or *Hamwic* but on a smaller scale (see below and Chapter 7). It would have been natural to have such a place on the Welsh border to regulate trade there just as London regulated trade with the Continent. The dealings between the Mercians and the Welsh were not all hostile. This central core site was apparently surrounded with a defensive ditch during the mid-ninth century perhaps in response to Welsh or Viking threats. This is an important site since it demonstrates that the combination of a trading settlement protected by walls was known in Mercia before the period of *burh* building at the very end of the ninth century.[20]

The impressive effort involved in the construction of Offa's Dyke appears to have silenced the Welsh for a good number of years and allowed Offa to devote more time to the extension of his authority among the other Anglo-Saxon kingdoms. It seems likely that Offa had restored his control over Kent by 785 when he issued a charter concerning lands in that kingdom. He had apparently deposed King Ealhmund the previous year and assumed direct control of the kingdom. Thereafter, he continued to issue charters involving Kentish lands until the closing years of his reign. This would appear to indicate that the new method of direct rule had proved reasonably effective while backed by strong military power. It will be seen later that it fared much less well in circumstances of weak rule.[21]

Another sign of the increasing sophistication of government in this period can be found in the appearance of a new royal sponsored and controlled coinage during the 770s and 780s. It replaced an earlier *sceatta* coinage minted in imitation of the late Merovingian silver *denier*. This had previously been used during the reign of King Aethelbald for the purposes of trade between the English kingdoms but more importantly with the Continent where it could be used in trade as a unit of exchange. It represented a medium of exchange for large scale international trade as witnessed by the pattern of archaeological finds which occur most frequently at major trading centres in England, on the Continent and on the borders between kingdoms. However, it remained a largely pre-literate coinage with almost no inscriptions. It therefore failed to fulfil an important propaganda function by carrying the royal name or title. The new coinage that now began to replace these *sceattas* was inspired by the new larger and thinner *deniers* first introduced on the Continent by Pepin, King of the Franks, in 755. In order to maintain their strong trading links with the Franks the Kings of Kent were encouraged to follow his lead and mint their own versions of these coins. They were designed to be of similar size, weight and silver content to facilitate their use as a means of exchange in trade with the Franks. These new coins, possibly the first Anglo-Saxon silver pennies, were struck in the 770s for Kings Heahberht and Egbert of Kent but in fairly limited numbers.[22]

King Offa was also keen to maintain trading links between his own great emporium at London and the Continent. This site lay beyond the River Fleet to the west of the old Roman city. At this time the ruined walls of the latter seem to have enclosed only the cathedral of the Bishop of London and a royal palace. The whole area around these sites had earlier been part of the independent Kingdom of Essex. It had been occupied by King Aethelbald of Mercia during the first half of the eighth century and swiftly became the main port for Mercian trade with the Continent. It was described by Bede in the 730s as: 'a trading centre for many nations, who visit it by land and sea.'[23] A fuller account of London during this period and later will be provided in Chapter 7.

Offa was probably anxious to adopt the new penny coinage himself and sought to do so as directly as possible by taking control of the Canterbury mint. Indeed, it is possible that this may have been one of the main reasons behind the resumption of his efforts to regain control of Kent at this very time. In 785 he had restored control over Kent, and immediately thereafter took over the minting of coins employing the same three moneyers who had previously worked for the local kings. Initially, he simply took over the existing operation and, although he increased the number of moneyers to six, the numbers of coins produced remained quite low. The new coins also had a powerful propaganda value since they carried his name and his title *Rex Merciorum* or King of the Mercians.[24]

King Offa was not content with this arrangement for long, however, and very soon decided to develop the process to a significant extent. He had the necessary wealth to do this as overlord and tribute-taker from much of central and southern England. He more than trebled the number of moneyers employed to twenty-one, he had far larger quantities of coins struck and he introduced a wide range of new designs. This rapid expansion and development of the coinage supported two major aspects of King Offa's policy. The first was a desire to foster trade with the Franks, something that becomes clear from his correspondence with Charlemagne. The availability of large numbers of coins for use in exchange with the Franks made such trade easier. The second was the need to demonstrate in a very visible way his power as the greatest king in the British Isles, the *Rex Anglorum* of some of his charters. The appearance of large numbers of such fine coins, bearing his name and, in the early stages of the new series, a handsome portrait unrivalled in Western Europe at the time, can have done no harm to his image and reputation wherever they were exchanged.

Silver penny of King Offa (obverse) with stylised portrait. (Copyright British Museum)

King Offa now sought to complete his increasing dominance over the other English kingdoms by extending his authority over the Church. The recovery of control in Kent in 785 allowed him to exercise more effective control over the Archbishopric of Canterbury and hence the other southern bishops. Initially, he appears to have sought to enforce this control by holding regular annual synods of the Church with the first taking place at Chelsea in that year. It is true that he had already held such a synod at Brentford in 781 but there is at present no record of any between then and 785. Indeed, the situation of rebellion in Kent during these years would seem to militate against the prospects of any synods in these years. What is clear from the surviving evidence is that King Offa summoned and presided over annual synods involving the Archbishop of Canterbury and all the bishops of his southern province from 785 until the end of his reign. These synods provided him with a useful opportunity to enforce a significant measure of political control over these men. He could inform them of his own priorities and instruct them about how he expected them to handle these. At the same time he could listen to their views, learn what were their concerns and respond to these in the way best calculated to preserve their loyalty to him. This is discussed further in Chapter 8.[25]

In the late 780s, King Offa was growing old and becoming conscious of the need to consider the fate of his kingdom after his death. He was well aware of the fate that had befallen the wider authority of many earlier Mercian rulers after their deaths, including his own direct predecessor Aethelbald. It is true that the latter apparently had no son to inherit this authority but even kings with heirs had sometimes found difficulty in transferring part or all of their power to these heirs. Offa decided therefore to take some important steps to try to preserve as much as possible of his own authority for his son and successor, Ecgfrith. The devotion of King Offa to this process is acknowledged by Alcuin who describes the young prince as 'born to the royal throne' in a letter of 786/7.[26]

There were two aspects to this problem and Offa set out in a very direct way to resolve them both. The first concerned how to ensure the succession of his son and heir, Ecgfrith, after his own death. He was apparently unwilling to leave this process to any natural inclination on the part of the Mercian nobles to support the succession of Ecgfrith as his nearest male relative. He wanted to insure against the possibility of any dispute over the matter. He chose to do this by following the precedent set by his Frankish neighbours; he had his son designated as his heir and consecrated king during his own lifetime. In 768 King Pepin had crowned his sons Carloman and Charles, the later Charlemagne, during his own lifetime in an attempt to secure his own new kingship. In this way the nobles would have to acknowledge the kingship of his son while he could ensure that they did so. As a result, the nobles would have found it difficult to do other than support the succession of this acknowledged king in due course.[27]

The process of consecration would require the participation of an archbishop and this brought out the second aspect of the problem. At this time Mercia was part of the archdiocese of Canterbury, and the Mercian kings relied on the services of its Archbishop. This situation had not caused significant problems to date since the Kingdom of Kent and the archbishops were normally susceptible to Mercian influence. However, King Offa had lost control over Kent for the period between 776 and 785 and had subsequently experienced a number of difficulties with Archbishop Jaenberht of Canterbury. This caused him considerable concern for the future. He must have wondered what might happen to the prospects for consecration of his successor in the face of an intractable archbishop or an independent Kingdom of Kent. The obvious, if somewhat radical, solution to this problem was to have an archbishop in Mercia who could perform the task.

This was by no means an easy process since any such major change in the hierarchy of the English Church would require the approval of the Papacy. However, King Offa was not easily daunted and an opportunity to progress this matter fortuitously presented itself. In 786, coincidentally, two legates, George, Bishop of Ostia and Theophylact, Bishop of Todi, toured the island of Britain to inform the local clergy about the latest decrees on Christian behaviour proclaimed by Pope Hadrian. They naturally visited King Offa at his court in Mercia soon after their arrival to secure his support for their mission and then accompanied him to a council meeting with King Cynewulf of Wessex. There the king was able to assist the legates by adding his own weight, as overlord of most of the English kingdoms, to their pleas for the latter's support. Thereafter, Bishop Theophylact went on to travel through Mercia and also visit the 'parts of Britain', probably Wales, under King Offa's protection. The king may have taken advantage of this golden opportunity to sound out this experienced and 'venerable bishop' about his plans. Subsequently, he summoned a synod at Chelsea, at which, in September 786, the legates were able to proclaim their reforming decrees to the whole southern English Church.[28]

It was probably in the wake of this great event that Offa finalised his plan. He composed a letter to Pope Hadrian in which he made a very solid case for the elevation of the see of Lichfield into an archbishopric. Unfortunately this letter does not survive but the thrust of its argument can be pieced together from the subsequent exchange of correspondence between King Cenwulf and Pope Leo III. According to a letter by Pope Leo, King Offa very astutely based his argument on the practical grounds of the growth of the Christian community of southern England and the consequent need for more archbishops to serve it. He naturally omitted to mention his contemporary personal difficulties with Archbishop Jaenberht. He also portrayed his request as the 'united wish and unanimous petition' of the whole English nation, which was soon to prove far from the case. The petition was clearly well pitched and its reception may have been facilitated by the payment of some 365 *mancuses* as the first instalment of a promised annual tribute to Rome. This payment is later referred to by Pope Leo and the survival of some contemporary coins bearing the legend 'St Peter' may imply that they were struck as part of this payment of alms. The letter and the tribute may have been delivered to Pope Hadrian in Rome by the returning legates. Indeed, the assistance and support provided to their mission by Offa would have left them with little reason to refuse such a reciprocal favour.[29]

This may not have been enough to secure papal sanction for such a significant change. There are signs that King Offa may have found it necessary to call on his influence with Charlemagne. At this time Pope Hadrian was heavily dependent on the latter's support in Italy and hence subject to his considerable influence. A rather interesting letter written by Hadrian to Charlemagne around this time appears to hint at the sort of pressure that might have been brought to bear to persuade the Pope to grant Offa's request. In this letter Hadrian speaks of rumours of plots involving Offa and Charlemagne and aiming at his own deposition. Charlemagne had apparently had to issue an official denial which loudly announced that they were 'certainly false'. In turn the Pope had declared that he was 'utterly assured' that there could be no truth in them. However, the very fact that the Pope felt that he had to express his concerns in writing strongly suggests a real feeling of unease, unfounded or not, on his part. What is certain is that, as per his stated intention in this same letter, he went on to receive the envoys of King Offa and to grant their requests. He did so in order to ensure the continued favour of Charlemagne.[30]

In 786, a political coup was mounted in Wessex when *Atheling* Cyneheard killed the current ruler, King Cynewulf. This appears to have been an internal struggle between rival branches of the West Saxon dynasty. King Cynewulf had earlier deposed Cyneheard's father King Sigeberht in 757 in order to seize the West Saxon throne himself. Of course, it is always possible that Offa had encouraged Cyneheard to act against Cynewulf. The latter already represented a threat to Offa's authority in England having previously worsted him at Bensington. The denouement of this dispute was a dramatic confrontation between Cynewulf and Cyneheard and their followers at *Meretun* in 786. This fight quickly become the subject of an Old English epic which later provided the basis for the account incorporated into the Chronicle under the year 757. The result of the dispute was that both of the rivals were slain in the fighting along with some 84 men. This double killing effectively removed the two leading candidates for the West Saxon throne and brought on a succession crisis.[31]

This was too good an opportunity to miss and it seems likely that Offa entered the contest in support of one of the emerging candidates, a man named Beorhtric. The Chronicle later claimed that 'his true paternal ancestry goes back to Cerdic' but the vehemence of this statement may in fact hide a rather shaky claim. There is no surviving record of any genealogy to demonstrate his claim although this may have been the result of the subsequent triumph of his rival. The latter was a man called Egbert who later claimed to be a distant cousin of King Cynewulf. The impact of Mercian intervention in this contest was to produce a clear victory for Beorhtric who became King of Wessex. The unsuccessful candidate, Egbert, was forced to flee the kingdom and seek refuge across the Channel at the court of Charlemagne.

This important intervention in West Saxon affairs secured immense advantages for Offa and the Mercians. It removed a significant threat from Mercia's southern border. It eliminated a major obstacle to Mercian overlordship of the English kingdoms. It left Mercia unchallenged in southern England. King Offa could now proceed to secure direct and close control over the remaining English kingdoms. In 789 Offa would further demonstrate his new influence over Wessex by arranging a marriage between King Beorhtric of Wessex and his daughter Eadburh. This marriage symbolised the dominance of Mercia and its ruler over this client kingdom. It also drew the client ruler into a close family relationship to his overlord and so placed him further in his control.[32]

In 787 King Offa finally received his reply from Pope Hadrian and it was all he could have wished. He summoned a synod to Chelsea which would be described in the Chronicle as 'contentious'. The reason for this clearly lay in what the Chronicle records that Offa proceeded to announce and carry forward at this synod. First of all, he announced the Pope's agreement to his request that the bishopric of Lichfield be raised into an archbishopric and this perhaps involved the actual presentation of a pallium to Hygeberht. This major coup in the clerical field was swiftly followed by its corollary in the secular sphere with the consecration of King Offa's son, Ecgfrith, as king during his father's lifetime. This was also the first recorded instance of the use of consecration in England during the Anglo-Saxon period. It may also have been the occasion for the issue of a unique series of coins bearing the name of Queen Cynethryth, the mother of the new king. This would have been a useful way of enhancing his status through advertising the status of his mother. The revolutionary nature of these events must have raised many an eyebrow and ruffled many feathers.[33]

King Offa was now established as *Rex Anglorum* or King of the English and his son recognised as his successor. He now apparently sought to secure this position and increase the prestige of his new dynasty by arranging a marriage alliance with Charlemagne. A single chronicle maintained at the Abbey of St Wandrille in France provides us with this information. Gervold, the abbot of this

The Angel, St Hardulph's Church, Breedon-on-the-Hill, Leicestershire. (Copyright Batsford)

house, was Charlemagne's superintendent of trade at *Quentovic*, the principal Channel port for the English trade, and as a result had developed close links with the English. This close relationship meant that Gervold often found himself employed as Charlemagne's ambassador to King Offa and he therefore developed what are described as 'strong bonds of friendship' with the Mercian ruler. Indeed, the latter would describe himself in letters as Gervold's 'dearest friend and intimate'. It was therefore Gervold that was employed to lead the important negotiations for this marriage alliance. Charlemagne appears to have proposed a marriage between one of Offa's daughters and his own son Charles. However, what Offa was interested in was a marriage between his own son and heir, Ecgfrith and Charlemagne's daughter, Bertha. This suggestion appears to have enraged Charlemagne so much that he not

A page from the eighth-century Offa Bible. (By permission of the Dean and Chapter of Worcester; photography by Christopher Guy)

only called off the negotiations but initiated a trade embargo. He may have considered that such a match bestowed too much dignity on Offa, especially since the only other marriage proposed for any of his daughters was with the Byzantine Emperor. According to Einhard, the royal biographer, Charlemagne wanted to keep his daughters near him at home and was very reluctant to part with them.[34]

It is not exactly clear why this family dispute resulted in a trade embargo. It is possible that there were wider causes of dissension between these men and their kingdoms which found a focus in trade. The spheres of influence of these two great rulers had crossed in Kent where increasing Mercian control after 785 may have disturbed the Franks. The consequences were clear as the chronicle of St Wandrille states and a letter written by Alcuin early in 790 confirms. A serious trade war broke out between these rulers whereby Charlemagne initiated a ban on merchants and shipping passing between their territories. In addition Charlemagne had been harbouring exiles who had fled from the tyranny of King Offa in fear of their lives. These men included fairly minor figures such as the unnamed followers of a nobleman called Hringstan, who had been banished by Offa and for whom Charlemagne sought to intervene and secure their return. More significantly, they also included Egbert of Wessex and a Kentish priest called Odberht or Eadberht, who was probably a tonsured member of the Kentish royal dynasty. The latter would both return after Offa's death to seize the thrones of Wessex and of Kent respectively, the latter as Eadberht *Praen*.[35]

King Offa could only be the loser in this dispute and he may have begun the process of rapprochement by soliciting the aid of the Frankish royal monastery of St Denis near Paris. In the very same year that the dispute erupted, 790, he issued a charter granting this monastery extensive rights in London and lands in Sussex. Naturally, these generous rights could only be profitable for St Denis if its Abbot could persuade Charlemagne to end the current trade war. This initial approach was probably the prelude to intensive negotiations on a wide range of issues in dispute between them. Thus, sometime between 793 and 796, Charlemagne wrote to Archbishop Aethelheard of Canterbury seeking his intercession in the restoration of political exiles, namely the followers of the recently deceased Hringstan, to Offa's favour. On this occasion the Frankish king appeared to anticipate failure. Ultimately, however, in spite of delays and set backs along the way these difficult negotiations, involving Abbot Gervold of St Wandrille and Alcuin, appear to have been successful. It seems clear that by 796 good relations between the two great rulers had finally been restored. In that year Charlemagne wrote warmly to King Offa describing him as a 'revered man' and his 'dearest brother', and referring to the restoration of the 'ancient pact' between them.[36]

The details of this treaty, as provided by Charlemagne in his letter, suggest that this was an agreement between men of equivalent status. They agreed to reciprocal arrangements for the protection and support of each other's merchants. They introduced mutual trading standards for particularly favoured goods – Frankish 'black stones' and English 'cloaks'. Charlemagne offered toll-free passage through his realm for English pilgrims, but in return Offa accepted that all such men who were found to be trading would be treated as merchants and pay tolls. However, Charlemagne was unable to secure the restoration of those English refugees in exile at his court, whom Offa clearly considered as oathbreakers and traitors. They had perhaps agreed to disagree on this matter, the sign of a certain amount of common recognition and mutual respect. There is nothing at all in this letter about a marriage alliance which perhaps remained too sensitive a subject to raise or had, just possibly, never been an important factor in the dispute. Charlemagne also presented rich gifts to Offa on this occasion including a 'Hunnish sword', probably part of the spoils from the great Avar treasure seized by the Frankish king in 791.[37]

In the meantime, King Offa continued the process of increasing his direct control over the other English kingdoms. In 792 he arranged the marriage of another of his daughters, Aelflaed, to the ruler of Northumbria, King Aethelred. The marriage, according to an entry preserved by Simeon of Durham, took place on 29 September of that year at Catterick in Yorkshire. This marriage, like that of King Beorhtric in 789, symbolised the dominance of Mercia and its ruler over this kingdom. It also drew its ruler into a close family relationship to his overlord and placed him in his debt. The current disputes over the throne within Northumbria ensured that individual rulers were usually too weak to oppose Offa and instead found themselves forced to accept his support in their attempts to retain power against their rivals.[38]

In 794 King Offa invaded East Anglia and deposed and executed its ruler King Aethelberht. The cult of his martyrdom was later celebrated at Hereford, which was perhaps also the location of his death. If so, it suggests a determination on Offa's part to prevent him from further influencing events in East Anglia. The particular ruthlessness of Offa's actions in this case suggests that Aethelberht may have attempted some form of rebellion against Mercian domination. The later account of this event by John of Worcester suggests that Offa's wife, Queen Cynethryth, had urged her husband to this end. However, there is no evidence to suggest that this is other than a popular fiction.[39]

On 29 July 796, King Offa died at the height of his powers, one of the greatest kings of Mercia and overlord of all the other English kingdoms. He was probably buried in the monastery at Bedford, where his widow Cynethryth would later preside as abbess. This is recorded only in the much later chronicle of Roger of Wendover and, although there is no surviving contemporary information, there seems no reason to doubt it. As intended, Offa bequeathed his kingdom and his wider authority to his son and heir, Ecgfrith. The latter issued a number of charters on his succession which indicate that he was able to call on his father's supporters. However, he was given little opportunity to demonstrate that he was no less a man than his father. He died on 17 December 796, only 141 days after his father and without heirs.[40]

What can we say about King Offa as a ruler? He was almost certainly the most powerful king ever to rule one of the English kingdoms of this period and well worthy of the style *Rex Anglorum* used in some of his charters. The extent of his dominion was greater than that of any of his predecessors including the direct rule of Mercia, Sussex, Essex, Kent and East Anglia and the overlordship of Wessex and Northumbria. He was treated with a great deal of respect by Charlemagne, the greatest ruler in Western Europe, who could be described as his 'faithful friend' and with whom he secured an advantageous trade agreement. Pope Hadrian was also described as his 'friend' and, perhaps after some persuasion, supported his attempts to introduce a Mercian archbishopric. The scholar Alcuin was impressed by his interest in education and in 795 sent him, at his request, one of his own colleagues as a tutor. Inevitably there was also a dark side to this powerful man. He had deposed and humiliated his client kings in Sussex and Kent. He dealt ruthlessly with direct

Section of an architectural frieze, St Hardulph's Church, Breedon-on-the-Hill, Leicestershire.
(Photograph by W. Walker)

opposition, most notably by executing King Aethelberht of East Anglia. He inspired fear for their very lives among those who fled abroad as a result of his 'unjust oppression'. Nevertheless, he could be described as 'protector of his country' and 'defender of the faith'.[41]

If King Offa's carefully laid plans for the succession had come to fruition and his dynasty had continued to rule would this ultimately have brought about a unified England under Mercian leadership? This is a question which is often asked and it is one for which there is no easy answer. There can be no doubt that King Offa had secured a remarkable degree of control over England. He had eliminated almost all of the former minor English kingdoms. He had reduced the former independent kingdoms of Kent and East Anglia to dependencies of Mercia. He had secured a much stronger overlordship than ever before over Wessex and Northumbria. In short, he was the most powerful English ruler until that time. The increasing sophistication of government and administration in this period appear to provide grounds for thinking that the centrifugal process whereby smaller polities were absorbed by larger ones could continue indefinitely. This scenario, of course, takes no account of the imminent but entirely unanticipated intervention of the Vikings. These Scandinavian raiders had already made their first appearance on the English scene some three years before Offa's death with their attack on Lindisfarne, although this first sally provided no measure of their subsequent impact. The intervention of these outsiders would initially severely disrupt and then radically transform the history of all of the English kingdoms including Mercia.

However, there are also some grounds for believing that even without this outside intervention there would have been no smooth transition from an expanding Mercia into a unified England. The relatively small size of the kingdoms of Kent and East Anglia made it almost inevitable that they would be absorbed by larger neighbours at some point but the same could not be said of Wessex or Northumbria. The latter had both been the centre of powerful hegemonies in the past and had the potential to be so in the future. There was nothing to suggest that their subjection to Mercia at this time was permanent but rather the result of a set of temporary circumstances. In a time when rule still remained very personal, the kind of hegemony enjoyed by King Offa still depended on strong personal leadership. A strong king was required to command and, where necessary, overawe his weaker subordinates. In this period when high mortality and early death were facts of life, the succession of a series of strong rulers in a particular kingdom could never be guaranteed. In this situation, whenever weakness appeared, for example through a disputed succession, the political bonds of society were loosened. This could happen to any kingdom at any time and would in Mercia following the death of King Ceolwulf I in 823.

What, then, can we say in answer to our earlier question? We can say that the rule of King Offa had suggested the possibility of English unity under one ruler but no more than this. We cannot say that it was inevitable even without Viking intervention. It seems likely that King Offa' s hands were too 'stained with blood' to permit him to become accepted as the founder of a dynasty to rule all the English kingdoms. He had been able to subdue and control the surrounding kingdoms, largely by force. However, he proved unable to ensure the continued maintenance of this power over time, or to convert initial confrontation and forced submission into acceptance and consent in kingdoms like Kent, East Anglia or Wessex. He had been able to manipulate and persuade the Church into conceding to his request for a Mercian archbishop. However, he failed to work within the traditions of the English Church and had instead been compelled to disrupt these traditions for his own ends. He proved unable to convince the Church to accept this change on a permanent basis and it would subsequently be overturned. Whether a unified England might have been formed by Mercian rulers will always remain one of history's many 'what ifs', but without the elements of co-operation and consent this seems unlikely.

CHAPTER 2

Dynastic Disputes and Decline

In 796, within the space of a single year, Mercia had been deprived of both the powerful rule of King Offa and the stability offered by the dynasty which he had intended should succeed him, in the person of his son Ecgfrith. The Mercian nobility found themselves, not for the first time, searching for a new ruler with some claim to royal blood from among their own ranks. In itself, this was not a new departure for them but it was unexpected at a time when Offa had been actively involved in a process of securing the throne for his own dynasty to the exclusion of all others. This process had probably involved the removal or exclusion of a number of rival lines. Indeed, a letter written by Alcuin to a Mercian *ealdorman* named Osberht in 797 condemns 'how much blood the father [Offa] shed to secure the kingdom for his son'. This made the selection of a new king with a reasonable claim to legitimate descent particularly difficult. The resulting uncertainty and lack of firm leadership undoubtedly encouraged those tributary kingdoms subject to Mercian rule to seek their freedom. Alcuin's letter to Osberht also expresses the fear that Mercia itself might descend into civil war like his native Northumbria.[1]

The loss of control by Mercia over its tributary states, whether temporary or permanent, meant more than a loss of prestige to the Mercian kings, it also meant the loss of the wealth they had previously provided in the form of tribute or conquered territory. In the absence of this tribute and land, the power of the Mercian kings to dispense rewards and patronage to their followers and supporters was significantly reduced. They were forced to look to their own lands for sources of wealth which meant increasing the levels of income from local dues and taxes. This situation naturally brought discontent and instability in its wake and, for a number of reasons, set a pattern which brought about a period of decline for Mercia.[2]

The combination of a new ruling dynasty with a weak claim and the loss of prestige and wealth resulting from the breakaway of former satellite kingdoms, encouraged some of the Mercian nobles to challenge the authority of the new kings. This resulted in a series of internal dynastic struggles which significantly undermined the ability of all Mercian kings to govern their own land. Instability at home also effectively prevented them from interfering beyond their borders to restore their position of overlordship. This process would result in a vicious circle where royal lack of power within Mercia hindered the projection of that power against other states and the lack of tribute from such states further weakened royal power at home and so on. This cycle would significantly reduce the importance of Mercia within the English polity for most of the ninth century. As a result, its kings ultimately proved less able to compete effectively with a resurgent Wessex or to defend their kingdom against a major Viking assault when it came.

However, this process was neither inevitable nor immediate but rather evolved gradually over a long period. In 796 King Cenwulf, a distant descendant of Pybba, the father of the seventh-century King Penda, and a distant cousin and *thegn* of King Offa, succeeded to the throne of Mercia. Initially, it appeared that Cenwulf's succession to power was unopposed within Mercia. In the absence of a descendant of the great Offa himself, he apparently proved an acceptable candidate. He and his family had probably been in royal service for some time (see Table 1, p.208, for this dynasty). It is almost certain that the Cuthbert, who appears as witness in a number of King Offa's charters, was his father and he himself is probably the man who is listed as a witness in a royal charter of 785. He appears to have secured the support of a number of Offa's leading *ealdormen* including Brorda, Esne, Aethelmund and Wicga. They had been leading witnesses in many of the charters of King Offa and continued to be such under Cenwulf. In his own charters Cenwulf referred to Offa as his predecessor and in one dated 803 he even endorsed one of the latter's earlier grants.[3]

King Cenwulf also appears to have continued to enjoy the support of the Mercian Church which, no doubt in the interests of peace and stability, actively endorsed and promoted his rule. He continued the practice introduced by his predecessor of holding annual synods of the whole English Church under his supervision. The first of these synods took place at *Clofesho* in 798 and involved discussion of an issue that would prove crucial to the future of Mercia and the English Church and to the future shape of England. In contrast to his predecessor, King Offa, Cenwulf actively sought to foster the support of the Church, probably as part of the measures intended to secure the succession of his new dynasty.[4]

As part of this process, King Cenwulf also sought to repair some of the damage caused to relations with the Church by Offa's creation of the Archbishopric of Lichfield in 787. Alcuin condemned what he called this 'partial split in the unity of the church' in a letter to Archbishop Aethelheard of Canterbury in 797. Cenwulf commenced the healing process immediately after his accession by sending an embassy to Rome under Abbot Wada who, however, proved totally unequal to the task by acting 'lazily' and 'foolishly'. It was following the synod at *Clofesho* in 798 that Cenwulf sent a letter to Pope Leo III carried by three of his most trusted men; Byrne, the priest and the *thegns*, Cildas and Ceolberht. In this letter he expressed the

Charter of King Cenwulf to Christ Church, Canterbury, 799. (BL Stowe Charter 7)

wish that the Pope might judge the case he presented and so bring the English Church to 'the unity of true peace'.[5]

The case that Cenwulf presented in this letter, which has fortunately survived, did not simply seek the views of Pope Leo but also tried to shape those views to a significant extent. He stressed that the original intention of Pope Gregory the Great had been to install two archbishops, one in each of the former Roman capitals at London and York. He highlighted the fact that the subsequent decision to base the southern archbishopric at Canterbury had been arrived at out of expediency when St Augustine was barred from entering London by the hostile pagan rulers of Essex. King Cenwulf suggested that Pope Leo should not simply abolish the Mercian archbishopric but, at the same time, relocate the archbishopric of Canterbury in London and so within his own kingdom of Mercia. In this rather clever way Cenwulf no doubt hoped to soothe the dissension caused by the creation of the Mercian archbishopric while at the same time providing an effective means of controlling the restored southern archbishopric itself. He also sent a sum of 120 *mancuses* of gold to accompany his letter and hopefully to ease the reception of his appeal. If the Pope acceded to his request that the southern archbishopric be moved from Canterbury to London, he would remain firmly in control of all appointments to the archbishopric. The contemporary situation in Kent would no longer hinder this control.

Unfortunately for King Cenwulf, Pope Leo readily agreed to restore the status quo by abolishing the new Mercian archbishopric and reducing Hygeberht to the status of a bishop. However, he rejected Cenwulf's suggestion that the southern archbishopric should be moved to London. This decision, communicated to Cenwulf in the Pope's reply of 798, must have been a blow to the former particularly as it was accompanied by a request that he resume Offa's promised annual tribute of 365 *mancuses*! Clearly Cenwulf's own donation of 120 *mancuses* fell short of what Pope Leo considered sufficient. The king may have attempted to appeal against this decision but if he did so no record of this survives. Ultimately, he was forced to accept Pope Leo's decision and undertake to abolish the Mercian archbishopric and this was finally done on 12 October 803 at a synod held at *Clofesho*.[6]

As mentioned, the smaller kingdoms previously subdued by Offa had been quick to test the mettle of his successors and, in particular, this new dynasty of Mercian rulers under Cenwulf. Indeed, Kent and East Anglia had already broken free of Mercian control under Eadberht *Praen* and Eadwald respectively during the brief reign of Ecgfrith, Offa's son. Eadberht *Praen* had returned from his Frankish exile and discarded his clerical status to wrest control of Kent from Ecgfrith and expel Aethelheard, the Mercian-sponsored Archbishop of Canterbury. In 797 Alcuin wrote to Aethelheard in his exile in response to a request for advice urging him to return to his post. He then wrote to the people of Kent reprimanding them for supporting the usurper and urging them to restore the archbishop. The mysterious Eadwald is known only from surviving coins struck in his name but it seems likely that he also secured control of East Anglia at this time. The response of King Cenwulf to these events demonstrated that Mercia was still a power to be reckoned with and one intent on preserving its dominance over the smaller kingdoms. King Cenwulf swiftly restored Mercian rule in both Kent and East Anglia. He ravaged Kent in 798, capturing Eadberht *Praen* and thereafter 'brought him in fetters into Mercia'. He then placed his own brother Cuthred in control there. On the evidence of the coinage, he also restored direct Mercian control over East Anglia expelling King Eadwald. He also appears to have reacted strongly to Welsh attempts to escape from Mercian overlordship and the Welsh annals record the death in 798 of Caradog, King of Gwynedd at the hands of the English near Offa's Dyke.[7]

In spite of Cenwulf's robust reaction to these smaller rebellions, the example of these minor tributary lands would soon be followed by the larger kingdoms. In 801 he faced an invasion of Mercia led by the weak King Eardwulf of Northumbria, a humiliating experience for the Mercian ruler. In response, Cenwulf was forced to lead a large army on a long campaign against Eardwulf before peace was finally restored and even worse was to follow. In 802, following the death of the Mercian-backed King Beorhtric of Wessex, Egbert returned from exile and seized control of the kingdom. This Egbert may have been the son of a man named Ealhmund, who had briefly been King of Kent in 784 until he

Lead seal of King Cenwulf, perhaps originally attached to one of his letters to the Pope in imitation of the Papal bulla. (Copyright British Museum)

was expelled by King Offa and forced to flee abroad. He was certainly the man who had previously attempted to seize the throne of Wessex on the death of King Cynewulf in 786 and who claimed descent from the line of Cerdic. However, as we have seen, he had instead been defeated and expelled by Beorhtric, who had become king of the West Saxons himself, with the backing of King Offa. By 802, therefore, Egbert already had good credentials as an opponent of both Beorhtric and his Mercian allies. He now reappeared to exploit West Saxon discontent with Mercian overlordship and take control of Wessex as its new king.[8]

In this same year, 802, the Chronicle records an event which may have represented an attempt by the Mercians to mount a swift counterstroke against Egbert. It notes an invasion of Wessex by *Ealdorman* Aethelmund, who crossed the West Saxon border at Kempsford with his forces. The speed with which King Cenwulf earlier recovered control over Kent and East Anglia suggests that this attack may also have been a similarly swift response to Egbert's recent coup. If so, it did not share the success of Cenwulf's earlier campaigns and Aethelmund was roundly defeated and killed by *Ealdorman* Weohstan and the levies of Wiltshire. As a result, there would be no restoration of Mercian influence in Wessex. Instead, the new King Egbert would be able to secure his hold on the West Saxon kingdom and thereafter to challenge Mercian domination of the other English kingdoms.[9]

It is probably no coincidence that it was within a year of this defeat by the West Saxons that King Cenwulf finally conceded the loss of the Mercian archbishopric at the Council of *Clofesho* in October 803. The opposition aroused by King Offa's imposition of this archbishopric on the English Church both within the Church and among the other English kingdoms had ultimately proved to be too great. From a position of strength, King Offa had been able to ignore this opposition but it had proved increasingly difficult for his weaker successors to do so. We have seen above that Cenwulf initially attempted to resolve the matter in a way favourable to himself in 798, but was unsuccessful. He then seems to have delayed acceptance of the unfavourable papal judgement for as long as possible, perhaps while he appealed. However, his loss of control over Wessex in 802 can only have brought home to him his inability to maintain an increasingly untenable position and so hastened his acceptance of the papal decision in the following year. The fact that he had in the meantime resumed control of Kent and so Canterbury may have made it easier for him to concede this advantage.[10]

The battle recorded in the Chronicle entry for 802 is interesting not only as the beginning of what became a gradual shift of power in favour of the West Saxons. It also records the death of *Ealdorman* Aethelmund, who may very well have been an ancestor of the later Aethelred, who would successfully steer Mercia through the darkness of the Viking conquest and so allow it to play a key role in the formation of

England. This Aethelmund was, almost certainly, *Ealdorman* of the *Hwicce* and, as such, based on Gloucester in the southern half of this former kingdom just across the border from Wiltshire. There he was in a key position to handle relations, whether friendly or hostile, with the neighbouring West Saxons and Welsh. The fact that Aethelmund was probably *ealdorman* of this area may also imply a relationship with the dynasty of King Cenwulf, which was also based in this former kingdom. The main focus of the royal dynasty, however, appears to have been in the northern half of this region around Winchcombe where the family monastery and the subsequent burial place of Cenwulf and his son Cynehelm was located.[11]

The family of this Aethelmund certainly had a long history of loyal service to the Mercian kings and had received their due reward in terms of land and office. A charter of Uhtred, sub-king of the *Hwicce*, reveals that Ingeld, Aethelmund's father, had been appointed by King Aethelbald of Mercia (716–57) to the position of *præfectus* or *ealdorman*. At that time, the Kingdom of the *Hwicce* was still an independent kingdom ruled by its own dynasty, although subject to Mercian overlordship. It seems likely that, by way of this appointment as an *ealdorman*, Ingeld was in effect being made the Mercian king's agent within this tributary kingdom. As such, his role was presumably to ensure that the overlordship of Mercia was enforced, that tribute was paid and that the tributary kings of the *Hwicce* fulfilled their obligations to their overlord in full. In the reign of King Offa, Aethelmund succeeded his father in this role. He first appears as the recipient of a charter, dated to 770, from Uhtred, Sub-king of the *Hwicce*, wherein the latter describes him as 'my faithful *minister*'. However, the charter also shows that Uhtred made this grant of five hides of land at Aston in Worcestershire to Aethelmund 'on the advice of King Offa' and thus perhaps acknowledges his direct link to the latter.[12]

It was probably at some point during the 780s that Aethelmund became the sole authority in the land of the *Hwicce* following the extinction of the native sub-kings under King Offa. He went on to witness many royal charters under Offa, Ecgfrith and Cenwulf. He was described by King Offa as 'his *minister*' in a charter of the 790s and by King Ecgfrith in a charter of 796 as 'his faithful prince'. It seems likely that it was he who rebuilt the church at Deerhurst in Gloucestershire and that he was later buried there. He married a woman called Ceolburh, who may have been related to King Cenwulf, and they had a son named Aethelric. She would later become abbess of Berkeley in Gloucestershire after the death of her husband in 802 and hold that position until her own demise in 807. Aethelric succeeded to his father's lands in 802 but does not appear to have succeeded him as *ealdorman*. It may be that his father's defeat in Wessex led to this loss of favour. In spite of this, Aethelric remained a powerful figure in the region and maintained close links with the families of two other *ealdormen*, Edgar and Esne, describing their sons as 'my close and most faithful friends' in a document of 804. He was a well-travelled man, who had visited the shrines of St Peter and St Paul in Rome at some point between 798 and 804. He endowed his father's church at Deerhurst with extensive lands in 804 for the benefit of the souls of his father and himself and in the hope that he also would be buried there. This Aethelric had apparently died by 824, when the monastery at Westbury-on-Trym that he had bequeathed to Worcester was the subject of a dispute recorded in a document of that year.[13]

On 12 May 805, Archbishop Aethelheard of Canterbury died. At this time Cuthred, the brother of King Cenwulf, ruled in Kent and so a Mercian named Wulfred was chosen to succeed to the archbishopric with Cenwulf's agreement. It must have seemed that this new archbishop would be sensitive to King Cenwulf's wishes but this was not to be the case. Archbishop Wulfred was a keen supporter of reform within the Church, and duly followed his own independent agenda. He sought to reform the lives of the Christ Church clergy. He actively pursued a policy of restoring the power and prosperity of the archbishopric through a re-organisation and consolidation of its lands. He also attempted to resume clerical control of appointments to local abbeys and churches, which had fallen into the hands of the king and his leading nobles. This activity eventually brought him into conflict with the king since some of his plans conflicted with existing royal interests.[14]

Record of the Synod of *Clofesho*, 803. (BL Cotton Augustus ii 61)

As early as 808, correspondence between Charlemagne and Pope Leo III mentioned conflict between king and archbishop. Archbishop Wulfred started to issue coins without the customary acknowledgement of the Mercian ruler on the reverse. In 814/15 he visited Rome to secure papal support for his reforms, perhaps as a counterweight to royal disapproval. In July 816, at the Synod of Chelsea, he passed a series of reforming decrees aimed at restoring clerical control of local monasteries and churches. This struck directly at royal interests since Cenwulf and members of his family currently controlled a number of important and wealthy abbeys. The rich monasteries of Minster-in-Thanet and Reculver in Kent, which were currently held by

Cwenthryth, the king's sister, quickly became the focus of this dispute. A clash was inevitable and in 817 or 818 Archbishop Wulfred was expelled from his see. He was unable to return until just prior to King Cenwulf's death in 821, when concerns about the succession may have prompted them to patch up their differences temporarily. In that year, Wulfred was restored but only at the price of surrendering his claims along with a large estate and a hefty fine.[15]

The process by which satellite states challenged Mercian overlordship under King Cenwulf's rule had not yet ended. As we have already seen, Cenwulf had proved able with some effort to regain control over Kent and East Anglia following their secession after the death of Offa. He continued to dominate Wales and, in 816, he was able to invade the provinces of Rhufoniog and Eryri deep in the heart of Gwynedd in North Wales and, two years later, to devastate Dyfed in the south. Nevertheless, he had been forced to concede the loss of Mercian influence in Wessex. This loss of domination over Wessex was to prove crucial in the long run since Wessex rapidly developed into the main rival of Mercia. It was natural that the new West Saxon king, Egbert, who had seized power there on the death of Beorhtric, would seek to strike back at Mercia in retaliation for his earlier humiliating expulsion. Fortunately, during most of Cenwulf's reign Egbert appears to have been absorbed in building up his own authority and control within Wessex. The Chronicle records his subjugation of the men of Cornwall in 815.[16]

It was in the period following King Cenwulf's death in 821 that Egbert first revealed himself as a formidable challenge to the Mercian kings. It is worth noting here that Cenwulf was the last Mercian ruler considered important enough for his death to be recorded in the *Annals of Ulster* until the Lady Aethelflaed in 918. Cenwulf had attempted to secure the future of his own dynasty by grooming his son Cynehelm to succeed him in Mercia and installing his brother Cuthred as sub-king in Kent. However, these plans were brought to nothing with the deaths, firstly of Cuthred in 807 and secondly of Cynehelm probably around 812. The latter, who was buried in the family monastery of Winchcombe, disappears from the record in that year. A later eleventh-century hagiographic legend would relate that he was murdered by his own tutor, a man called Aescberht, in Clent Forest in Worcestershire, which may be true. However, this account also portrays him as aged seven, and firmly places the blame for his death on his own sister Cwenthryth, Abbess of Winchcombe, Minster-in-Thanet and Reculver. The details of this account are highly improbable and were possibly invented much later to enhance the enormity of the crime and therefore Cynehelm's own subsequent status as a saint. The fact that Cynehelm was subsequently buried at Winchcombe makes it unlikely that its abbess, Cwenthryth, was involved in his death. It is possible, however, that behind this legend lies the suspicion that he had been murdered at the instigation of a rival from within his own family, perhaps his relative Ceolwulf who eventually succeeded to the throne. This may therefore be evidence for the sort of internal rivalries that would ultimately weaken the kingdom as a whole.[17]

King Cenwulf was forced to alter his succession plans as a result of these premature deaths. He may have attempted to enhance the status of his new dynasty by having his murdered son elevated to sainthood. At a more practical level, Cenwulf may have appointed one of his remaining kinsmen, Ceolwulf, to succeed him. The latter may have been the same man who witnessed one of his kinsman's charters in 814. When King Cenwulf died some seven years later, in 821, he was buried in the church he had founded at Winchcombe back in 811, and Ceolwulf duly succeeded to his rule over both Mercia and Kent. The record of Ceolwulf's consecration by Archbishop Wulfred on 17 September 822 is preserved in a charter issued on the same day. It appears that Ceolwulf was not as popular or successful as his predecessor, perhaps as a result of suspicion about possible involvement in the murder of young Cynehelm. Indeed, he was probably conscious of this unpopularity and perhaps sought to counter it by leading a successful military campaign. He apparently selected the Welsh as his victims and probably threw the entire weight of his forces against them. In 822 he proceeded to enforce Mercian overlordship in Wales by destroying Degannwy in Gwynedd and taking direct control of the kingdom of Powys. However, this success while clearly important in itself was apparently not enough to secure Ceolwulf's kingship. In 823, within a year of this victory and only two years after his succession, the Chronicle records that Ceolwulf was deprived of the kingdom. The rulers of Powys were soon able to recover their kingdom following his downfall.[18]

This abbreviated reign and its abrupt end sowed the seeds of disputes that were to disrupt the kingdom of Mercia for the next fifty years or more. The clashes undermined the power and authority of the Mercian kings, leaving them less able to intervene in other kingdoms and even open to similar intervention themselves. Already, only two years later in 825, people would look back on the relatively long reign of King Cenwulf as a golden age. In that year, one of those present at a synod held at *Clofesho* could declare that 'after the death of Cenwulf, King of the Mercians, many quarrels and innumerable disputes had arisen between important men of all kinds – kings, bishops and ministers of God's churches – concerning a multitude of secular affairs'.[19]

The man who replaced Ceolwulf in 823 was one of his own *ealdormen*, named Beornwulf. He had previously appeared in last place among the *ealdormen* who witnessed the last surviving charter of Ceolwulf's short reign, dated to 26 May 823. He appears to have represented a discontented faction among the Mercian nobility currently on the fringes of power but which harboured its own designs on the kingship. King Beornwulf was the first of a number of men who would occupy the

Mercian throne during the ninth century, whose names alliterate on the letter B and who were probably all members of the same kin-group. (They will be referred to hereafter as the 'B' dynasty to distinguish them from Cenwulf's 'C' dynasty, who appear to have favoured names that alliterate on the letter C). If this assumption is correct, they may have represented a rival dynasty that provided an alternative focus for those dissatisfied with the rule of Cenwulf's line. A number of men, who may have been members of this group, had been present among the witnesses to the charters of earlier Mercian kings, including Beornwulf himself and, perhaps, Brorda and Beornmod.[20]

Unfortunately, we have no firm information on the origins of this kin-group which would allow us to establish the location of their power base. There is a possibility that they represent descendants of a certain Beorhtwald, a nephew of King Aethelred of Mercia, who was granted lands in the region of the Middle Angles in the 680s (see Table 2, p. 209, for this dynasty). They were more certainly linked to the man named Beornred, who had contested the throne with Offa following the death of King Aethelbald in 757. If so, they may just possibly have been located in this same general area of the central East Midlands. This location is perhaps also suggested by the fact that following the Viking occupation of much of that region in the 870s, some members of the 'B' dynasty would be found in close alliance with the Vikings. However, this may simply have been an alliance of convenience and we cannot be certain that this was indeed where this 'B' dynasty was based.[21]

The origin of King Beornwulf's rule in a coup undoubtedly meant that he lacked the full support of the Mercian nobility. Indeed, a significant change in the witnesses to royal charters on his succession appears to reflect almost a 'purge' of the senior Mercian nobility in which he removed his opponents from positions of authority and replaced them with supporters. In the space of a single year between 26 May 823 and 824, the charters reveal a dramatic change in personnel among the ranks of the *ealdormen*. The last surviving charter of Ceolwulf in 823 records ten *ealdormen*, excluding Beornwulf himself, three of whom, Aelfwald, Eadferth and Muca, disappear immediately thereafter. The fate of only the last of these men is known for certain and will be discussed below. In the first surviving charter of Beornwulf in 824, they are replaced by seven new *ealdormen*: Cuthred, two by the name of Eadwulf, Ealdred, Ecgberht, Ludeca and Uhtred. In this document they are listed alongside seven survivors from Ceolwulf's reign: Beornnoth, Bofa, Eadberht, Ealhheard, Mucel, Sigered and Wulfred, who managed to span the change of dynasty. The survival of Beornnoth and Bofa may be explained by their being related to the new king and, indeed, the former became his leading *ealdorman*. The result of this process may have been the introduction of a much more narrowly focussed base of support for the new kings. In turn, this reduced base of support may have made the new ruler's position more insecure than that of both his immediate predecessors. In spite of this, he was apparently able on the evidence of surviving coins, to appoint a man named Baldred, probably a brother or cousin, as sub-king of Kent.[22]

The Chronicle contains a cryptic entry under the year 824 which may provide another fragment of evidence for the sort of factional struggles that fuelled dynastic change during this unstable period. This simply records that two *ealdormen* named Burghelm and Muca were killed. The latter appears as a prominent witness to both the existing charters of King Ceolwulf as noted above. He was almost certainly an appointee of that king and hence probably one of his close supporters. It seems likely that he lost influence at court when his own candidate Ceolwulf was deposed in 823. *Ealdorman* Burghelm is otherwise unrecorded but it seems natural to assume on the basis of his name that he was a supporter and possibly a relative of King Beornwulf and his 'B' dynasty. If these suggestions are correct then the killings of 824 could be interpreted as examples of factional violence spilling over in the wake of dynastic change. The changes in the kingship incurred the consequent gain or loss of power and influence among the nobility and these men were clearly prepared to fight for what they had. It seems likely that these men were not the only losses in this process given the known changes to charter witness lists. The fact that they are seldom mentioned in the Chronicle leaves us largely in the dark about them.[23]

Detail from a decorated cross, St Michael's Church, Cropthorne, Worcestershire. (Photograph by W. Walker)

The new king, Beornwulf, actively sought to secure support and legitimacy for his new dynasty from the start. In 824, at a synod held at *Clofesho*, he sought to resolve, once and for all, the long-running dispute with Archbishop Wulfred of Canterbury. He may even have employed the assistance of the Pope to broker a deal, as suggested by the presence of a man called Nothelm, who is described as a papal 'messenger', in the documents recording the final settlement reached. The immense significance of this particular synod for contemporaries is evidenced by its inclusion in the Chronicle entry for that year. In the following year, 825, another synod, once again held at *Clofesho* and under the presidency of King Beornwulf, finally resolved the bitter dispute over control of the monasteries of Minster-in-Thanet and Reculver in Kent. Cwenthryth, the sister of King Cenwulf, was permitted to retain her position as abbess of these houses for her lifetime in return for recognition of Archbishop Wulfred's authority over them and the surrender of extensive lands in Middlesex and Kent. In this way, King Beornwulf probably hoped to secure the support of the archbishop for his kingship at the expense of his 'C' dynasty rivals.[24]

King Beornwulf could not base his rule on clerical support alone, he also needed to secure secular support. He appears to have decided to attempt to bolster his rather insecure position by seeking success in war and the rewards in tribute and prestige which would follow this. This was a common strategy adopted by rulers who considered themselves insecure at home. If this was Beornwulf's intention then unfortunately he selected the wrong target for his aggression. In 825 the Chronicle records that Egbert of Wessex fought with the army of Beornwulf at a place called *Ellendun*, now identified as Wroughton in Wiltshire and completely defeated him. The much later account of Henry of Huntingdon may preserve the remnant of an Old English poem on this battle which makes clear the bloody nature of the encounter. It says that: '*Ellendun*'s stream was reddened with blood, was blocked with the fallen and filled with the stench.'[25]

The location of the battle shows that King Beornwulf was the aggressor, who had invaded West Saxon territory. As a direct consequence of his victory, Egbert was subsequently able to ravage a largely undefended Mercia in reply. He went on to drive the Mercian sub-king, Baldred, out of Kent in 826 and bring that area under West Saxon control by installing his own son, Aethelwulf, in his place. The costly defeat inflicted on the Mercian royal army meant that they were unable to interfere with Egbert's actions. In turn, the West Saxon victory encouraged the East Anglians to throw off Mercian rule and in this same disastrous year of 826 Beornwulf would meet his death in an attempt to prevent this. The immediate result was the loss of Mercian control over East Anglia, where a man named Athelstan became king, issuing his own coins independent of the Mercians.

The longer term result of the defeat at Wroughton and the consequent loss of control in Kent and East Anglia was to further weaken Mercia itself. The rivalry for the Mercian throne between the 'B' and 'C' dynasties, and the disruption and disunity which this had fostered, had brought a major decline in the power of the kingdom. As a result, it had lost its position of pre-eminence and its hold on its satellite kingdoms. This was the beginning of a process of decline which would in time undermine the prestige of the Mercian kingdom while enhancing that of its main West Saxon rivals. Increasingly, King Egbert of Wessex would be looked on as the foremost ruler in England and the man to whom satellite kingdoms should offer their tribute.

In Mercia itself, the supporters of Beornwulf appear to have tried to retain their hold on power after his demise by securing the succession of one of his *ealdormen*, Ludeca. This man had featured ninth in the list of *ealdormen* who witnessed two charters of King Beornwulf in 824. The first and only time Ludeca appears as king is in a Chronicle entry for 827 which records that he met his death in battle along with no less than five of the *ealdormen* who supported him. He was defeated by a force under a man called Wiglaf, who then seized the throne. This battle was most probably part of an internal power struggle between the rival groups of nobles which had formed around the 'B' and 'C' dynasties. In this context, Ludeca and his five unnamed *ealdormen* clearly represented supporters of the 'B' dynasty since he, almost certainly, owed his appointment as *ealdorman* to Beornwulf. In contrast, Wiglaf and his forces represented the supporters of the 'C' dynasty, since he was related to the former king, Ceolwulf, through the marriage of his son Wigmund to Ceolwulf's daughter Aelfflaed. The kin-group to which Wiglaf belonged, and which may be called the 'W' dynasty, appears to have been based on the territory of the *Tomsaete* as revealed by the location of their chosen family burial place at Repton.[26]

The succession of Wiglaf did not resolve the dynastic rivalry within Mercia, although the losses suffered by the supporters of the 'B' dynasty in 825, 826 and 827 temporarily relegated them from any significant influence in Mercian affairs. There was another significant change among the witnesses of royal charters after Wiglaf's succession. The deaths of five of King Ludeca's *ealdormen* in battle undoubtedly contributed to this transformation but it probably also reflects a purge of 'B' dynasty supporters. In the space of six years between the last surviving charter of Beornwulf in 825 and the first of Wiglaf in 831, no less than seven *ealdormen* disappear from the record. They were presumably the five who fell with King Ludeca and two others; namely, Beornnoth, Cuthred, Eadberht, Eadwulf, Ealhheard, Ecgberht and Uhtred. In 825 a total of eleven *ealdormen* are listed under Beornwulf but only four of these men survived to serve King Wiglaf: Cyneberht, Eadwulf, Ealhhelm, Mucel and Sigered. In 831 the first charter of Wiglaf lists three new *ealdormen* – Aelfstan, Aethelheard and Tidwulf – and later documents add four more: Aethelwulf, Ealhhelm, Hunberht and another Mucel, probably the same man identified by Asser as Aethelred Mucil.[27]

The bloody circumstances surrounding this further change of dynasty also provided King Egbert of Wessex with a fresh opportunity to exploit Mercian weakness. He was quick to do so and in 829 he invaded Mercia, conquering the whole kingdom and driving Wiglaf into exile. He even went so far as to issue a few coins minted in London and bearing the legend *Rex M{erciorum}* or King of the Mercians. Subsequently, he went on to lead his victorious army northwards right across Mercia to the river Dore where he received the submission of the Northumbrians. This demonstrates clearly how thoroughly Mercian opposition had been crushed and represents a dramatic transformation since the death of King Offa. In 796 Mercia had dominated the other English kingdoms and Egbert was an exile with the Franks but now the tables had been well and truly turned with Egbert the master and the Mercian king in exile. In a little over thirty years Mercia had been brought low by the scourge of bitter internal rivalries.[28]

The decline of Mercia had begun gradually but in the wake of the disasters of the last few years had developed exponentially. The first effect had been to encourage rebellion among its satellite kingdoms which led to the loss of Wessex. This had drawn the Mercian armies into a number of campaigns of subjugation designed to restore their authority. In turn these campaigns dissipated their strength and, in the case of Wessex, proved completely ineffective. The costs of retaining control had increased but conversely the tribute needed to defray such costs had been reduced significantly. This put a strain on the finances of the kingdom and so on relationships between the king and his nobles. The most aggrieved among the latter gathered around the rival 'B' dynasty who appeared to offer an alternative. The tension and open warfare between these rivals absorbed the energy of the Mercian nobles and distracted them from the real task of dealing with Wessex and the satellite kingdoms. This led to further rebellion by the satellites combined with attacks on the weakened kingdom by newly independent Wessex. This vicious circle had brought Mercia by 829 down to a position as a tributary of Wessex, reversing the situation at the end of Offa's reign.

This complete reversal of fortune did not last long however as Egbert of Wessex proved unable to maintain control of Mercia directly or to find a suitable local puppet ruler. As a result, within a year King Wiglaf had managed to fully restore Mercian independence. He threw off West Saxon overlordship and re-established his authority in Mercia in 830. Already in 831 he was able to issue a charter to Archbishop Wulfred which shows that his authority extended into Middlesex by that date. It is possible that this grant was intended to secure the Archbishop's support following the Mercian loss of control in Kent. In 836 King Wiglaf was able to hold a synod at Croft in Leicestershire which was attended not only by Archbishop Ceolnoth but by all of the southern bishops. It was during Wiglaf's reign that the Vikings began to pay increasing attention

Charter of King Wiglaf to the Minster of Hanbury and Mucel, son of Esne, 836. (BL Cotton Augustus ii 94)

to England making a number of attacks in coastal areas. The Chronicle records almost annual assaults against the coasts of Wessex and Kent from 835 but this largely West Saxon source probably fails to record many similar attacks which must have occurred along the coasts of Mercia. It does record attacks on Lindsey in 838 and 'a great slaughter' in London in 842 and these are unlikely to have been isolated examples. The Vikings were well versed in detecting and exploiting division and weakness wherever they found it and these were certainly present in Mercia at this time. In spite of the increasingly alarming scale of these assaults, King Wiglaf continued to rule the Mercian kingdom for a further ten years and, perhaps surprisingly, was apparently followed on the throne by his son Wigmund. It was only in 839 at the very start of the latter's reign that the 'B' dynasty showed signs of revival.[29]

The rival 'B' dynasty had been slowly restoring its influence after the disastrous losses it had suffered in the defeats of the three years 825, 826 and 827. In 839 their plans came to fruition following the death, probably from natural causes since there is no record of any upheaval at this time, of King Wiglaf and the succession of his inexperienced son, Wigmund. In any case, the 'B' dynasty took full advantage of their opportunity and were able to restore their fortunes with King Beorhtwulf succeeding to the throne. He was presumably related to the earlier King Beornwulf, although exactly how is unknown. He had appeared in twentieth place among the witnesses to one of his predecessors charters in 836. The apparently less violent nature of the transfer of power on this occasion may be reflected in the less drastic changes in the witness lists of royal charters at this point.[30]

It is difficult to be sure on this score, since the gap of four years between the last charter of Wiglaf in 836 and the first of Beorhtwulf in 840 is long enough for the small number of changes which are apparent to be due to natural causes. Thus only two *ealdormen*, Ealhhelm and Tidwulf, disappear between these dates and only a single new *ealdorman* named Dudda replaces them. Although these changes may be entirely the result of natural wastage there does seem to be some evidence of changes in status at court related to the change in dynasty. The disappearance of Tidwulf from the lists and his replacement in the leading position by *Ealdorman* Hunberht, who has made a spectacular rise from seventh place, is suggestive of the victory of one faction over another. The close association of this same Hunberht with King Beorhtwulf in a charter of 848 relating to Breedon-on-the Hill in Leicestershire, where he is described as *princeps* and in turn acknowledges Beorhtwulf as his 'lord' may support this.[31]

The newly installed King Beorhtwulf soon faced an immediate challenge, apparently from the Vikings, when they attacked London in 842. This event is recorded in the Chronicle but may also be evidenced by the discovery of a hoard of coins in Middle Temple dated to *c*. 840 and probably buried to prevent it falling into Viking hands. This appears to have been part of their pattern of increasingly violent and successful attacks on important economic targets on or near the coasts. Indeed, the same Chronicle entry that records this attack also records the burning of Rochester in Kent and *Quentovic* in France. However, it was not until the very end of Beorhtwulf's reign that the Viking threat began to assume a really significant scale. Beorhtwulf appears to have been secure enough to enforce Mercian overlordship in Wales and, in 849, would kill Meurig, King of Gwent, in the process of maintaining it. In spite of this, success against the Welsh, the restored 'B' dynasty probably remained insecure and continued to need to be on its guard against its rivals. It is possible that this need led King Beorhtwulf to enter into some form of limited co-operation with the West Saxon rulers at this time.[32]

The coinage issued by King Beorhtwulf during his reign uses the same reverse design as that issued by his contemporary King Aethelwulf of Wessex. It has been suggested that this indicates some form of co-operation between these two rulers but whether it amounted to the political alliance suggested by some remains to be seen. There are no independent indications of such an alliance in contrast to the evidence to be found in the Chronicle for the later alliance between Burgred and the West Saxons. It is possible that the common design of this currency indicates no more than a desire on the part of these rulers to ease the process of economic exchange between their realms, in effect, an effort to encourage trade between their kingdoms. It is true that this suggests a certain amount of co-operation, but perhaps no more than is involved in one king copying the coin design of the other. The possibility that moneyers may have moved between the kingdoms, perhaps tempted by better conditions, means that they themselves might have been the means of transfer for these designs.[33]

The notion of an alliance between Mercia and Wessex at this time appears to be contradicted by evidence of continued rivalry between the two antagonists. Thus it was apparently during King Beorhtwulf's reign that Berkshire, which had probably been in Mercian hands since 779, was lost to the West Saxons. A charter of 844 shows Ceolred, Bishop of Leicester, granting land at Pangbourne to King Beorhtwulf, who then passed it on to *Ealdorman* Aethelwulf. The latter part of this grant itself may have been part of a last-ditch attempt to persuade Aethelwulf to remain loyal since within five years he had transferred his allegiance to Wessex. In 849, when the future West Saxon King Alfred was born at Wantage, the shire was clearly under West Saxon control. During this same interval, the name of *Ealdorman* Aethelwulf disappears from the witness lists of Mercian charters and reappears in those of the West Saxons. He did not entirely forget his Mercian origins however and, following his death in battle near Reading in 871, his body was taken north to Derby for burial on his native soil.[34]

An ornate pillar from the crypt, St Wystan's Church, Repton, Derbyshire. (Photograph by W. Walker)

Whatever the policies followed by King Beorhtwulf, the 'C' dynasty, in the person of Wiglaf's grandson, Wigstan, waited in the wings for an opportunity to recover the throne. The tension between these rival dynasties and their supporters gradually built up as Wigstan grew to manhood before finally exploding into violence in 849. In that year Beorhtfrith, the son and heir of King Beorhtwulf, perhaps fearful that Wigstan might attempt to deprive him of his inheritance, murdered Wigstan on 1 June at a place subsequently called Wistowe in Leicestershire. The later hagiographical account of this incident relates it to a proposed marriage between Beorhtfrith and Aelfflaed, Wigstan's widowed mother and a daughter of King Ceolwulf I, and Wigstan's opposition to this alliance. Beorhtfrith is reported to have invited his rival Wigstan to a parley to discuss the matter, only to murder him. It is possible that this story, though late, contains a kernel of truth. It may be that this proposed marriage was simply intended to reinforce the claim of the 'B' dynasty by linking it directly to the 'C' dynasty. It may even have been intended to settle the long-running dynastic dispute through a marriage alliance involving the two parties. In either case, it was obvious that Wigstan himself would be the loser and he therefore probably sought to prevent the match and paid the ultimate price for this. He was buried alongside his grandfather in the family monastery at Repton and a cult of sainthood quickly developed around his tomb. Subsequently, this cult was probably encouraged and fostered by the supporters of the 'C' dynasty under King Ceolwulf II to reinforce the legitimacy of their restored rule.[35]

This second murder of a representative of the 'C' dynasty might seem to imply that they got the worst of this struggle and had all the martyrs. However, there exists a small scrap of evidence which suggests that this may not, in fact, have been the case. A very late and extremely confused tradition records the commemoration by c. 900 of a St Beorhthelm at Stafford and subsequently at Runcorn. The specific legend associated with this saint has unfortunately been confused with the legend of an entirely unrelated French saint with a similar name and is therefore entirely worthless in terms of helping us to identify him. However, in light of our knowledge of the kingdom of Mercia and of other Mercian saints from this period, for example, Cynehelm and Wigstan, some of the background to this unknown saint can perhaps be suggested. The name Beorhthelm itself suggests that he was probably a member of the 'B' dynasty and that he therefore represents their own saint and martyr. He would in effect be their equivalent of Cynehelm and Wigstan. He does not feature among the witness lists to any surviving charters but this does not mean he never existed. It would not be surprising if he had been a member of the 'B' dynasty who fell victim to their rivals during one of their many disputes and was subsequently commemorated by his family at Stafford.[36]

The immediate effect of Wigstan's murder was, as intended, to remove the threat from his party to a 'B' dynasty succession. However, this further outbreak of dissension in the Mercian kingdom also had an unanticipated consequence. It once again drew the attention of predatory Viking raiders to the weakness of the kingdom. In 851 the Chronicle notes that a force of 350 ships entered the mouth of the Thames. This fleet had spent the previous winter of 850-851 on the Isle of Thanet in Kent. This was the first Viking force to winter in England and it clearly portended a substantial increase in the scale of Viking activities both in terms of the numbers of men involved and in the planning of their operations. The winter spent in Thanet allowed their leaders to reconnoitre suitable targets and they selected the two richest sites in the immediate area, London and Canterbury. They sailed up the River Thames and stormed the great Mercian port of London. This assault on the main emporium of Mercia was a major event which must have produced shock waves

Silver penny of King Beorhtwulf
(obverse). (Ashmolean Museum,
Oxford)

throughout the kingdom. It certainly reached the ears of chroniclers across the Channel where it featured in the *Annals of St Bertin*. It also provided an early taste of what would lay in store for Mercia in the future.[37]

King Beorhtwulf of Mercia, alerted by the earlier presence of the fleet in Thanet probably made preparations to summon an army to protect the south-east of his kingdom. When the attack came, he proved unable to prevent the storming of London itself, which was too easy to reach from the sea for his land force to be able intervene. Nevertheless, he responded positively by marching on London to counter-attack the Viking force. In the battle that followed, however, Beorhtwulf and his Mercian army were defeated and put to flight. This defeat was not the result desired but it appears to have at least succeeded in deflecting Viking attention from Mercia to Wessex since their army next crossed the Thames into West Saxon territory in Surrey. They then proceeded to raid through Wessex until defeated in battle by King Aethelwulf of Wessex at *Acleah*. The battle with Beorhtwulf may have resulted in significant losses to the Viking army, which caused them to divert their attack and perhaps even contributed to their subsequent defeat.

King Beorhtwulf died in 852, the year following this defeat, but when this happened it was not his son, Beorhtfrith, who benefited from the earlier murder of Wigstan. It is possible that revulsion against his involvement in the murder made Beorhtfrith's succession politically unacceptable, but it is much more likely that he simply pre-deceased his father, perhaps falling in the battle outside London. In either case, Beorhtwulf was succeeded as King of Mercia not by his son but by Burgred, who was probably a younger brother or cousin. He had already appeared in third place among the *ealdormen* witnessing one of King Beorhtwulf's charters in 845. It would be this King Burgred who was to be faced with the greatest challenge in the history of the Mercian kingdom. This was the arrival of the 'great raiding army' in England and its subsequent attempt to conquer and subdue each of the individual English kingdoms in turn. He faced this challenge unsure of the loyalty of many of his nobles who were supporters of a rival line and without any allies among the other English kingdoms. This challenge would make or break all of the traditional English kingdoms and Mercia would be tested with the rest.[38]

The period between the deaths of King Offa and King Beorhtwulf clearly witnessed a decline in the power and influence of the Mercian kingdom. By 850, the

Mercian kings had lost their earlier political influence over Wessex, Northumbria, East Anglia, Kent and Sussex. A glance at the reign lengths of the individual kings during this period reveals an important part of the reasons for this. After a series of long and stable reigns – Aethelbald (forty-one years), Offa (thirty-nine years) and Cenwulf (twenty-five years) – there came three rulers who, following each other in rapid succession, barely managed two years each. They were succeeded by Wiglaf, who managed only one year before his deposition by Egbert of Wessex in 829. The expulsion of the West Saxons in 830 was followed by a more creditable ten years for Wiglaf and twelve for Beorhtwulf. However, it was not really until the reign of Burgred, who ruled for twenty-two years, at the close of this period that some stability was finally restored. The short reigns experienced during this time had made it difficult for kings to establish their authority, which depended very much on close personal contact with their nobles.

The fact that many of these kings succeeded members of a rival dynasty with very different policies and priorities, and often in violent circumstances, only made the situation worse. The frequent shifts of policy and personnel that such changes brought in their wake could only increase the general instability and further weaken any ruler's hold on the kingdom. The associated rise and fall of the supporters of these rival kings extended this instability down the social structure. In these circumstances, the kings were unsure of their support and the nobles were unsure about their kings. This was not an atmosphere conducive to the smooth operation of royal government and it is hardly surprising that Mercia itself lost a great deal of its power and influence as a result.

In order to provide a contrast to this picture of decline it is instructive to look at the situation in Wessex during the same period. Following the death of King Beorhtric in 802, Wessex was ruled by a series of kings with long reigns: Egbert (thirty-seven years), Aethelwulf (nineteen years) and Alfred (twenty-eight years). Although the last two of these kings were separated by three others – Aethelbald, Aethelberht and Aethelred, each with relatively short reigns of between two and six years – these men were all brothers and so might therefore be expected to demonstrate a greater element of continuity than unrelated rivals. In addition, all these kings were drawn from the same dynasty and hence provided far greater stability than could possibly be the case in neighbouring Mercia. This pattern of succession in Wessex contrasts sharply with that in contemporary Mercia and explains much about the relative rise and decline of these states at this time. However, it is important to note that this difference was, to a significant extent, the result of individual dynastic fortunes rather than any planning. The succession in Wessex before the reign of King Beorhtric had shown many of the signs of instability witnessed in Mercia during this later period.[39]

Most historians have interpreted this decline in Mercian power as complete and irreversible, leaving the kingdom virtually dependent on Wessex and ripe for Viking conquest. This interpretation is, however, an exaggerated one. The evidence shows that Mercia remained a powerful kingdom with the potential to challenge Wessex. The longer reign of King Burgred presented an opportunity for stability that had been absent before. The kingdom had suffered no major loss of territory and remained larger than Wessex even after the latter had absorbed Sussex and Kent. The West Saxons had failed to subdue Mercia, aside from the space of a single year under Egbert in 829/30, in contrast to the reverse achieved under King Offa. The West Saxons had established their control over Sussex and Kent but, once again unlike Offa, were unable to secure similar control over East Anglia. The Mercians continued to retain their overlordship in Wales in spite of West Saxon power. All of this indicates that Mercia was very far from being a spent force at this time. When the Vikings arrived in force in 865 they would be faced with two powerful English kingdoms rather than one.

CHAPTER 3

The Great Raiding Army

When King Burgred commenced his reign in 852 the Vikings had already emerged as a significant threat to the coastal areas of Mercia and the other English kingdoms. As early as 792, a charter of King Offa had mentioned the need to defend Kent from these pirates. In 807 King Cenwulf had ransomed a priest from their clutches. We have already noted some other signs of their activities. According to the Chronicle, what must have been fairly large raiding parties had already attacked Lindsey in 838 and sacked London in 842. They must also have carried out many other attacks that went unrecorded in the West Saxon inspired text of the Chronicle. For example, we only know that a Viking force was raiding in the area of the later Shropshire in 855, deep within Mercia, because the fact is mentioned in a surviving charter. Most spectacularly, the Vikings had stormed London in 851 and put Burgred's predecessor King Beorhtwulf and his army to flight. On this occasion, the resistance put up by Beorhtwulf and his force proved sufficient to divert the Viking army into West Saxon territory and subsequent defeat, but the menace from Viking raiders remained an increasingly potent one.[1]

The origins of these notorious sea raiders lie in Scandinavia and in the early medieval history of that region. They first burst onto the wider European scene in the latter part of the eighth century with their spectacular assault on the great Northumbrian monastery at Lindisfarne on 8 June 793. This event shocked many people across Western Europe, partly because of its violence and the sacrilege involved but mainly because it seems to have come as a surprise. It seems hardly credible that the Anglo-Saxon settlers had not maintained links with their Continental homelands after their arrival in England. It is well established that they retained strong links with the German lands on the north-west coast of Europe which proved instrumental in the conversion of these lands to Christianity. Scandinavia was only a short sea journey northwards from these German lands. The inclusion of Scandinavian manufactured luxury goods in the royal burial at Sutton Hoo shows that trade with that region continued into the seventh century at least. The later accounts of trading voyages provided by the Norwegian Ottar and the English Wulfstan to King Alfred also suggest that earlier contacts between these regions were by no means unlikely. It seems highly probable that traders from Scandinavia were a familiar sight in the English kingdoms. Indeed, the well-known case of mistaken identity recorded in Aethelweard's Chronicle under 789, when a West Saxon official mistook an early group of these raiders for peaceful traders, with fatal results, supports this view.[2]

If we accept the familiar presence of pagan Scandinavians as peaceful traders in the seventh and eighth centuries then it was clearly their transformation into ruthless and violent raiders that came as such a shocking surprise. The contemporary words of Alcuin, a native of Northumbria then living on the Continent, appear to confirm this, when he writes: 'never before has such an atrocity been seen in Britain as we have now suffered at the hands of a pagan people.' What had caused this transformation? There has been much ink spilt on this subject and I do not propose to review it in detail here. In the context of the different focus of the current work, it must suffice to highlight some of the main reasons proposed for the Viking phenomenon and to offer a few thoughts of my own.[3]

The main reasons put forward to explain the great upheavals of this period are extremely varied. They extend from climatic and economic factors to political and technological changes. It has become apparent that none of these factors, individually, offers a particularly satisfactory explanation for the timing, scale, pattern or purpose

Viking raiders from a grave stone from Lindisfarne. (Copyright English Heritage)

of the entire sequence of events usually known as the Viking Age. It seems most likely that it was, in fact, a complex combination of a number of these factors that was responsible for this outburst of activity. The reasons why so many individuals became involved in this activity may have varied quite significantly. The events that constitute the Viking Age are not in themselves uniform. The first manifestation of the period was a series of small-scale seasonal raids by a few ships on rich but largely undefended coastal sites, usually churches. This was followed some thirty years later by a series of more extended raids by larger groups of thirty or forty ships aimed at rich trading centres some of which were defended. Thereafter came raids by even larger forces, in hundreds of ships, capable of striking far inland and seizing political power. This pattern of escalation really argues for a series of Viking Ages.[4]

It is much easier to be sure about the purpose or aims of these various phases of raiding, and this in turn may throw more light on what prompted them. They were all intended to secure wealth for their participants. This becomes obvious when we consider the reported activities of the various groups of Vikings involved in raiding during this period right across Europe. In the early stages, this wealth was usually portable, in the form of slaves, bullion or coins. In later stages, it often took the form of land or political power. The search for this wealth was the mainspring for all their activities during this period. They clearly preferred portable wealth in the early period when they intended to carry it away for use at home or in trade. They are regularly recorded as seeking out the most portable wealth available. They were always willing to ransom captives or even holy relics in exchange for bullion or coin which were easier to transport and to exchange. They readily destroyed works of art or manuscripts to get at the precious metals or jewels lavished on them. In addition if they were paid in bullion or coin they would often stop raiding and move on. The later raiders who became actively involved in local politics were able to consider land as an alternative source of wealth and hence settlement became their aim. It was wealth in whatever form that would allow these raiders to improve their own lives or to gain power and influence over others.

This search for wealth through raiding did not make the Vikings at all unusual in this period. In all of the kingdoms they attacked across Europe exactly the same activity was going on. The rulers of the English and Frankish kingdoms also led their followers on regular military expeditions with the aim of securing wealth either in plunder or in land. Indeed, the Franks held an annual muster of their army at the Marchfield before deciding where to direct their aggression for that year. The campaigns mounted by these kings can sometimes seem more organised and more political in their origins because of their larger scale and their direction against other kingdoms. In Mercia, for example, these campaigns were usually aimed at traditional targets; the Welsh, the men of Kent, the Northumbrians and the West Saxons. In spite of this, however, they remained at heart raiding expeditions intended to secure wealth for their participants. If these target kingdoms recognised the overlordship of their potential attacker and paid tribute they would not be attacked.[5]

In essence the Viking leaders were doing no more than any other rulers in Europe during this period by seeking wealth through warfare beyond their borders. What then made them stand out from the crowd? There were two main features of the Viking assault which made them different. The first was their lack of respect for the Christian Church which was a natural consequence of their paganism and lack of understanding of Christianity. There has been a great deal of argument about the extent of their depredations in this respect. However, it surely cannot be denied that, as pagans, they had no aversion to targeting Christian sites and no fear of the wrath of God. In contrast Christian rulers, whatever their individual failings in particular cases, were generally aware of the sanctity of the Church and fearful of the effects of divine punishment. The other peculiarity of the Viking raids was symptomatic of their origin in a classic confrontation between a sea power and land powers. The Vikings proved so successful in their raids all across Europe because they usually held command of the sea. They were able to strike at their land-based opponents at almost any point they chose while remaining largely immune across the sea to any counterattacks. In contrast their land-based opponents found themselves overstretched attempting to defend all of their long coastlines and river systems and almost completely unable to retaliate. It took them a long time to adjust to this new situation and a change in the pattern of Viking activities before they could turn the tables.

In the end the lack of contemporary Scandinavian sources mean that we will probably never fully know the precise circumstances behind the descent of these sea raiders on the coasts of Western Europe. My own view, for what it is worth, is that a combination of factors contributed to the initially spectacular appearance of the Vikings. The Scandinavians had been developing their seafaring skills through trade over a long period. The recent subjugation of the Frisians and the Saxons by Charlemagne had effectively removed important rival naval powers from the North Sea. The decline of the once powerful Kingdom of Northumbria into political chaos following the murder of King Aethelred in 795 offered the prospect of easy targets for raiding particularly in the form of rich and undefended coastal monastic sites. The similar decline of Frankish naval power and the later internal tensions within the Frankish kingdom itself also offered them potential targets. The occupation by Norsemen during the previous fifty years or so of the Northern Isles of Scotland provided convenient staging posts on the route to the coastlands of eastern England or the Irish Sea. All of these factors probably contributed to the initial decision of some Norsemen to try their hand at raiding isolated coastal monasteries in Northumbria and Ireland in search of easy gains.[6]

The initial seasonal raids, which appear to have consisted of small numbers of raiders, mostly Norwegian, with a few ships at most, probably brought immense wealth to the individuals involved and allowed them to enhance their status and power at home. In turn the leaders of these first raiding parties were able to attract or employ greater numbers of men for subsequent raids. The larger raids that followed secured more wealth and the cycle resumed. The process gradually drew in other leaders who were unwilling to be left behind in this rush for wealth. Inevitably more important local rulers became involved from perhaps around 810 onwards in an attempt to control and channel this new growth industry to bolster their own power at home. This process gradually brought larger fleets and more men into the raids, which consequently brought about a significant extension in the range and scale of the raiding activity. This is reflected in contemporary chronicle accounts which provide clear evidence of the increasing scale and range of attacks until from 830 onwards substantial fleets of around thirty ships were involved.

This process was encouraged by the civil war in the Frankish Empire from 830 onwards and the contemporary internecine warfare both within and between the various English kingdoms. The disruption of local opposition that resulted from these distractions made it possible for increasingly larger raids to be mounted and important trading sites like London to be targeted. The increased numbers of raiders also exploited this weakness to winter on the territory of their victims and so extend their raiding time into the next year and beyond. The leaders of these larger raiding parties were now important enough to be named in Western European sources and sometimes to become a factor in local politics. The increasing tempo of these operations and their success encouraged some of the more important leaders of these groups to consider the possibilities for even more ambitious raiding. This was the background to the formation of the *micel here* or so-called 'great raiding army' which would arrive in East Anglia in 865.

It seems likely that the common threat presented by the attacks of these Scandinavian raiders that caused the rulers of both Wessex and Mercia to consider what would previously have been unthinkable. The recent experience of these men and their kingdoms at the hands of these heathen raiders may have encouraged them to consider the possible advantages of military co-operation. In 851 the ease with which the Vikings had been able to switch their attack from West Saxon territory in Kent to Mercia and once again to Wessex, while inflicting significant damage on each, showed the urgent need for a co-ordinated response. This represented a significant change from previous relations between these kingdoms which had largely been based on rivalry and hostility. King Burgred of Mercia and King Aethelwulf of Wessex broke with this tradition and reached out to each other in order to face a common threat.[7]

The first fruits of this developing relationship appeared early in 853 when the Chronicle records that King Burgred and his *witan*, or royal council, sought West Saxon participation in a campaign into Wales. King Aethelwulf agreed and led his army through Mercia to link up with the forces of Burgred. They invaded Welsh territory together and brought the Welsh to heel so that they submitted to Mercian overlordship. This was probably the first time in history that a joint campaign had been undertaken by these previously hostile armies. It had not been directed against the Vikings perhaps because they apparently failed to make an appearance in this year. In the absence of any activity on their part it may be that a conscious decision was made to direct the new alliance against the Welsh instead. It was perhaps felt essential that the new co-operation should be tested in practice and the Welsh provided a convenient target. It should be noted that, in spite of fairly strong West Saxon hints in the Chronicle that their own King Aethelwulf was the stronger partner in this alliance, it was Aethelwulf who was called on to aid King Burgred and not vice versa. This might imply that the West Saxon ruler was in fact the junior partner in this arrangement.[8]

This joint expedition was apparently a great success and probably led to the decision to turn this limited co-operation into a more permanent alliance. As a result, after Easter 853 the formal alliance of the two kingdoms was sealed when King Aethelwulf gave his daughter, Aethelswith, in marriage to King Burgred at his palace of Chippenham in Wiltshire. This appears to have been the first marriage between the dynasties of Mercia and Wessex which did not imply some form of overlordship but an alliance of independent rulers. In the past, such marriages had usually involved the submission of one ruler to another and were accompanied or followed by close supervision of the subordinate ruler by his overlord. This particular instance was different since both Aethelwulf and Burgred continued to function as independent rulers. In this context, it is interesting to note the difference in interpretation placed on the events of 853 by different versions of the Chronicle. The 'A' version, which was compiled in a West Saxon context, appears to interpret the co-operation between Burgred and Aethelwulf as being led by the latter. In contrast, the 'D' version, which has gone through a Northern or Mercian filter, interprets these same events in a more balanced way.

Silver penny of King Burgred (obverse). (Ashmolean Museum, Oxford)

It has also been suggested that the design of the coinage issued in Mercia and Wessex around this time provides further evidence of the increasing co-operation between these two former rivals. In the 860s the coinages of King Burgred of Mercia and his contemporary King Aethelred of Wessex, the son of Aethelwulf, adopted a common 'lunettes' design for the reverse of their coins. Indeed, a leading authority has gone so far as to speak of this as 'a single uniform coinage for both Wessex and Mercia'. This clearly has implications for economic co-operation and the improvement of the process of trade and exchange between these kingdoms. Indeed, the discovery in widely separated surviving hoards of a mixture of these West Saxon and Mercian coins suggests that this was successfully achieved. Whether it also implies anything in terms of the political alliance between these rulers is less clear.[9]

In subsequent years, however, it appears that the new alliance was not activated. In 855 the Vikings were active, as recorded in a contemporary charter, in the Wrekin area of Shropshire, a region far from the sea and close to the heart of Mercia. This force was probably the same as that which had attacked the coast of North Wales from the Irish Sea under the leadership of a man named Orm. The progress of their raid can be followed in the pages of the Welsh and Irish annals. They are first recorded in 853, when they laid waste the Isle of Anglesey off the north Welsh coast. In 854 Cynan, King of Powys, died in Rome, possibly exiled from his kingdom by these same Vikings. It was certainly only a small step from Powys or even from North Wales to the Wrekin in Shropshire. In 855 King Aethelwulf of Wessex was undertaking a pilgrimage to Rome and in his absence his son Aethelbald was seeking to usurp his father's kingdom. In these circumstances it is not perhaps surprising that no one in Wessex was willing to assist King Burgred under the terms of the alliance. Instead, it was left to the Welsh themselves under Rhodri *Mawr* to defeat this Viking force and kill its leader in 856 as noted in the Irish annals. Otherwise, the Viking raiders of these years may simply have confined themselves to fairly small scale attacks. It is possible that the Mercians and West Saxons were able to defend their kingdoms against these attacks with their own forces. There is certainly no record of any West Saxon requests for Mercian assistance or vice versa.[10]

The event that finally triggered full military co-operation between the allies was the arrival in England of the *micel here* or 'great raiding army' in 865. This army clearly represented a major escalation of Viking activities both in terms of scale and organisation. Its very name signifies that it represented a very significant escalation on previous Viking expeditions. This army was almost certainly more than a coastal raiding force and more apparently than the force of reportedly '350 ships' which stormed Canterbury and London in 851. It was certainly designed and equipped to remain in England not just over a winter but, if necessary, for a number of years. It also paid close attention to the local political scene showing an uncanny ability to target and exploit division and weakness wherever it was to be found. The intelligence gathered by the Scandinavians during their years of trading and on their previous raids clearly provided them with unrivalled information on the political and military strengths and weaknesses of each of the individual English kingdoms.[11]

In 865 this 'great army' landed first not in Mercia or Wessex but in the smaller and weaker kingdom of East Anglia. The sheer size of their force proved sufficient to overawe King Edmund and the East Angles, who according to the Chronicle immediately 'made peace with them', in this case probably a euphemism for swift and abject submission. The latter is made clear by the subsequent actions of the East Angles. They not only provided the Viking army with quarters over the winter but also, in the spring of the following year supplied them with horses to allow them to mount an effective land campaign in England. They probably also provided up-to-date intelligence information on the political situation in the various English kingdoms. It was probably this information which provided the Vikings with their next target.

In the autumn of 866 the Viking army moved swiftly northwards through Mercia and across the river Humber into the ancient kingdom of Northumbria. They probably left behind a small garrison to watch over their interests in East Anglia. They were drawn north by the knowledge that Northumbria was in the throes of a period of the most bitter civil strife. The throne was currently in dispute between two rival candidates, Osberht and Aelle, and their respective supporters. The legitimate but unpopular King of Northumbria, Osberht, had recently been overthrown by a powerful group of nobles, who had then elevated Aelle to the throne. The latter could offer no legitimate claim himself but, nevertheless, had powerful support. However, neither candidate had been able to eliminate his rival or gain complete control of the kingdom, which remained dangerously divided between the rival factions. In this condition, Northumbria was clearly vulnerable to outside intervention and the Vikings intended to exploit this opportunity to the full.[12]

As a result of the disunity in Northumbria, the 'great army' was able to occupy the key city of York on 1 November 866 without opposition. A heathen army had seized control of what was to all intents and purposes the capital of the kingdom and one of the great Christian centres of England virtually unopposed. The Northumbrians appear to have been stunned by this dramatic turn of events. Indeed, it had sufficient impact to cause the previously bitter rivals, Osberht and Aelle, to finally put aside their differences and negotiate a truce. This took some time and it was spring of the following year before the rivals were able to combine their forces and prepare to oppose the Viking army.

The joint Northumbrian army, which assembled in spring 867, was a large one and its leaders apparently felt confident that they could deal with the Vikings. This is evident from their decision to attack the Viking force although it had retreated behind the refuge of the repaired Roman fortifications of the city. This put the

Northumbrians at a considerable disadvantage in assaulting a fortified position which the Vikings had had time to prepare for defence. In spite of this, the Northumbrian army managed to penetrate the walls and enter the city itself. In the process, however, they suffered such immense losses that the Vikings were able to turn the tables on them. As a result, the Northumbrian army was completely defeated and destroyed and both of the rival kings and eight of their *ealdormen* were killed. This disaster occurred on 23 March 867 and placed the now defenceless kingdom at the mercy of the Vikings. In the aftermath, the Northumbrians were obliged to submit to their enemy, who spent the summer of 867 raiding unhindered through Northumbria as far north as the river Tyne. According to later accounts, the Vikings then appointed a man named Egbert to rule the kingdom in subordination to their overlordship. The origins of this man are unknown but it seems likely that he was a member of the local nobility with a following of some size other-

Viking warrior from a cross face, St Andrew's Church, Middleton, N. Yorkshire. (York Archaeological Trust)

wise he would have been unable to serve his new masters effectively. He was clearly expected to keep the Northumbrians quiet and ensure that they provided the Vikings with whatever they wanted. Once again a small garrison was probably left in York to keep an eye on him.[13]

The prominence given to these events in the Chronicle clearly indicates that they were a completely new and sinister departure in the history of the English kingdoms. One of the major English kingdoms, one with a long and glorious past, had to all intents and purposes been conquered by this Viking army. This development must have been viewed with anguish and concern in the other English kingdoms, and particularly in neighbouring Mercia. Indeed, the Mercians were well advised to be concerned for they themselves would very shortly be facing the menace presented by this victorious army.

In 868 the Viking army left a ravaged and subdued Northumbria behind them and entered Mercian territory. The Mercians were apparently unable either to block their progress or to bring them to battle before they reached Nottingham on the river

Trent. The Vikings proceeded to set up winter quarters in that fortress. Whether this was an existing Mercian fortress built to defend the border with Northumbria and similar to that excavated at Hereford on the Welsh borders, or a new construction by the Vikings themselves is unclear. In light of the disastrous experience of the Northumbrians, King Burgred wisely decided not to tackle this powerful force alone in its secure base. Instead, he and his *witan* met and invoked military assistance from his brother-in-law, King Aethelred of Wessex, under the terms of the alliance made with King Aethelwulf. Undoubtedly, he hoped that the combined forces of the two kingdoms would be able to defeat the Vikings where the Northumbrians alone had failed. King Aethelred, accompanied by his younger brother Alfred, duly brought his West Saxon army northward through Mercia to Nottingham.[14]

King Aethelred and his forces linked up with King Burgred and his Mercian army outside the Viking fortress at Nottingham. As they had done at York in the previous year, the Vikings remained within their fortress and dared the English forces to attack them. However, on this occasion the English kings, reasonably enough, chose not to attempt to storm the strongly fortified position but instead settled down to undertake a siege. It is not clear how long this siege lasted, perhaps until the autumn, but in the end it proved inconclusive. The Chronicle says only that there was 'no serious fighting' and that the Mercians made peace. Why had all the efforts of the two allied kingdoms apparently come to nothing in this way?

It seems most probable that the siege of Nottingham went on for some time and assumed the aspect of a stand-off. The Viking army could not risk venturing out of the fortress while the English forces would not risk assaulting it. This situation could not continue indefinitely and one side or the other must eventually have run short of supplies. The Vikings probably had the smaller force and, although they could no longer forage for supplies, had perhaps been able to secure sufficient from the surrounding region before the siege began. The combined English armies were probably significantly larger and, although they had greater access to supplies, many of their men had obligations on their own lands at home. As a result, it seems most likely that the allied armies began to break up first, especially if the siege ran on into autumn. The men involved would then have needed to return home to gather their own harvest and could not be retained any longer. It would, in many ways, not be surprising if it had been the West Saxons who withdrew from Nottingham first. They were, after all, operating further from their own homes and in defence of the lands of men, whom many probably considered as foreigners and some as enemies.

We will probably never know the precise situation but it seems likely that King Burgred, abandoned by his allies and with his own forces dispersed, made peace with the Vikings. He could not expel them by force but nor could he simply leave them where they were. It seems most likely that they remained quiet thereafter and returned the following year to York. Although there is no direct evidence for this, the Vikings presumably agreed to withdraw in return for some form of payment in cash or kind. This also apparently allowed them to replenish their supplies and recover from their losses over the winter before heading back to their base at York. In return they presumably undertook to withdraw without further damaging Mercian territory. It is even possible they may have agreed not to return to Mercia for a year since they remained quiescent in Northumbria for a period of more than a year after their withdrawal. Of course, this may simply have been a result of the need to replenish any losses due to starvation and disease suffered during the siege. In the short term, Burgred's action resolved his immediate difficulty but in the longer term it may simply have encouraged the Vikings to try their luck again in the hope of further payment.

On this occasion, the West Saxon alliance was probably an important factor in preserving the Mercian kingdom from more widespread devastation and possibly from conquest. It initially helped to keep the Viking army bottled up in Nottingham and thereafter contributed to persuading them to retreat. The allies had failed to defeat the enemy but they had at least avoided the fate suffered by the Northumbrians and East Anglians before them. It was in this same year, according to Asser and John of Worcester, and perhaps during this joint campaign, that a further marriage took place between these allies. *Atheling* Alfred of Wessex married Ealhswith, daughter of Aethelred Mucil, *Ealdorman* of the *Gainas*. This second marriage was probably intended to reinforce the bonds between the allies since Aethelred Mucil is probably the same man, who can be found as a prominent witness under the name Mucel in a number of King Burgred's charters. However, it is also possible that this campaign sowed the first doubts about the value of this alliance in the minds of some in Mercia. Doubts that would ultimately undermine it completely. Indeed, the effect of a West Saxon withdrawal from Nottingham, if such occurred, must have caused some to reconsider an alliance which had encouraged them to oppose the Vikings only to abandon them

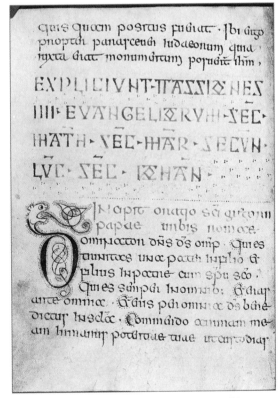

Page from the Book of Nunnaminster, possibly owned by Ealhswith, the Mercian wife of King Alfred. (BL Harley 2965, f. 16v)

later to buying them off. Undoubtedly, those opposed to King Burgred and the alliance in the first place would have exploited this opportunity.[15]

In 870 the Viking army resumed its raiding activities after a year of rest and recuperation at York. They must, by now, have severely depleted the available supplies in Northumbria especially after the devastation inflicted in 867. On this occasion, although the Vikings once again entered Mercian territory, they did so only in order to pass through it to reach their real target, the kingdom of East Anglia. It is possible that King Edmund of East Anglia had rebelled against his Viking overlords and that he therefore had to be dealt with. The apparent frustration of the Viking assault on Mercia in 868 may have encouraged him to take such a step. It is also possible that the tough resistance presented by the combined forces of Mercia and Wessex at Nottingham had convinced the Vikings themselves to look for a softer target. In this context East Anglia, which had had four years to recover from the effects of the Viking occupation of 865, provided a convenient alternative.[16]

The Viking force successfully managed to pass through Mercian territory unscathed on their way to East Anglia. The reason for this may have been that, on this occasion, the Mercians were not provided with enough warning to enable them to mobilise their forces to oppose them or that they may simply have been reluctant to do so without West Saxon support. Alternatively they may have agreed to permit them passage on the understanding that they left Mercian territory untouched. The East Anglians had made a similar sort of deal in 865 although in their case a significant element of coercion was involved with the Vikings actually in occupation of the land at the time.

In any case, the Viking army took up winter quarters at Thetford on the borders of the Fens. It seems clear that on this occasion, King Edmund of East Anglia elected not to make peace or submit to the army but to oppose them. This perhaps lends credence to the notion that he had already rebelled against their authority although it might simply be a response to their return to plunder his already ravaged kingdom once again. He apparently attempted to catch them unawares by attacking them in their winter camp at Thetford. However, as the Northumbrians had discovered at York in 866, the Vikings were formidable opponents when safely ensconced behind fortifications. The resulting battle was a disaster in which King Edmund and his army were utterly defeated and the king himself slain. The Vikings were now free to raid at leisure throughout East Anglia.[17]

In the following year, 871, the Vikings moved from East Anglia to invade Wessex, advancing up the Thames to Reading in Berkshire and probably building a fortress there. They again crossed Mercian territory in order to reach their objective but once again whether this was done with Mercian consent or by default we do not know. The West Saxons sought to oppose the Vikings militarily and initially attempted to target their foraging parties. The immediate results of this sensible strategy were promising, with a small force of Vikings under two *jarls* surprised and defeated at Englefield by a local West Saxon force under the former Mercian *ealdorman*, Aethelwulf of Berkshire. In the wake of this minor local victory, however, King Aethelred may have become overconfident as he now chose to bring up the main West Saxon army to assault the Viking fortress at Reading. In light of earlier Northumbrian and East Anglian experiences, the result was disappointingly predictable; a West Saxon defeat and the death of *Ealdorman* Aethelwulf. Thereafter, the Chronicle records that the West Saxons fought a series of engagements with the Vikings and the impression is given that the former had the latter on the run. This appears to be a rather partisan account of what was probably, in fact, a rather unsatisfactory and frustrating campaign from the West Saxon standpoint which resulted at best in a stalemate. In almost all of the engagements that are recounted in any detail it is stated that the Vikings either won or 'held the field of slaughter', the latter phrase usually carrying the implication of victory. The single exception to this pattern is the battle of Ashdown which is recorded as a West Saxon victory. However, even this struggle went on until nightfall and, if victorious, may have been a rather pyrrhic victory.[18]

In the end, it is admitted in the Chronicle that the West Saxons had to make peace with the Vikings like others before them. This suggests that most of the battles in this campaign amounted to little more than skirmishes, with the exception of Ashdown, and that the West Saxons were, in fact, far from having the upper hand. The fact that the Vikings had received significant reinforcements during this year in the shape of a 'great summer army' – probably led by the three kings, Guthrum, Osketel and Anwend, and arriving at Reading either from the Continent or direct from Scandinavia – makes the West Saxons lack of success all the more understandable. It seems likely that their constant harrying of the Viking army resulted at most in encouraging them to withdraw from Wessex to try their luck elsewhere.

The sudden wealth of information provided in the Chronicle text about Viking activities in Wessex in 871 and on the defensive measures adopted to oppose them should set alarm bells ringing about the nature and origins of this source. It contrasts vividly with the relative dearth of information about their earlier activities in East Anglia, Northumbria and Mercia. A reading of the Chronicle text reveals quite clearly that it is, quite legitimately, essentially only interested in portraying events occurring in Wessex and usually in a way positive to King Alfred. It only reveals the barest details of events elsewhere and in this process may omit a great deal of what actually happened. In light of this fact and its general acceptance among historians, it is surprising how many of the latter continue to write as though Wessex was the only

English kingdom to significantly resist the Viking onslaught. It seems most unlikely that this should be the case. Indeed, there are hints in the later account provided by Roger of Wendover, that this was not so. In most cases, however, we have no alternative sources for events and it is unlikely that we will ever recover them. It is therefore important to keep in mind that the Chronicle seldom reveals the whole story of this period.

In all of the West Saxon campaigns during 871 there is no indication of any Mercian involvement. What had happened to the alliance between Mercia and Wessex which had promised so much? Is it simply the case that the West Saxon Chronicle text fails to record the Mercian contribution to West Saxon defensive efforts? This is possible but perhaps unlikely since the same account makes no reference to West Saxon aid for Mercia in the following year. It seems more likely that the possible early withdrawal of the West Saxons from Nottingham in 868 had made the Mercians reluctant to aid the former now. It would seem that the alliance, which had been the foundation for many hopes of resistance to the Vikings had, in fact, quickly crumbled. It should be noted that the sort of internal tensions, existing within Mercia and previously exploited by rival claimants, had not disappeared but remained just under the surface ready to break out at any time. It seems likely that many Mercian nobles were disenchanted with the policies of King Burgred. He had after all proved unable or unwilling to oppose the Vikings effectively but had instead offered a humiliating and no doubt expensive tribute to buy them off. Staunch supporters of the 'C' dynasty had probably opposed him from the start. The lands of many others particularly in the eastern part of Mercia may have suffered from the passage of Viking armies in recent years. Others still may have resented being tied to an alliance with their West Saxon rivals which had proved unable to deal with the Viking problem. The ranks of such discontented men had perhaps grown large enough to oppose any direct action in support of Wessex.

In the following year, 872, the Vikings moved back down the Thames crossing from Wessex into Mercia and occupied London. If the collapse of the alliance with Mercia had indeed already happened, with the Mercians failing to support the West Saxons in 871, it seems highly unlikely that the West Saxons would wish to aid the Mercians now. Even if this were not the case, the West Saxons must still have been licking the wounds suffered during the many battles of the previous year. In either event, the Mercians could probably no longer expect any help from the West Saxons. In the absence of his West Saxon allies, King Burgred of Mercia chose, once again, to make peace with the Vikings and to permit them to occupy London unopposed. It is on this occasion that a charter of Bishop Waerferth of Worcester records the collection and payment of an 'immense tribute' to buy off the Vikings in London. It is worth noting here that until this date the Viking army had not invaded Mercia directly since their advance to Nottingham in 868. Instead, they had limited their activities against the kingdom to taking passage through its border regions around Lindsey and London to reach other kingdoms. This situation would change in the next couple of years as the Vikings began to sense a weakness in the Mercian body politic but, for the moment, events in Northumbria caused them to return north.[19]

In 872, according to northern annals preserved in the thirteenth-century chronicle of Roger of Wendover, the Northumbrians followed the tragic example of the East Angles and rebelled against Viking overlordship. They drove out King Egbert and Archbishop Wulfhere of York, who had led the puppet government submissive to Viking demands. They were obviously not prepared to lead such a revolt and instead sought refuge with King Burgred in neighbouring Mercia, where they were honourably received. At first sight it is difficult to understand why Burgred received these exiles so favourably since they had been supporters of his Viking foes, albeit reluctant ones. He may have felt a great deal of sympathy for their plight as a man similarly forced to compromise while under increasing pressure to resist the Vikings more actively. It may also perhaps be suggested that he hoped to curry favour with the Vikings, who posed an increasingly dangerous threat to his own kingdom, by sheltering their supporters in this way. It was certainly becoming increasingly important and necessary for Burgred to reach some kind of understanding or accommodation with the Vikings now that he could no longer rely on the West Saxon alliance. If this was Burgred's hope then sadly it would prove ill-founded.[20]

In 873 the Viking army moved north from London, probably through Mercian territory, and perhaps under an agreement made with King Burgred as part of his efforts to pacify them. They probably entered Northumbria and crushed the rebellion there, temporarily restoring their candidate King Egbert to his throne and securing the recall of Archbishop Wulfhere. The restoration of these men is noted by Roger of Wendover and Simeon of Durham although neither says how this was achieved. Thereafter, the Vikings based themselves at Torksey in Lindsey for the winter from where they could monitor their recent conquests in Northumbria and East Anglia and directly threaten Mercia. This placed them in occupation of part of Mercia and induced King Burgred to make peace with them yet again. If he was indeed now pursuing a policy of appeasement towards the Vikings this was no doubt an attempt to avoid antagonising them. This policy carried distinct dangers in terms of presenting the Vikings with an image of weakness and an invitation to attack but perhaps there was now no alternative. Burgred seems to have hoped that the Vikings could continue to be induced into attacking other kingdoms by his own submissive posture. What had brought him to this position?[21]

The failure of the West Saxon alliance was clearly a major factor in undermining Mercian ability to resist the Vikings. They clearly felt unable to offer effective military resistance without West Saxon aid. The early fall of the kingdoms of East Anglia and Northumbria had deprived the Mercians of other possible allies. On their own they were naturally reluctant to provoke a Viking attack but should still have been in a position to offer some sort of defence. The reason that they did not attempt this was perhaps the revival of the old rivalry with the 'C' dynasty. The latter had found a new champion in a man named Ceolwulf, whose relationship to previous members of the dynasty is unfortunately unknown (see Table 1, p. 208). In view of recent events, it seems likely that many Mercian nobles were unhappy with the lack of action against the Vikings on the part of King Burgred. The lands of some of these men may have suffered from the passage of Viking armies in recent years. Others may have resented being tied to an alliance with their West Saxon rivals which had proved ineffective. These men and others discontented with their lot under King Burgred would have gravitated towards the party gathered around Ceolwulf. They probably presented a significant factor in undermining Burgred's authority within Mercia and therefore in his reluctance to antagonise the Vikings.

In 874 King Burgred was finally forced to recognise that his new strategy had failed completely. The Viking army advanced from Torksey directly into the heartland of Mercia and seized the royal mausoleum at Repton. This must have been a shattering blow to Mercian morale and to King Burgred in particular. If any resistance was offered it was apparently considered unworthy of record. The kingdom of Mercia now submitted completely to the Vikings, like East Anglia and Northumbria before it. King Burgred was deposed and driven into exile, probably initially in Wessex and thereafter on the Continent. He journeyed across Europe to Rome accompanied by his wife Aethelswith, the symbol of his defunct alliance with Wessex. It is fortunate that a contemporary record of these exiles has been preserved in the *Liber Vitae* of the monastery of S. Salvatore in Brescia in Northern Italy, which lay on the route taken by English pilgrims to Rome. This book recorded the names of important people who wished to be remembered in the prayers of the monks. It records the names of King Burgred and Queen Aethelswith and of five men and three women of their party. It seems that King Burgred had taken to heart a letter sent to him by Pope John VIII a year earlier which had attributed his misfortunes to his sins and those of his people. He now sought out the shrines of St Peter and St Paul in order to receive absolution, and perhaps the restoration of his fortunes. In fact, Burgred remained in Rome until his death, which may have occurred fairly soon after this, and he was buried in St Mary's Church in the English quarter. It appears that his widow, Queen Aethelswith, lived on in Rome for fourteen years and, according to the Chronicle, she died and was buried in Pavia in 888. It is usually assumed that she

Ring of Queen
Aethelswith. (Copyright
British Museum)

was living there by this time, but it is also possible that she was on her way home to England, perhaps with the intention of ending her days there.[22]

What had happened to Mercia following King Burgred's departure? The Chronicle says that the Vikings 'gave' the kingdom to Ceolwulf, 'a foolish king's *thegn*'. The implication is that they had appointed a subordinate ruler for Mercia just as they had earlier appointed Egbert to rule Northumbria on their behalf. This account of the events of this catastrophic year for the Mercian kingdom makes it appear that the Vikings dealt with Mercia as they wished. However, there are perhaps grounds for suggesting that the Mercians had an involvement in directing at least some of these events. The Chronicle is compiled from a West Saxon viewpoint and its account of this year in particular appears to have been heavily influenced by this. The clue to this lies in the extremely derogatory references to Ceolwulf which carry the clear inference that he was not a legitimate ruler. In contrast, the evidence of surviving Mercian charters and the coinage indicates quite clearly that the opposite was the case. King Ceolwulf II was clearly regarded as a legitimate ruler of Mercia and recognised in Mercia itself as such. There can surely be little doubt that he was a member of the 'C' dynasty of Kings Cenwulf and Ceolwulf I and hence carried a valid claim to the throne. West Saxon efforts to undermine his status were perhaps inspired by his dismissal of their former ally King Burgred and his rejection of the policy of alliance with Wessex.[23]

This knowledge casts a very different light on the events of 874 as recorded in the Chronicle. It seems certain that it was the Viking invasion which brought about the deposition of King Burgred but it is less certain that it was the Vikings that actually deposed him. It is perhaps more likely that the Viking assault caused the entire Mercian nobility to lose faith in Burgred. He had now demonstrably failed in his efforts to protect the kingdom and they now abandoned him. Instead, they turned to the rival 'C' dynasty. If this scenario is correct then it was the Mercians themselves who deposed Burgred and drove him into exile. The Vikings provided the catalyst for political change within Mercia itself rather than themselves bringing about that change. The Mercians probably hoped that, in the future, a more positive response to the Vikings would be the eventual result. In the immediate circumstances of 874 this was clearly impossible and the new king had little option but to submit to the overlordship of the Vikings.

It has been suggested that the appearance of common designs on the coins of King Ceolwulf II and King Alfred signifies that he was an ally of Alfred, like his predecessor King Burgred. Thus the so-called 'two emperors' and 'cross and lozenge' coinages were minted in the names of both of these kings. However, in contrast to the case with Burgred and Alfred noted above, the evidence of the Chronicle strongly suggests that this was far from the case. The venom and contempt contained in its references to Ceolwulf II make it clear that, when these entries were composed, the West Saxons considered him to be no friend of theirs. It seems far more likely that these coins were minted to the same design in an attempt to ease the process of exchange and to encourage trade rather than to signify any political arrangement. The fact that a coin exists showing this same design but bearing the name of Halfdan, the later Danish king of Northumbria, suggests that this was the case. The latter was certainly no ally of the English but he was attempting to gain the same trading advantages as his English neighbours by mimicking their coins.[24]

During this period, the political situation in London, where these coins are believed to have been minted, is almost completely unknown. It is possible that it remained under Viking control: it could equally have returned to Mercian control or have fallen under West Saxon control. It is also possible that it remained under no direct political control but was left to fend for itself in the debatable zone between the rival spheres of influence of these three parties. In these circumstances it is difficult to be sure how its moneyers were able to continue to operate their mints. They may have fled to safer areas taking their skills with them or they may have continued to operate from London on a freelance basis minting coins to a required design for anyone who could supply the necessary bullion. Either of these scenarios might explain the common designs in use by London moneyers for coins minted in the names of three different kings. King Alfred may have minted these coins using moneyers who had fled from London into Wessex to escape the attention of the Vikings. The same designs were then adopted by King Ceolwulf for the economic reasons noted above and minted by other moneyers who had also fled from London but this time into Mercia. Finally, the design was again borrowed by Halfdan, newly settled in Northumbria, in an attempt to establish a presence in the English trading system also using experienced London moneyers, perhaps captured during Viking raids on London.

What is clear is that, in 874, the Mercian kingdom had been reduced to a miserable condition. It had been compelled to submit to Viking overlordship. Its new king had had to swear oaths of allegiance and give hostages to the Viking leaders and agree to assist and serve them. A Viking army was stationed in the heart of the kingdom freely raiding its rich lands and monasteries. The picture was not entirely black, however, and there remained a number of factors which foreshadowed the survival of the kingdom. The Mercians had probably replaced their own ruler rather than allowing the Vikings to do so, which suggests that they retained some control over their own affairs. In addition, there remained large areas of the kingdom, in the south and west particularly, which still lay beyond Viking reach and hence relatively unscathed. This left some grounds for hope that the kingdom might somehow survive its present circumstances to rise once again.[25]

In 875 the Viking army finally abandoned their camp at Repton, no doubt encouraged in this process by the significant losses they had suffered

Replica of a Mercian decorated grave slab, St Wystan's Church, Repton, Derbyshire. (Photograph by W. Walker)

from disease while based there. This time instead of the entire force moving on to their next target the army divided into two groups under different leaders. The first under Halfdan marched north to Northumbria and after camping on the river Tyne for a year dispersed to settle on the land in 876. The second force, under the three kings Guthrum, Osketel and Anwend, moved south-east to Cambridge and took up quarters there over the winter while raiding the surrounding countryside. It is not certain but it seems likely that these leaders separated because they represented different groups of Vikings with their own priorities. The force under Halfdan were probably mainly survivors of the original 'great army' of 865 now reduced by warfare and disease to a shadow of its former self. They had clearly had their fill of plunder and were now ready for a more permanent reward in terms of land. The group under the three kings was probably part of the 'great summer army', which had only arrived in England in 871 and was therefore still fresh and ready for more raiding.[26]

The crisis was still far from over, and the fate of the English kingdoms still hung in the balance. The Vikings at Cambridge probably drew tribute from Mercia again during their stay there. King Ceolwulf was being compelled by the active presence of the Viking army to follow very similar policies to those of his predecessor. He may have attempted to resist them but if so we have no record of it. He may even have had to abandon areas of eastern Mercia to them. This could not have been a very satisfactory result for those Mercians who had supported Ceolwulf in place of Burgred. Nevertheless, it was perhaps a wise course to follow and almost certainly a necessary one. A measure of hope was perhaps restored the following year when the Vikings decided to focus their attention once again on Wessex. Indeed, it is possible that this action may have been encouraged by Ceolwulf both as a means of removing the Vikings from Mercian territory but also as a way of inflicting damage on his West Saxon enemies. The personal nature of the hostility shown towards him, by the West Saxon compiler of the Chronicle, may have seemed sufficient justification for such a response. Alternatively, the origins of this personal animosity towards Ceolwulf in the Chronicle may lie in what could be seen as a treacherous act by a fellow Christian.

In the years 876 and 877 the Vikings invaded Wessex and based themselves in Dorset and Devon, inflicting great damage on the local area and twice forcing King Alfred to make peace with them. As in 871, the Chronicle provides a great deal of detail about the campaigns and about the peace terms arranged on these occasions. It hints that the peace terms were in some way 'special' and that they involved new concessions on the part of the Vikings. This is no doubt intended to demonstrate King Alfred's superiority over other English rulers and particularly his superior abilities in dealing with the Vikings. How far can we rely on the statements made by the Chronicle on these matters?[27]

In 876 the Vikings traversed Wessex, easily avoiding the West Saxon army to reach Wareham without loss. Thereafter, there is no record of any subsequent battle or siege at Wareham but simply the statement that Alfred made peace with the Vikings there. There is no immediately apparent difference between the circumstances facing Alfred on this occasion and those facing Burgred of Mercia in 872 or 873. The specific reference in the Chronicle to the Vikings offering hostages and agreeing to swear oaths to secure the peace terms may be a new concession but might equally have accompanied previous such agreements. Certainly, such actions were fairly standard elements of the guarantees surrounding treaties during this period. It is difficult to see what purpose there was in accepting a peace treaty which was not accompanied by some such guarantees. If it was the intention to demonstrate that Alfred had secured additional guarantees which would make the peace terms effective then this is undermined by what immediately follows. The Vikings demonstrated the worthlessness of these 'new' concessions by instantly breaking them and occupying Exeter.

It was at Exeter in 877 that King Alfred did achieve a success of some sort. He pursued the Vikings to Exeter and probably besieged them there although this is not specifically stated. The most important factor in his success, however, was undoubtedly the loss of a major proportion of the Viking fleet in a storm off Swanage. It was this which probably persuaded the Vikings to strike a deal with Alfred and to stick to it. Once again however, this was probably not a spectacular breakthrough by Alfred but rather another mutual agreement between the parties concerned. The crucial factor was that this time the Vikings, in the face of the loss of their fleet, had to leave the West Saxon kingdom and hence they returned to Mercia. It would become clear within the space of a year that this was no more than a temporary setback for the Vikings. King Alfred had not defeated them but only bought himself a little time.

In 877, then, the Viking army returned to Mercia and, according to the Chronicle, divided the kingdom between themselves and King Ceolwulf. This may be a simplification and compression of events that may have been more complex and taken place over a longer time scale. We have already seen how the Vikings had occupied London in 872, Torksey in 873, Repton in 874 and Cambridge in 875. It is notable that, with the exception of London, each of these places falls within the area of Danish settlement in Mercia later covered by the Danelaw. It is possible that when the main Viking army left each of these districts for pastures new they did not entirely abandon them but left small garrisons behind to safeguard their interests. They had probably done the same in East Anglia and York in earlier years. In 877, therefore, it is possible that what happened was that they returned to settle areas already monitored by their garrisons. This settlement may have been a carefully prepared one like that which took place under Halfdan in Northumbria. It was possibly undertaken under the leadership of either Osketel or Anwend, who both disappear from the records at around this time. This would have left Guthrum alone to lead the Viking army to Gloucester and into Wessex the following year. There is no evidence in surviving sources for the Mercian reaction to this carve-up of their kingdom. There may have been no resistance at all; it may have been ineffectual; or it may have been just enough to secure the continued independent existence of the remainder of Mercia. It is worth noting that while the Vikings would settle all of East Anglia and all of Northumbria south of the Tyne, they would ultimately only settle the north-eastern portion of Mercia. Of course, this difference might simply reflect the relative size of the Viking force involved, which could not absorb any more territory, but it could also have been a concession to Mercian resistance.[28]

How had this Viking army managed to overwhelm three English kingdoms, two of them large and well resourced, in such a short space of time? There has been a great deal of argument about the exact physical size of this 'great army', with calculations ranging from 600 to 4,000 men. Sawyer's earlier warnings to be cautious about possible exaggeration of the numbers involved in these raids according to contemporary accounts remains useful but should not force us to disregard any large number quoted simply because it is large. Many contemporary writers could count and could therefore recognise a tenfold increase in ship numbers when they saw it. A few numbers are clearly exaggerations but these are usually fairly easy to spot and should not prevent us from trusting the many others which show no obvious signs of this. The increase in the numbers of ships recorded by contemporaries both in England and on the Continent between the 800s and the 830s is not imaginary but is reflected in the increasing impact of the forces involved. They had expanded from small largely coastal hit and run attacks into more extensive attacks against larger centres and sometimes on inland sites. In addition, it must be remembered that Viking armies did not remain a consistent size for any length of time. They were able to divide up quite easily, as in 875, and were sometimes reinforced, as in 871. They often left garrisons in conquered districts, and crews with their accompanying fleets. They suffered almost continuous losses through a mixture of military action and disease. In these circumstances it would not be surprising to find a great deal of variance in estimates of their numbers.[29]

The arguments for a small 'great army' have been rendered increasingly untenable by recent archaeological discoveries at Repton in Mercia. The discovery there of a mass grave containing no less than 245 bodies close to the Viking fortress constructed on this site in 874 has finally provided us with some tangible evidence. These bodies consisted mostly of males aged between fifteen and forty-five, who were almost certainly Viking warriors buried in company with an important leader. The latter may possibly have been Osketel or Anwend, who both disappear from the records at around this time. The bodies showed no obvious signs of wounds and therefore probably represent victims of hunger or disease. If the army present at Repton in 874/5 could afford to lose 250 men to disease and then divide into two groups, each individually large enough to undertake the settlement of Northumbria and the assault on Wessex respectively, it was surely larger than the few hundreds envisaged by Sawyer. It almost certainly consisted of thousands rather than hundreds of men.[30]

Whatever the exact figures, it seems unlikely that the Vikings could ever have projected and maintained across the North Sea forces larger than those that the three major English kingdoms of Mercia, Wessex and Northumbria could have brought against them. It was not therefore a simple superiority in numbers that achieved these remarkable results, except possibly in the case of the smaller kingdom of East Anglia, but rather a superiority in organisation. The answer to the question, in fact, lies in the mobility and flexibility of the military organisation of the Viking army. It was these vital ingredients that enabled them to outwit, outrun and, where necessary, outfight the opposing English forces. All too often, individual English forces found themselves outnumbered, outflanked or outfaced by their often more experienced opponents.

The most important of these factors was probably mobility, whether by land or by water. This factor allowed the Vikings to strike without warning, inflict maximum

Viking mass grave from Repton.
(© Copyright Martin Biddle)

damage on their often unprepared opponents and then escape without significant losses. Not surprisingly in face of their skill as seamen, they made great use of their fleets of shallow-draught warships to mount rapid strikes against any point along the coastline or on a navigable stretch of river. This placed a large part of England within easy reach, while the rest could be covered on horseback. The Vikings could usually seize horses from their victims either in the form of tribute or booty, as in 865, but sometimes, as in 892, they brought them with them in their ships. The Vikings were also more mobile than their opponents because of their relative lack of encumbering baggage. They lived off the land and therefore did not require the sort of cumbersome supply train that would have reduced their mobility significantly. This mobility allowed them to avoid pitched battles except in the most favourable circumstances as at York in 867. The booty and captives that they collected while raiding could readily be left for safekeeping either with their fleet or in a fortified base camp. They could also, in cases of dire necessity, be abandoned or slaughtered to permit escape. This left their raiding force free to range at will, largely untrammelled. In addition, the Vikings of these early years knew that their own families and lands were safe from retaliation at home in Scandinavia. Consequently, they were free to campaign as ruthlessly as they wished against their victims in the certainty that their own loved ones and property were largely immune from attack.[31]

The other key factor in the success of the Viking army was their flexible organisation which allowed them to adapt readily to different circumstances. Each Viking army consisted of a series of smaller warbands each commanded by its own independent leader, the *hold* or *jarl*. They were probably bound together by oaths of fellowship like those of a later period, and certainly pledged by oath to follow their leader. The evidence for these small bands, which are variously called 'brotherhoods' or 'fellowships', can be found not only on later Viking runestones but also in contemporary annals. Runic inscriptions at Hedeby and Sjorup in Denmark record that those commemorated were *felagi*, or fellows, of those who raised and inscribed the stones. In 860 the *Annals of St Bertin* record that a large Viking force under Welland split up according to their *sodalitates*, or brotherhoods. These independent warbands were, in turn, gathered into a larger army by means of their individual leaders being pledged by oath to follow more important commanders or kings, like Halfdan or Guthrum.[32]

This arrangement made the Viking army extremely flexible. It could readily be broken up into its smaller component units and then be reconstituted in the same form or a different form as required. In this way, Viking forces could disperse to escape encirclement, as in 892, to forage, as in 871, or divide to tackle a number of different tasks, as in 875. They could just as readily combine with other forces into a larger army to form a concentrated force in preparation for a major operation such as a battle or siege. This flexibility also made it much easier to absorb reinforcements – as with the 'great summer army' of 871 – and to shed satiated or discontented elements, such as the Northumbrian settlers of 876 or those who left for the Continent in 896. Such manoeuvres might have left other armies in complete disarray but appear, in spite of some disruption, to have left the Viking army well able to maintain its fighting power.[33]

The individual Viking soldier was also very adaptable in a way which enhanced the overall flexibility of their army. He had the advantage of a wide range of useful skills learned from his rural background at home in small isolated hunting, farming and fishing communities. He possessed sufficient basic ship-handling skills or familiarity with ships and the sea to enable him to offer unrivalled abilities as a seaman. He had a familiarity with domestic animals that allowed him to handle horses for riding or pack transport and to slaughter cows, sheep or even horses for food. He could quickly construct earthworks for protection. He was equipped with the necessary fighting skills and in most cases these had already been honed over a number of years of active raiding throughout Europe.

In contrast to this the English armies of this initial period of Viking assaults lacked the same mobility and flexibility. This is not to suggest that contemporary English armies were either obsolescent or incompetent but rather that they were adapted to and equipped for a very different kind of warfare. The individual English soldiers possessed most of the same skills as their opponents since they came from a similar rural background, although specifically military skills were probably less well developed. The majority of Englishmen were landsmen from areas far from the sea and, as such, were completely lacking in the skills associated with seafaring. The English armies were designed to undertake regular, usually seasonal, offensive or defensive land campaigns against neighbouring kingdoms. In terms of defence, they had almost no experience of raids from the sea and all their defensive preparations were based on their land borders and designed to face familiar Welsh or English opponents. In attack, they normally faced opposing forces very similar to their own and their favoured tactic was to ravage their opponents' lands to force their submission while seeking to prevent them raiding their own lands. This style of warfare favoured the use of relatively large forces to maximise the extent of the ravaging while also allowing for reserve forces to prevent retaliation.[34]

In their initial operations against the Vikings, the English found themselves deprived of their customary target and ill-equipped to catch the smaller swift-moving Viking armies with their slow-forming and slow-moving larger forces. They had no defence against the sudden assaults undertaken by the concentrated might of the 'great army'. The defence forces of the local area - the only forces able to group quickly enough to oppose the initial attack – were too small to inflict more than

The Abingdon Sword. (Ashmolean Museum, Oxford)

minor losses on the Viking army. There was simply not enough time to gather the size of army that was necessary to bring the Vikings to battle and defeat them. Once formed, however, this larger English army was to prove too unmanageable and cumbersome to catch the Viking force when it had moved on to raid other areas. On the few occasions when English forces were able to catch up with the Viking army, the latter retreated behind fortifications that the English were either unwilling to assault as in 868 or unsuccessful in doing so as in 867 and 871. The English attempts at siege warfare were usually abandoned when the supplies needed for their large forces ran out or the term of service of their troops ended as in 868. The English were not trained or equipped to deal with such a mobile enemy in the field or to assault defended fortifications of which there were relatively few in England. They were also unable to strike back at the Vikings' own lands or people since they were far away across the sea. In short, they faced an impossible task trying to deal with this new threat with armies neither designed nor equipped for the purpose. In this context the initial success of the Vikings is not perhaps so surprising. If the English could adapt, then things might be very different but first they had to survive.[35]

It was now a question of transforming the English military forces into smaller but better equipped and more flexible units, the kind of units capable of pursuing and catching the Viking raiders and defeating them in battle. This process required time and if Mercia and Wessex could not survive long enough for this reorganisation to be completed successfully, they would succumb to Viking occupation just as East Anglia and Northumbria had before them. They had to continue the struggle for as long as possible and using any means, including treaties and tribute payments, to give themselves breathing space to reorganise. Only time would tell if either of them would succeed.

CHAPTER 4

The Struggle for Survival

In the year 877 the kingdom of Mercia appeared to be on the brink of collapse, a mere shadow of its former glory, ripe for Viking conquest and destined to be snuffed out as surely as Northumbria and East Anglia before it. In contrast, by 911 it had risen like a phoenix from the ashes to stand alongside Wessex as one of the springboards for the recovery of the English kingdoms and the reconquest of Viking-occupied territory. How was this remarkable turnaround achieved?

The short answer is that we simply do not know for certain. This period of Mercian history is particularly obscure, and for the first half of it almost no sources survive from Mercia to shed even a faint shaft of light on events. The focus of the sources from this period on King Alfred and Wessex is readily apparent from the large number of books historians have written about him. How then can we understand what happened in Mercia during these years? The best that we can do is to look at the few facts that do survive about events in Mercia at this time and consider these in light of what happened in other lands under Viking assault. This process can at least offer us some suggestions as to how Mercia may have survived through this period as a cohesive entity.[1]

First, we need to consider the origins of the man who probably masterminded this transformation, Lord Aethelred. He was a royal *ealdorman* whose power base lay in the south-west of Mercia in the former kingdom of the *Hwicce* around Gloucester. He may have been the man of this name who witnessed charters of King Burgred in 866 and 869, and who was granted land by this same king at Lydney in Gloucestershire. He had close connections with Berkeley Abbey and with the city of Gloucester itself and its ancient minster of St Peter. He would build a splendid new minster church, initially dedicated to St Peter, in the city and would later be buried in it. He would also translate the relics of the great Northumbrian royal saint, Oswald, to this new minster, which would be known thereafter as St Oswald's. On the evidence of his Gloucester associations, Aethelred can be identified with reasonable confidence as *Ealdorman* of the *Hwicce*.[2]

He can also, although somewhat more tentatively, be seen as a relative and successor of the earlier *Ealdorman* Aethelmund and his family (see Table 3, p. 210, for his

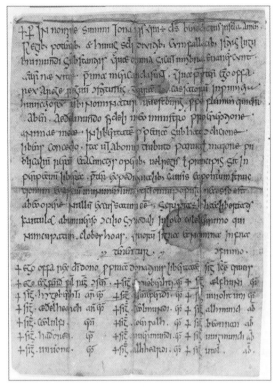

Charter of King Offa to his faithful minister
Aethelmund, an ancestor of Lord Aethelred?, 790s.
(BL Add. Charter 19790)

connections). The evidence for this link is mainly circumstantial and rests on a number of associations between these men and their families. The alliteration between their names Aethelred, Aethelmund and the latter's son Aethelric is suggestive but given the relative abundance of these names is not in itself enough. The fact that both men held the position of *ealdorman* of the *Hwicce* makes it possible that they are related and that the post descended through the family. However, such posts were royal appointments and therefore not necessarily held by a single family and so this cannot be certain. Both men shared an interest in St Peter's Minster in Gloucester and in the cathedral at Worcester, which they endowed with lands. This is interesting but not conclusive since any *ealdorman* of this region might be expected to patronise these important local churches. Perhaps the most interesting connection between the two men relates to land at Stoke Bishop and the Abbey of Berkeley both in Gloucestershire. In 804 Ceolburh, the widow of Aethelmund, was abbess of Berkeley when their son Aethelric made arrangements to grant land at Stoke Bishop to support her during her lifetime with reversion to Worcester at her death. In 883 Aethelred was granted land at Stoke Bishop by Berkeley Abbey in exchange for certain privileges and went on to grant this land to one of his *thegns* with reversion to Worcester after the latter's death. Is it possible that this indicates Aethelred was restoring a pledge made by his relatives nearly eighty years before? In the current state of our knowledge it is impossible to be certain but it is an interesting possibility. In summary we have only circumstantial evidence for this connection but cumulatively it looks quite impressive.[3]

We have seen in Chapter 3 that, in August 877, the Chronicle records that a Viking army, which was withdrawing from Exeter in Wessex, invaded Mercia and apparently enforced a partition of the kingdom on King Ceolwulf II. In the version of the Chronicle compiled by *Ealdorman* Aethelweard of Wessex in the tenth century can be found the following account of this year: '[the Vikings] . . . ravaged the kingdom of the Mercians . . . and with one involved movement encamped in the town of Gloucester.' This entry offers the possibility that it was Viking control of Gloucester which may have forced King Ceolwulf to accept this partition of Mercia but it also had another important consequence. If this was the case, it would effectively have placed a Viking army in control of the probable home base of Lord Aethelred of Mercia. In such disastrous circumstances, what happened to Aethelred himself? We know that he survived to fight another day but not how he did this. If we consider the reactions of other rulers faced with the sudden presence of an unwelcome and hostile Viking army on their territory a number of possibilities present themselves.[4]

It is probably fairly safe to assume that Aethelred did not actively oppose the Vikings on this occasion. It seems very likely that had he done so he would have met a similar fate to that endured by the rulers of East Anglia and Northumbria. They had chosen to engage the Viking army in open battle with disastrous results. They were utterly defeated in the fighting that followed and killed into the bargain. In view of his own limited resources it would have been folly for Aethelred even to attempt this.

It is possible that Aethelred made peace with the Vikings and paid them to leave his lands. As we have already seen, the payment of what was in effect 'protection money', whether in cash or in kind, was a fairly common response to Viking assaults. This policy had been followed by the people of Kent in 865, those of East Anglia in 866, and those of Mercia itself in 868, 872 and 873. We have already seen King Burgred raising funds to buy off the Viking army in 872. This sort of measure could be very effective in the short term as a means of deflecting Viking attention onto other targets. It worked well in East Anglia in 866 and in Mercia in 868 and 872 although it failed to achieve its aim in Kent in 865. In the longer term, however, the relatively easy profit it offered tended only to draw the Vikings back again in search of more of the same.[5]

It is also possible that Aethelred was forced to simply abandon his lands and flee either into hiding or into exile abroad. The former fate would shortly befall Alfred of Wessex when the Vikings forced him to seek refuge in the marshes around Athelney in Somerset. The latter fate had fallen on the Welsh leader Rhodri *Mawr* of Gwynedd who fled to Ireland in this very year of 877 and would subsequently befall Alan of Brittany in 919. In such circumstances there are a number of places where Aethelred may have sought refuge, including Wales, Wessex or even Ireland. The possibility of a flight to Ireland may seem the least likely option, partly in terms of convenience and partly because the level of contemporary Viking activity in Ireland must have rendered it a rather unsafe haven. The circumstances of Rhodri *Mawr*'s own flight to Ireland make it unlikely that Aethelred would have found refuge in North Wales. In contrast, neighbouring South Wales may have been free of Vikings at this time and could have offered Aethelred a convenient bolthole, although the traditional hostility between Mercians and Welsh might have precluded this. He may equally have sought refuge in neighbouring Wessex, the only English kingdom to remain free of Viking control at this time. This last option is perhaps the most attractive since it could provide an ideal opportunity for the origins of the later close relationship between Aethelred and Alfred of Wessex, which would subsequently bring them into alliance against the Vikings.[6]

There is another possible way, although perhaps a less savoury one, that Aethelred may have avoided destruction at the hands of the Viking army. This option was to submit to the Vikings and offer them tribute and/or assistance in planning their conquests elsewhere in return for being left unmolested. This may seem a rather 'cowardly' response to Viking attack but it was nonetheless effective in many cases and was widely adopted by the English. It had been employed by the East Angles in 866, by the Mercians in 869, 871 and 872. This alternative has the advantage that it might explain Aethelweard's reference to the Vikings having 'built booths' in Gloucester. This is the more literal translation of the phrase rendered by Campbell in the quotation above as 'encamped' and in the original Norse speech of the Vikings can signify trading activity. This may imply that the Vikings traded with the West Mercians while in Gloucester and perhaps that they even purchased supplies for their subsequent campaign in Wessex. Although such action would probably result in damage to fellow Englishmen in other kingdoms, we should not consider it in some way underhand. It should be remembered that all the English kingdoms had a long history of rivalry and conflict sufficient to excuse almost any action against each other. They may all have spoken dialects of one English language and considered themselves members of one English Church and, for some purposes, members of an English race but, first and foremost, they still thought of themselves as Mercian, West Saxon or Northumbrian. The Vikings in East Anglia in 866 had been given horses which they then used to invade and conquer Northumbria.[7]

What is not disputed is that, in the mid-winter of 878, the Viking army moved out of Gloucester and crossed the border into Wessex. They intended to catch King Alfred unawares and then occupy and settle Wessex just as they had already done in Northumbria, East Anglia and parts of Mercia. Shortly after 6 January, the Viking army advanced stealthily on the West Saxon royal palace at Chippenham in Wiltshire. They narrowly failed to capture the King, who was forced to flee with a small party to the temporary refuge provided by the Isle of Athelney in the Somerset marshes. The West Saxons, effectively deprived of their leader, finally submitted to Viking overlordship. At this point, it must have seemed to many that the Christian English were now doomed to live under pagan rule. This did not happen because of two vital episodes of survival, one well known and the other less well known, in the next few years. The first was the survival of King Alfred and the second the survival of part of the former kingdom of Mercia under Lord Aethelred. The story of Alfred's survival and the recovery of Wessex are well known, if not legendary. The story of Aethelred and the survival of Mercia is almost unknown, largely because it is unrecorded.[8]

We know very well that King Alfred held out behind fortifications he had built on the Isle of Athelney and struck back at the Viking occupiers of Wessex. He gradually built up his support in Wessex and spread the West Saxon resistance to the Vikings into Wiltshire and Hampshire. Finally, almost two months after Easter 878, he emerged to lead the men of Somerset, Wiltshire and West Hampshire against the Vikings under Guthrum. He defeated them in a battle at Edington in Wiltshire and forced them to flee to the fortress they had built at Chippenham. He went on to besiege them there for two weeks before hunger forced them to come to terms with him. The result was that Guthrum agreed to withdraw his army from Wessex and submit to Alfred's overlordship including accepting baptism. The formal submission took place some three weeks later at Wedmore, where Guthrum and twenty-nine of his leading followers were baptised – Guthrum adopting the name Athelstan – and swore oaths to their overlord Alfred. The incorporation of baptism into this ceremony suggests that it may have involved genuine concessions on the part of Guthrum as this is not known to have been accepted by members of this army as part of a treaty before this time. However, it would be an exaggeration to suggest as some have done that this ceremony was a surrender since we know that the Vikings remained at Chippenham rather than withdrawing immediately. Indeed, they did not withdraw from Wessex until the following year which suggests a mutual agreement between the parties rather than a surrender by Guthrum.[9]

The immediate consequence of this agreement was the withdrawal of the Viking army from Wessex the following year but a more lasting result was to follow. In 879 the army withdrew across the border to Cirencester in Southern Mercia and wintered there but in 880, it suspended its raiding activities altogether, withdrew into East Anglia and dispersed in order to settle the land. It had been raiding for nearly nine years now and had suffered considerable losses during that period. They were also no doubt ready, like Halfdan's men before them, to settle down on some of their new-won land. It was probably this as much as their defeat by King Alfred which persuaded them to settle in East Anglia, since they appear to have made no effort to continue their raiding in Mercia while at Cirencester. The preoccupation of the Viking army in Wessex from 878 to 879 and its withdrawal to East Anglia to settle on the land in 880 provided crucial breathing space for the Mercians.[10]

In Mercia, King Ceolwulf II struggled to maintain authority over his much reduced kingdom during this period. He appears to have retained authority in the west and north of the former lands of Mercia although he may have temporarily abandoned

Silver penny of King Ceolwulf II (reverse), showing two emperors. (Copyright British Museum)

south-western areas of Mercia to the Vikings in 877. The retention of his authority in the north-west is suggested by the record in the Welsh and Irish annals of the death of Rhodri *Mawr* of Gwynedd and his son Gwriad at the hands of the English in 878. In the circumstances of that year, these English can only have been the Mercians and were presumably either led or directed by Ceolwulf. The Northumbrians were now under Viking rule and in no position to interfere in North Wales and the West Saxons too distant to do so. The temporary abandonment of south-western areas of Mercia appears implied by the freedom afforded to the Vikings to occupy Gloucester in 877 and Cirencester in 879.[11]

The subsequent fate of Ceolwulf is unknown but there are a few clues which may point to what may have befallen him. The Welsh annals for 881 contain a notice of a battle at Conway in North Wales, described as 'vengeance for Rhodri at God's hand'. This phrase implies that this battle succeeded in avenging Rhodri's death in some way. It could simply signify that on this occasion the Welsh were victorious over the English but it may perhaps mean more than this. There could be no more apt revenge for the death of Rhodri than the death of King Ceolwulf himself. We know that Ceolwulf disappeared from the record sometime between 877 and 883 but have no firm evidence for when or how this happened. He may simply have died of natural causes. The only scrap of information that we have is contained in the text of a Mercian regnal list recorded in an eleventh-century manuscript from Worcester. This gives Ceolwulf II a reign of only five years, which would place his death in 879. This is some two years before the battle of Conway but it does come from a later source and may not be entirely accurate. We simply do not know how or when Ceolwulf finally met his end.[12]

The Viking preoccupation with Wessex and their subsequent settlement of East Anglia certainly allowed Lord Aethelred to recover. Once again there is no surviving record of how he may have achieved this but we can perhaps offer a surmise. Probably, in the circumstances of the initial abandonment of south-west Mercia by King Ceolwulf in 877 and more certainly after the latter's death, sometime in the period 879–81, he presumably assumed rule over what remained of the former Mercia starting from his own region, the later counties of Gloucestershire and Worcestershire. Initially this may have begun as a temporary expedient, the most powerful surviving *ealdorman* leading those of his people who still remained free, against their enemies. However, it soon blossomed, after the death of Ceolwulf, into an assumption of royal power. It was royal authority alone that would enable him to offer fully effective resistance to the invader, and as an *ealdorman* he would already have been familiar with many aspects of royal power.

Aethelred certainly resumed control of his own region of the *Hwicce* perhaps driving out any Vikings left behind to monitor or subdue it. Thereafter, he probably extended his influence to those neighbouring areas either by assuming the authority of any missing *ealdormen* or more probably by reaching agreement with other surviving *ealdormen*. He could offer them support and protection from his relatively intact and undamaged region in return for their agreement to submit to his leadership and direction. Many *ealdormen*, whose regions lay more exposed to or had in fact already suffered from Viking attack or occupation, must have welcomed such an approach. As the surviving Mercian *ealdormen* combined in this way their joint power increased and they found themselves better equipped to resist the Vikings that surrounded them. He therefore began in gradual stages to fulfil the role of a king by offering support and protection in return for service and loyalty. In this way, Aethelred restored the remnants of the former Mercian kingdom to a condition which allowed it once again to play a significant role in English affairs.

It was also during this period of recovery that Aethelred managed to achieve an arrangement which provided his reconstructed West Mercia with a powerful ally against the hostile powers that surrounded it and prevented it from being isolated and destroyed. This was the alliance between himself and King Alfred of Wessex. Whatever the previous relations between Mercia and Wessex and in spite of any aid that Aethelred may possibly have provided to the Vikings in 877, the experiences of the last few years had brought both men to the conclusion that unless they stood together it was unlikely either would survive. The dramatic importance of this sea change in English politics cannot be overstressed. The great rival powers of the pre-Viking period concluded a firm and solid alliance against their joint enemies.

This alliance would prove vital in securing the future of both the kingdoms involved and later in enabling them to strike back at the Vikings and restore the losses suffered at their hands. In spite of appearances and the relative power of the parties involved it seems to have been very much an alliance of equals. In contrast to the position under Burgred and Aethelwulf or his son, Aethelred, the Mercians and West Saxons now needed each other much more and so proved able to co-operate very closely with little or no apparent friction. The fact that this alliance of two unlikely bedfellows worked and worked well is a tribute to the two men, Aethelred and Alfred, who first negotiated it and then made sure that it worked in practice. They would both demonstrate a great deal of sensitivity and respect for each other's positions during their period of collaboration. This was a key factor in their success, in the recovery of their respective kingdoms and ultimately in the forging of a sense of common English identity. In the short term this alliance may have proved sufficient to dissuade the Vikings from further invasions of English territory for they remained absorbed with raiding on the Continent for the next ten years.

In 883, when Lord Aethelred finally emerges from the shadows into documented history, he had already established himself as the ruler of what remained of the former Mercian kingdom and forged the important alliance with Wessex. A charter which survives from that year clearly reveals Aethelred acting as the lord of Mercia and the ally of Alfred of Wessex. In this document, Aethelred grants the monastic community at Berkeley in Gloucestershire exemption from certain royal dues and rents in return for twelve hides of land at Stoke Bishop and thirty *mancuses* of gold. He does this as someone acting of right as a king. The transaction is witnessed by two *ealdormen*, Aethelfrith and Aethelwold, and two bishops, Waerferth of Worcester and Deorlaf of Hereford, and the whole *witan* of Mercia. It is also endorsed by Aethelred's ally King Alfred of Wessex.

Interior of St Mary's Church, Deerhurst, Gloucestershire, showing Saxon architectural features. (Photograph by W. Walker)

This charter reveals Aethelred functioning as a king of Mercia although he is addressed in the text we have only as *ealdorman*. He grants Berkeley a general exemption from royal dues and rents as only a king could. The priority of Aethelred in this text is, not surprisingly, on military affairs and he is careful to specifically reserve the three necessities of military service and fortress and bridge construction. He uses the land received from Berkeley Abbey to reward a man named Cynewulf, son of Ceoluht, who was almost certainly one of his *thegns* or military retainers. He probably also used the gold to help finance his military effort against the Vikings. These are clearly the actions of a king and the fact that the Mercian *witan* endorses this charter emphasises the royal nature of the actions undertaken by Aethelred therein.[13]

In 884 another surviving charter of Aethelred, which grants five hides of land at Himbleton in Worcestershire to *Ealdorman* Aethelwulf, was issued at a meeting of the *witan* held at Princes Risborough in Buckinghamshire. The witnesses on this occasion included a total of three bishops, six *ealdormen* and five *thegns* but there is no endorsement by King Alfred. This document provides further confirmation of both the extent of Aethelred's authority in the former Mercian kingdom and its royal nature. He grants land in Worcestershire with exemption from royal taxes and tolls and does this at a meeting of the *witan*, which he has summoned to meet in Buckinghamshire. He demonstrates authority in areas well beyond those covered by his own authority as *ealdorman* of the *Hwicce*, and close to Viking-occupied territory. Thus the charter is granted at a meeting held in Buckinghamshire and Bishop Wulfred of Lichfield in Staffordshire is among the witnesses. This document also demonstrates that Aethelred was winning over members of the old nobility since the *Ealdorman* Aethelwulf to whom he granted land in this charter was a relative of the former King Cenwulf of Mercia.[14]

An example of the practical effect of the new close co-operation between Aethelred and Alfred occurred in 886. In that year, King Alfred led an army into the lower Thames valley and occupied the city of London. This action offered him the potential to monitor and control future access by Viking fleets up the river Thames into the heart of Wessex or Mercia. A friendly garrison in the city could effectively bar travel upriver to small groups of raiders. Although larger forces might force a passage, the bypassed city garrison would still pose a threat to the retreat of such groups following a defeat or some similar reduction in strength. However, Alfred, by taking London, had trespassed into the territory of the former Mercian kingdom and this carried with it the potential for tension and dispute with the Mercians. It was, after all, their city and its occupation by the West Saxons might be resented by many. He realised the sensitivity of the situation and defused it by immediately handing the city over to Aethelred to garrison on behalf of them both. Thus Alfred gained an important element of security on the West Saxon border but at the same time preserved his vital alliance with Aethelred by his respect for Mercian rights. The subsequent restoration of London by Alfred and Aethelred is related in Chapter 7.[15]

It is notable that in the surviving documentary sources Aethelred of Mercia never employs the royal title and it seems that he issued no coinage in his own name. As a result, it has been fairly widely assumed, on the model of earlier practice, that this signifies Aethelred's complete submission and by extension the direct submission of Mercia to King Alfred. Indeed, at least one historian has gone so far as to call him the 'Alfredian governor' of Mercia. Unfortunately, this carries a clear implication that Alfred actually appointed him to govern Mercia and could also therefore dispense with him. There is absolutely no evidence that this was the case. Indeed, there are a number of indications that Alfred could not simply command Aethelred but had to respect his authority. He recognised Aethelred's historic rights in London, he issued no separate charters for Mercia but rather endorsed those issued by Aethelred himself and, on the evidence of Aethelweard, left Aethelred in command of the Mercian army. This behaviour would appear to indicate the respect due to an ally rather than the exploitation of a subordinate.[16]

It is true that there are many examples whereby formerly independent kings of the *Hwicce*, Sussex and Kent lost their royal titles and their right to mint coins under King Offa. However, there is an important and fundamental difference between those earlier arrangements and this particular case. It is clear that Mercia, after its territorial losses to the Vikings, was the weaker partner in this alliance. The recognition by Aethelred of King Alfred's superiority in terms of power and authority had been achieved by negotiation and agreement rather than by force of arms. This is an important point which should be acknowledged. It was one of the reasons that this rapprochement between former rivals thrived while earlier enforced submissions had fostered resentment and fuelled rebellion. There was no West Saxon invasion and conquest of Mercia but rather a mutual agreement by two rulers which recognised the appropriate extent of each others authority. The significance of the term 'King of the Angles and Saxons or Anglo-Saxons', which was first employed by Alfred at this time, is a key to this. It discarded the old labels of Wessex and Mercia to recognise a new order but it avoided the hint of hegemony often associated with earlier use of the term *Rex Anglorum* or 'King of the English'. It is clear that Alfred was the senior partner but it is also clear that Aethelred was not simply one of his *ealdormen*. The precise nature of Aethelred's status and of his relationship with King Alfred and his successor will be further explored in Chapter 7.

One sign of this agreement can perhaps be seen in the coinage at this time. There are no surviving coins bearing the name of Aethelred and no evidence that any such were ever minted. Aethelred had clearly conceded his right to mint coins in recognition of King Alfred's greater power and perhaps of the fact that Wessex, which now also held authority in Kent, dominated Mercian trade routes with the Continent. However, coins were minted bearing the name of King Alfred in Mercia at Gloucester, Oxford and London and Alfred's coins circulated throughout Aethelred's area of authority. This contrasts sharply with the position under King Ceolwulf, who had issued coins with the same designs as Alfred but under his own name. This was an important concession by Aethelred but it was also the culmination of a trend. As far back

Silver penny of King Alfred, minted at Gloucester (reverse). (Copyright British Museum)

as the reigns of King Beorhtwulf of Mercia and King Aethelwulf of Wessex coins with the same designs had been issued to assist the process of trade and exchange while still retaining the propaganda value of carrying their own names. This had been continued by their successors when they minted coins with standard designs but different names and titles. The rulers concerned clearly valued the appearance of their names on these coins as part of their struggle against a rival. As a result of their solid alliance, Alfred and Aethelred no longer had any need for such a device and a standard coinage was adopted and minted in both kingdoms.[17]

Another example might be found in the actions of the Welsh rulers. In his *Life of King Alfred*, Asser recounts how the rulers of South Wales sought Alfred's support against Anarawd of Gwynedd and 'the might and tyrannical behaviour of *Ealdorman* Aethelred of the Mercians'. This comment shows that Aethelred was already pursuing his own Mercian agenda of enforcing his authority in Wales. The Welsh clearly expected Alfred to intervene with Aethelred and curb his aggression towards their kingdoms. However, it seems unlikely that Alfred would be willing to intervene forcefully against Mercian interests in Wales in view of his own need for Aethelred's support. The alliance with Mercia was too important to Alfred for it to be compromised by any significant concessions to the Welsh. It is notable in this context that Asser provides no specific details of the alleged advantages gained by the Welsh kings from their association with Alfred. In 894 Aethelred would join Anarawd of Gwynedd in ravaging Ceredigion and Ystrad Tywi in central Wales without apparent objection by Alfred. Similarly, in 915 Lady Aethelflaed would harry Brycheiniog without reference to King Edward.[18]

It was at some point during the 880s, perhaps after the occupation of London, that a formal marriage alliance took place between Mercia and Wessex which would ultimately have tremendous and unforeseen consequences for both. It was the immediate need for a united front against the Vikings that had first brought Aethelred of Mercia and Alfred of Wessex together. This threat had for the moment subsided but the activities of Vikings on the Continent, which were being monitored by the Chronicle, showed that it was by no means over. The traditional way to make an expedient military alliance, such as currently existed between Aethelred and Alfred, more permanent was through a marriage alliance between the two families. This would involve the marriage of Aethelred with Aethelflaed, the eldest daughter of King Alfred and his wife Ealhswith, who was herself descended from Mercian royalty. Aethelflaed may have been aged around eighteen in 886 and so, as Asser's *Life of King Alfred* remarks, ready for marriage. This marriage provides further confirmation of Aethelred's status in Alfred's opinion since it seems to have been customary for the daughters of Alfred's family at this time to marry other independent rulers rather than mere *ealdormen*.[19]

This marriage followed in an ancient tradition of attempts to forge links between peoples through those between ruling dynasties. It does not appear to have been seen as a marriage of submission where an overlord attempted to assert his control over a lesser ruler by binding him into his family circle. Instead, it reflected the earlier marriage in 853 of King Burgred of Mercia to Aethelswith, daughter of Aethelwulf of Wessex, which sealed an alliance between two formerly rival kingdoms. Ultimately, it might have proved as ineffective in its purpose as many earlier marriages – including that of King Burgred and Aethelswith. It was a combination of the surrounding circumstances and the characters of the individuals involved which would transform this particular marriage into an effective alliance between kingdoms. An alliance which would establish such a close relationship between the two kingdoms and their nobles that it provided a key element towards the process of the future unification of England. This possibility, however, lay far in the future and in the short term this marriage carried no more than the potential for cementing the alliance between Mercia and Wessex.

The potential threat to Wessex and Western Mercia from the Danish settlers in East Anglia receded further sometime after 886, when King Alfred negotiated a treaty with their ruler, King Guthrum. The text of this treaty has survived and it is clearly an attempt to stabilise and formalise relations between what was, in spite of a reference to rule by the 'army', increasingly being viewed as a newly emerging Danish kingdom of East Anglia and the established English kingdoms. It dealt with such formal international concepts as territorial boundaries, procedures for dealing with legal disputes, extradition and trade relations. It is clear from the boundary clause that this particular treaty was one between the English and those Danes under Guthrum's authority and so included the Mercians in its provisions. In spite of some inherent risks, this arrangement seems to have proved temporarily effective. Thus King Guthrum, or Athelstan to give him his baptismal name, appears to have kept the oaths he had sworn and remained quiescent in East Anglia for his remaining years. However, this treaty alone could not provide any final resolution to the problem of security for the English kingdoms. The Danes settled in East Anglia remained free to resume their raiding activities against their new English neighbours at any time. More dangerously, the official recognition this treaty accorded to the Viking seizure of rich lands in England would, almost inevitably, encourage the leaders of other Viking bands to try their luck. Indeed, both of these risks would become a reality in the years following the death of King Guthrum in 890.[20]

The English leaders were not ignorant of the risks that they were running and it was probably during this period of relative peace that Alfred and Aethelred began to make changes that would prove to be key to defeating the Viking menace. These were the reorganisation of the army along the lines set out in Chapter 7 and the policy of building fortresses or *burhs* in order to provide secure bases from which they could oppose future Viking raids. This combined strategy is usually credited to King Alfred but it should be remembered that the Mercians had a well-established tradition of fortress construction stretching back at least to King Offa. A contemporary document known as the *Burghal Hidage* describes how these fortresses were maintained and garrisoned by drawing manpower from the surrounding area. It lists all the *burhs* built across Wessex and the amounts of land from which they drew their garrisons but makes only indirect reference to Mercia. It does show that the *burh* at Worcester in Mercia, one of only three Mercian *burhs* included in the text, drew support from 1,200 hides of land, the equivalent of the modern county of Worcester. Based on the calculations contained in this document, this area would have supplied the *burh* with sufficient men to garrison 4,950 feet of wall at four men every 5½ yards. Quite remarkably, recent excavations have suggested that the circuit of the walls of the *burh* at Worcester is about 4,650 feet.[21]

There is no evidence as to when this policy of building *burhs* was started. It cannot have been until the immediate threat from the Vikings had been removed in 880 with the final withdrawal of Guthrum into East Anglia. Prior to this, all of the resources of the English rulers must have been completely devoted to coping with the Vikings' physical presence. They were probably therefore not in a position to act on any strategy for the future even if they had developed such. It is extremely fortunate, then, that a charter of the period 889-899 survives which shows Aethelred of Mercia ordering the construction of the *burh* at Worcester for 'the protection of all the people'. A further charter of 904, by which Bishop Waerferth of Worcester grants a tenement inside the north wall of this *burh* to Aethelred and his wife, demonstrates that its construction had probably been completed by this date. Some of these fortresses or *burhs* were certainly in position before the next large-scale Viking assaults from 893 onwards and they are increasingly referred to in the accounts of this and the following years. It seems likely therefore that construction of these *burhs* began during the decade 880-890 and proceeded on into the early tenth century.[22]

However, in 890, while this policy remained in its infancy with many *burhs* still under construction, King Guthrum of Danish East Anglia died and his successor, King Eric, clearly did not feel obliged to observe the Treaty of Wedmore, especially when faced with the prospect of further loot. At the same time, a large Viking army, which had been raiding in Northern France since being expelled from Kent in 885, found itself faced with a terrible famine and was looking round for richer pickings. Thus the Viking threat to Mercia and Wessex quickly re-emerged in a particularly formidable form. In the winter of 892 this Continental army crossed the Channel and landed in England. In order to hasten their departure, they had been provided with sufficient ships at Boulogne, no doubt by anxious locals, to transport both them and their horses. This army appears to have been very large and it arrived in England in two separate groups. The first and main portion, consisting of around 200 ships, landed at the mouth of the river Lympne in Southern Kent and stormed one of the English *burhs*, which was still under construction at Appledore on the edge of Romney Marsh. The second and smaller force of around 80 ships under a leader named Haesten entered the Thames Estuary, landed in northern Kent and built a fortress at Milton Regis. The death of Guthrum and the arrival of this new army would test the efficacy of the Treaty of Wedmore and find it wanting.[23]

Early in the following year, 893, King Alfred responded to this new threat by leading an army into Kent in an attempt to prevent the Vikings advancing into Wessex itself and, if possible, drive them away in emulation of his previous success in 885. He appears to have had insufficient forces to besiege both Viking groups closely and instead had to try and block any advance into Wessex from a more distant covering position between the two Viking bases. This presented the Vikings at Appledore with an opportunity to evade the West Saxon army. They first sent their ships around the coast of Kent to Essex, which was then subject to the Danes of East Anglia, where they found refuge at Benfleet in spite of the Treaty of Wedmore. They then divided their army up into small units, infiltrated through the West Saxon blockade and broke out into Wessex.

Recombining there, they began to raid through eastern Wessex with West Saxon forces in pursuit. They were finally caught loaded with booty by a West Saxon force led by *Atheling* Edward, the son of Alfred, at Farnham in Hampshire. They were severely mauled and forced to flee after abandoning their booty. They fled across the Thames into Mercian territory and sought refuge on the island of Thorney in the river Colne in Hertfordshire. The Chronicle states that their unnamed king had been wounded at Farnham and could not be moved any further. It is also possible that they assumed that having left West Saxon territory and entered Mercia they would be safe from pursuit as

Badly damaged page from the manuscript of the Chronicle of Aethelweard. (BL Cotton Otho A x, f. 4v)

had often been the case in the past. Unfortunately for them, this was no longer the case and they were very soon besieged by a joint Mercian and West Saxon force under Lord Aethelred and *Atheling* Edward. Aethelred had brought his army from London, where he had no doubt been guarding his frontier against this new threat in neighbouring Kent.[24]

Rather ominously, *Atheling* Edward's West Saxons soon had to withdraw, due to lack of provisions and the ending of their term of service. In spite of this, Aethelred continued the siege with his own force, hoping for support from King Alfred. The Northumbrian and East Anglian Danes chose this precise moment to launch a maritime raid on Devon. This was perhaps a coincidence but it seems more likely that it was planned and intended to divert attention from their Viking colleagues trapped at Thorney. This raid which flagrantly breached the Treaty of Wedmore caused Alfred to redirect the bulk of his West Saxon forces to defend Devonshire leaving only a small remnant to support Aethelred. In the absence of strong West Saxon support Aethelred wisely resisted any temptation to storm the fortress in the face of its large garrison. He was however able to prevent their escape and according to Aethelweard they were forced to come to terms. They surrendered hostages to Aethelred and swore to leave his kingdom. They were then permitted to leave and join their colleagues at Benfleet in Essex where the latter had built a fortress. This treaty effectively removed the immediate threat from this Viking force but did not resolve the problem and could not have been intended as any more than a temporary expedient.

Indeed, Haesten, the commander of the force at Benfleet, set out on a raid into Mercia with a large force soon after this. It was only now that reinforcements arrived from Wessex to join Aethelred and *Atheling* Edward in London. Thus reinforced, the English commanders resolved to attack the Viking base at Benfleet. They selected an opportune moment for their attack probably as a result of good intelligence, with Haesten absent on his raid with a large part of the army. This left the fortress at Benfleet undermanned and the joint English force was able to storm the defences. They slaughtered the Viking defenders and captured their booty, ships and families. They broke up or burnt the greater part of the Viking fleet and towed the rest to London and Rochester. They also carried off the recovered spoils and the more important captives including Haesten's wife and sons. Although important hostages, the two boys were later returned to their father since Alfred and Aethelred had earlier stood sponsors at their baptism perhaps early in 893. This was the first time that an English force had successfully taken a Viking fortress and the first time that Viking families had been successfully targeted.

When the main Viking force under Haesten returned to Benfleet they found it ruined and empty. They were forced to build a replacement fortress at nearby Shoeburyness. Haesten responded to this disaster by launching a savage retaliatory assault into Mercian territory. He recruited additional support for this action from the Danish kingdoms in East Anglia and Northumbria. He entered Mercia with his revitalised army and initially advanced up the Thames valley. He then appears to have struck northwards across country deep into the heart of Mercia.

Lord Aethelred responded to this threat by calling out forces from throughout Mercia and by requesting aid from Wessex. The Mercian forces appear to have consisted of two major elements, one summoned from north of the Thames, roughly the region between the Thames and the Severn, and the other summoned from west of the Severn and including allies from Wales. The West Saxon force sent to his aid consisted of the forces of Somerset and Wiltshire led by their *ealdormen*, Aethelhelm and Aethelnoth, respectively. In the absence of King Alfred, still occupied in Devon, it seems almost certain that Aethelred assumed overall command of these allied forces. On this occasion we have evidence that the English armies were mounted in order to pursue their opponents more effectively. The Chronicle account makes this clear later in the year when it refers to the English using their horses to consume the corn supplies. Probably due to this extra mobility, the English were able to catch up with the Viking army at Buttington on the upper Severn near the border with Wales. The springing of this trap may also have involved a Mercian and Welsh force from west of the Severn cutting them off from Wales and trapping them against the pursuing Mercian and West Saxon forces coming from east of the river.[25]

The cornered Viking force built a fortress at Buttington where they were besieged by Aethelred who posted his forces on both banks of the river. The siege lasted for many weeks and hunger reduced the Vikings to eating their horses. In spite of this, drastic expedient large numbers of warriors died of starvation and disease. In desperation they eventually attempted to break out of the Mercian encirclement and reach the safety of Danish-held territory in the East Midlands. However, the English force on the east bank of the Severn were ready for them and secured a crushing victory in the ensuing battle. They slaughtered a large number of the Vikings and only a few escaped to reach safety in the east. Lord Aethelred and his combined force had achieved another important victory.

The remnant of this defeated Viking army appears to have managed to recruit fresh reinforcements from Danish-occupied eastern England. They apparently intended to mount a more carefully planned assault on Mercia, than that which had ended in disaster in the summer, during the winter period. They certainly proved much less bold and much more circumspect in their intentions than earlier in the year. This was perhaps a reflection of a reduced scale of the forces involved. They left their families, their ships and their plunder behind in East Anglia for safekeeping. This had the effect of increasing the morale and the cross-country mobility of their army. They entered Mercia and made a rapid march by day and night apparently without any major detours or extensive pillaging. They reached the apparently deserted and partly ruinous Roman fortress of Chester and occupied it, no doubt refurbishing its defences.

The speed of this well-planned and directed advance appears to have caught Aethelred by surprise. As a result, Mercian forces proved unable to intercept the Vikings before they reached Chester. Nevertheless, Aethelred was still able to isolate the Viking army within its fortifications and lay close siege to it. This siege lasted for two days and involved the very effective use of a scorched earth policy. The Mercians seized all the cattle in the area, burnt or consumed all the corn and killed any Viking foragers. These tactics proved highly effective, forcing the Viking army to abandon their fortress and withdraw into North Wales. In the following year, 894, when the Vikings sought to return from Wales it is notable that they chose to travel through Danish occupied Northumbrian territory rather than risk any further encounters with Aethelred's forces.

The successful campaigns of 893–4 against the Vikings under Haesten and his colleagues were in the main undertaken by Mercian forces under Aethelred. They had certainly enjoyed some limited West Saxon support under *Atheling* Edward and various *ealdormen* but the bulk of the West Saxon forces under King Alfred had been occupied in the West Country from mid-893 until 894, dealing with a large Danish fleet drawn from Northumbria and East Anglia. The leadership of Aethelred of Mercia had proved consistently successful during these campaigns. He had led his largely Mercian forces to victory at Benfleet and Buttington against major Viking forces. In the former case, he had, for the first time, successfully stormed and reduced one of their defended fortresses. He had also successfully cornered and besieged highly mobile Viking forces on three occasions at Thorney, Buttington and Chester. In the last case, there is clear evidence that he employed a scorched earth policy to force them out and it seems likely that such tactics were more commonly employed in these situations. The Chronicle accounts of starvation among the Vikings at Thorney suggest as much.

This significant Mercian success against forces, which were initially seen by the Chronicle as substantially larger (at 280 ships) than those faced by King Alfred in Devonshire (140 ships), has perhaps not been sufficiently appreciated. It proves the substantial contribution of Aethelred and the Mercian army to the overall English success during these years. Indeed, it was Lord Aethelred's great victory at Buttington that would be recorded in the contemporary Irish annals rather than those achieved by King Alfred elsewhere. It is true that Aethelred enjoyed some West Saxon assistance in achieving these successes but the West Saxon-inspired Chronicle itself admits that this aid was not substantial. It reveals that it was an 'inconsiderable portion' of the West Saxon army which joined in Aethelred's assault on Benfleet. It records that the West Saxon forces present at Buttington were led by two *ealdormen* and therefore probably included the men of their shires only. Indeed, at Chester Aethelred proved able to defeat the Vikings without any recorded West Saxon help. This shows that Aethelred was much more than a junior partner of the West Saxon king. He was a powerful ally, well able to act independently to frustrate Viking plans and ambitions.[26]

In the summer of 894 Aethelweard records, in his version of the Chronicle, a raid by *Ealdorman* Aethelnoth into Danish-occupied territory between the rivers Welland and Kesteven around Stamford. It seems highly probable that this raid also involved the participation of Mercian forces under Lord Aethelred. The location of the area ravaged makes this likely since any West Saxon force would have had to cross Mercian territory to reach it. In view of the fact that these men had already demonstrated close co-operation in the campaigns of the previous year it seems virtually certain that Mercian forces took part. This retaliatory action would have provided an ideal opportunity for them both to strike back at their tormentors. The English forces involved, whether they included Mercians or not, laid waste a wide area of the later Rutland. This was no doubt intended to discourage the Danish settlers in these areas from joining any further invasions of Mercia or Wessex. It may even have been a factor in causing the Viking force raiding in Wales to return home in response to this threat to their families. The sequence of events in the different Chronicle accounts and the relationships between them, if any, are far from clear.[27]

In the late autumn of 894 the Viking army from Shoeburyness, which was now based on Mersea Island in Essex, advanced by ship up the Thames and into the river Lea, where they constructed a fortress, possibly at Hertford. The garrison of London was unable to prevent their passage upriver on this occasion because of the width of the river and the strength of the Viking fleet. The Vikings were able to spend the winter in their new fortress, largely unmolested. The English response to this latest invasion did not come until the following summer. An army drawn from the London garrison and other, possibly local, forces rather rashly attempted to capture this new Viking fortress. The assault, like many before, failed with considerable losses among the English attackers, including some, probably West Saxon, royal *thegns*.[28]

However, on this occasion, defeat did not discourage the English, who probably managed to maintain a watch on the fortress until a more formidable offensive could be mounted in the autumn. At that point, King Alfred brought a large army to besiege the fortress closely and prevent the Vikings from seizing the local harvest. Once again, it seems likely that Aethelred and his forces participated in this venture although this is not recorded in the West Saxon-influenced Chronicle. The English leaders also planned to cut off the retreat of the Vikings by blockading the river Lea behind them. They therefore built two fortresses, one on either bank, perhaps on the model of those constructed by the Frankish king, Charles the Bald, between 862 and 870 at Pont de l'Arche on the river Seine in France. The intention was to prevent escape by ship downstream to London. An ambitious construction project like this would have required the diversion of considerable manpower from the English armies. As a result, it appears that the Viking force was able to break through the thinned English siege lines and advance directly across Mercia to Bridgnorth on the river Severn. There the Vikings built another fortress and no doubt raided the surrounding area.[29]

An English force had pursued them but the composition of this force is not made clear in the sources. It seems unlikely that it was the main West Saxon royal army which had already completed its period of service. It was certainly not the London garrison which remained behind to seize and destroy the abandoned Viking fleet. It seems more likely that it was a Mercian or mixed Mercian and West Saxon force and therefore one under Lord Aethelred's command. The English force, whatever its composition, invested the Viking fortress at Bridgnorth through the winter. The Welsh annals record the harrying of Ceredigion and Ystrad Tywi at this time by Anarawd of Gwynedd and the English. This may have been part of the measures taken by Aethelred to prevent supplies or help reaching the Vikings at Bridgnorth or it may be an unrelated action. On this occasion no attempt was made to capture the fortress and the Viking force was apparently able to survive a long siege. In the summer of 896 the Viking army at Bridgnorth finally dispersed and withdrew to Danish-occupied areas in East Anglia and Northumbria. Their campaign had clearly not been as successful as they had hoped. They had lost all of their ships and probably returned almost empty-handed. Indeed, a number of them appear to have decided to cut their losses and withdraw from England to try their luck on the Continent.[30]

The Chronicle's comment, that this latest Viking army, which had first landed back in 892, had not affected the English people greatly, clearly reflects a West Saxon view since their impact on Wessex itself had indeed been limited. The main impact of their activities had fallen on Mercia, which had, in contrast, suffered more severely during these years. Nevertheless, the impact of the Vikings on Mercia had been restricted by the resolute actions of Aethelred and his West Saxon allies. The Vikings had been unable to conquer any new territory and had largely been prevented from raiding freely across Mercian territory. They had been diverted or repulsed from their objectives on a number of occasions and had been defeated several times with considerable losses. Much of the credit for this success should probably be attributed to Lord Aethelred's leadership and the skills of his Mercian troops. This success brought a return to peace in the following years when the remaining English kingdoms of Wessex and Mercia remained relatively free from Viking attack. The next upheavals they faced would arise as a consequence of the death of King Alfred in 899.

When King Alfred died on 26 October 899 a succession crisis swiftly developed in Wessex which threatened to undermine all that he and Aethelred had achieved together. The king was survived by two sons by his Mercian wife, Ealhswith, sister of *Ealdorman* Aethelwulf. The elder of these, *Atheling* Edward, was recognised as the principal beneficiary in Alfred's will, which dealt with succession to his family or private property. Edward clearly intended to succeed his father as king of Wessex also, but in this case the succession arrangements were not so clear cut. In Wessex at this date there were no firmly established rules as the earlier succession of Alfred on the heels of three older brothers had shown. It was generally recognised that it was more important to select a competent adult male as king than to preserve any specific line of descent. Such males were usually selected from among the descendants of previous kings and where a choice between brothers did exist the eldest was usually preferred. In 871, when Alfred's elder brother, King Aethelred, had died, his two sons, Aethelwold and Aethelhelm, had simply been too young to succeed him and so Alfred had ascended the throne instead. The position had changed by 899. The sons of Aethelred had grown to manhood and the elder, *Atheling* Aethelwold, was older than either of Alfred's sons. He therefore had a claim to the throne which was at least as strong if not stronger than that of Edward, and he clearly intended to advance it.[31]

In late 899 or early 900, therefore, Aethelwold and Edward both sought to make good their respective claims to the throne and to have these recognised in Wessex. The Chronicle account of this period is clearly biased, it implies that Edward succeeded his father as of right and makes no concessions to Aethelwold's claim. It is certainly likely that Edward was better placed, in terms of position in his father's counsel and as the leader of West Saxon armies, to take up the reins of power. He could also draw on support from his mother's kin, including *Ealdorman* Aethelwulf, and from his brother-in-law Lord Aethelred of Mercia. It was this last relationship which provided the basis for the close alliance between Wessex and Mercia in face of the Viking threat and Aethelred therefore had to support Edward in order to preserve this.

However, *Atheling* Aethelwold had no intention of allowing his cousin Edward's succession to proceed uncontested. He therefore occupied royal residences at Wimborne in Dorset and Christchurch in Hampshire. He also secured the allegiance of a number of important men although their names and significance are nowhere recorded. It should be noted that Wimborne Minster was the burial place of his father King Aethelred and therefore perhaps a centre of family power or a potent symbol of his own royal descent. He also appears to have attempted to marry a consecrated woman. This lady is also unnamed, although it seems likely that she was an important woman who could offer some assets to Aethelwold in terms of royal descent or noble support to enhance his prospects. In any event Aethelwold was clearly not entirely without support in pressing his claim.

In this struggle for support, *Atheling* Edward's advantages appear to have secured him the greater degree of support. He was able to employ the royal army to besiege and isolate his cousin at Wimborne before he could further increase his support and to seize the woman the latter had selected as his intended bride. Initially it appeared that Aethelwold intended to fight but in face of the odds against him he, rather judiciously, chose to fight another day. He slipped away during the night to seek refuge in Danish-ruled Northumbria. It is clear from this that neighbouring Mercia was as unsafe for him as Wessex itself. He now needed support from outside to restore his fortunes in the absence of sufficient support within Wessex itself.[32]

It was to be nearly two years later, in 902, before Aethelwold returned bringing a Danish fleet recruited in Northumbria by sea to Essex, where he secured further support from the Danish rulers of East Anglia. The Danish rulers recognised Aethelwold's claim to the throne of Wessex and undertook to support him in pursuing it. The Chronicle's suggestion that the Northumbrian Danes handed over their kingdom to him is frankly unbelievable although his name still appears in some lists of the rulers of York or even of East Anglia at this time. The Danes no doubt hoped to secure considerable riches for themselves in return, either in booty collected during the fighting or in land secured by his success. Aethelwold was taking a risk by leading Viking raiders into English territory since this could potentially alienate many in Wessex who might otherwise have been persuaded to support his claim. He clearly considered this a risk worth taking in terms of the potential prize although the fact that he initially directed his attack against Mercia perhaps suggests a wish to avoid antagonising potential supporters in Wessex.

Aethelwold had also developed a strategy intended to deal with any interference from Lord Aethelred of Mercia. He recruited a dissident faction from within Mercia led by a man named Beorhtsige, a son of *Ealdorman* Beornnoth. This man is described as an *atheling* by the Chronicle and so was presumably related to one of the last Mercian kings of the old 'B' dynasty (see Table 2, p. 209). *Ealdorman* Beornnoth, himself, appears to have been loyal to Aethelred, being among the witnesses of a number of his charters up until 884. He appears to have died at some point between that date and 902 when he may have been succeeded by his son, Beorhtsige. If so, Beorhtsige clearly harboured wider ambitions than a simple *ealdorman*'s authority, stretching to the restoration of his families' previous royal status. These were ambitions that threatened Aethelred's own position as ruler of Mercia and therefore he could only oppose them.[33]

In late 902 a Viking invasion of the far north-west of Mercia took place under a man named Ingimund. The Irish had expelled the Vikings from Dublin in 902 and many of them were forced to seek refuge elsewhere. A group of them led by this Ingimund attempted to seize control of Anglesey but were driven off by the Welsh. They next landed in Mercian territory in search of a refuge in the Wirral, an isolated peninsula to the north of Chester. This was an area distant from the centres of

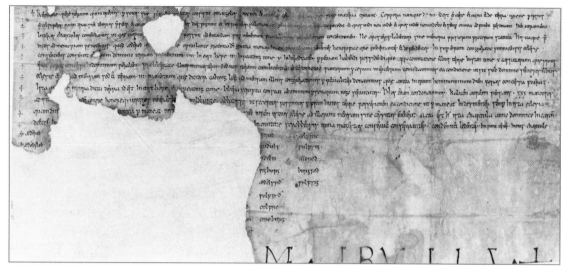

Charter of Lord Aethelred and Lady Aethelflaed to Much Wenlock, 901. (BL Cotton Charter viii 27)

Mercian power in Gloucester and close to a disputed border with the lands occupied or controlled by the Northumbrian Danes. In face of this new invasion it seems likely that Aethelred had been forced to travel north to confront these invaders. Indeed, it may have been around this time that he constructed the *burh* at Shrewsbury to protect it from Viking incursions. It is unlikely, however, that this invasion was part of a concerted plan arranged with Aethelwold and his Danish allies. The Vikings of Dublin were rivals and would soon become open foes of the Danes of York and are therefore unlikely to have assisted them. Nevertheless, this northern invasion must have caused Aethelred to divert his forces from watching his eastern borders and so eased the task of Aethelwold.[34]

It was probably this northern distraction that left Mercia exposed to attack by the dissidents and their Viking allies. In 902 Aethelwold led an army largely made up of his Viking allies from Essex deep into central and south-west Mercia. They harried widely, no doubt targeting the lands held by Aethelred and his supporters, and almost reaching Aethelred's capital at Gloucester. They then crossed the Thames at Cricklade and entered Wessex. They ravaged the area around Braydon in Wiltshire and carried off a great deal of plunder. The defection of Beorhtsige and the recent deaths of *Ealdorman* Aethelhelm of Wiltshire in 897 and *Ealdorman* Aethelwulf in 902 and Aethelred's absence in the north-west had probably weakened and undermined Mercian and West Saxon defences. The invaders did not pursue their invasion any further, however, perhaps because Aethelred and Edward had called out forces against them. In the face of this they prudently withdrew to East Anglia, managing successfully to avoid interception by the English forces.[35]

In reply, King Edward of Wessex invaded East Anglia and harried the area between the Dykes and the river Ouse. It was as the West Saxon army withdrew after this raid, that a section of it consisting of the men of Kent fell behind the main host and was set upon by a force led by Aethelwold and King Eric of Danish East Anglia at Holme in Huntingdonshire. The battle that followed on 13 December 902 appears to have been a victory for the larger Viking force, which held the field at the end of the day. However, it proved disastrous for Aethelwold's cause. There was a tremendous slaughter on both sides but it was the deaths among the leaders which proved decisive. *Atheling* Aethelwold and Beorhtsige both died along with Eric, the Danish king of East Anglia. This resolved the succession dispute in Wessex quite conclusively and removed Aethelred of Mercia's rival at the same time. It also left the Danish kingdom of East Anglia severely weakened after the loss of its king and large numbers of its fighting men. The sacrifice of the men of Kent had secured the futures of Edward and Aethelred and enhanced their alliance to the benefit of both. The importance of this victory for Mercia can be seen in its featuring in the text of The Mercian Register even though it had probably involved no Mercian forces.[36]

It would seem probable that the conflict with the Danes lost much of its heat after this battle. Certainly, no major actions are recorded in English sources after this date. A few years later, in 906, the Chronicle records that King Edward finally established peace with the Danes of East Anglia and Northumbria at Tiddingford in Buckinghamshire near Watling Street. The location of this meeting on Mercian territory suggests that this was not only a treaty with Wessex but with Mercia as well. The peace established provided an opportunity for both Aethelred and Edward to restore their authority in their kingdoms after the disruptions of the recent war of succession.[37]

In Mercia, Lord Aethelred used this peaceful interlude to re-establish his authority in the far north-west of his lands. The recent invasion of Ingimund and his Viking followers from Ireland had undermined what Mercian authority had been restored to this area after the Danish occupation of Chester in 893. It is clear from place-name evidence that Ingimund's followers had not been driven out by Aethelred after 903. Instead, they had been allowed to remain in this area, a fact supported by a late Irish source. This settlement may be evidence for the adoption in England of a policy also being followed by Charles the Simple, King of the Franks at this time. This involved allowing one group of Vikings to settle in a vulnerable coastal area in return for their undertaking to defend these areas against other Vikings. This arrangement carried the risk that they might renege on the deal and use their new settlement as a base for attacks on other areas. The late Irish source which records this episode suggests that something along these lines was in prospect with Ingimund casting covetous eyes on Chester itself. However, in 907 Aethelred led an army north to Chester where he had the Roman walls restored and the resulting new *burh* garrisoned. This brought what had been a semi-independent Viking enclave in the Wirral under firm Mercian control and also provided a strong defence for the northern and western frontiers of Mercia.[38]

It must also have been during this peaceful interlude that King Edward and Lord Aethelred initiated a process intended to assist them in the future recovery of territories occupied by the Danes. This involved them in encouraging individual nobles to use their own money to purchase lands in the Danish-occupied territories. This provided them with a stake in an area which they could only fully exploit when the area had been brought back under English rule. A later charter of King Athelstan reveals that Edward and Aethelred had commanded their faithful *thegn* Ealdred to buy land worth £10 at Chalgrave and Tebworth in what was later Bedfordshire from the local pagan Vikings. This land would subsequently be brought under English rule and in 926 Athelstan would confirm Ealdred in his possession of it. This process provided opportunities for enrichment to those who were prepared to take part in the recovery of this lost land and proved to be a vital catalyst in enlisting enthusiastic support for the process.[39]

In 909 Edward and Aethelred conducted a joint campaign into territory subject to the Northumbrian Danes in the region of Lindsey. The Chronicle attributes this venture to Edward alone but indicates that the invasion involved both Mercian and West Saxon forces. This suggests the likelihood of participation by Aethelred which is confirmed by the independent Mercian Register. The joint army spent some five weeks ravaging the land 'very severely', killing and capturing men and cattle. The Mercian Register records that at some point during this campaign Aethelred took the opportunity to remove the body of the Northumbrian royal saint, Oswald, from his shrine at Bardney in Lincolnshire. It had been buried there shortly after his death in battle against the pagan Penda of Mercia in 641. This sacred relic was then transported by Aethelred to his own seat of power at Gloucester. There he laid it to rest in a new church foundation which he subsequently dedicated to the saint. It may be that he hoped to gain the favour of this saint against the Vikings who were the new pagans. Equally he may have hoped that the presence of the relics of this great Northumbrian saint would encourage the surviving English of Northumbria to look favourably on the prospect of Mercian rule.[40]

In the following year, 910, the Northumbrian Danes responded to this English raid on their territory by invading Mercia. They made their move while King Edward of Wessex was in Kent collecting a fleet possibly to attack East Anglia. They apparently intended to strike at Lord Aethelred of Mercia when he was unable to call on significant West Saxon aid. They advanced through central Mercia to the River Avon and then turned north and crossed the Severn into the heart of Mercia. They ravaged the land and amassed a great deal of plunder. Then, loaded with spoils, they began their withdrawal using the Severn crossing at Bridgnorth. They had apparently managed to avoid any encounters with Mercian forces and no doubt thought the West Saxons were far away. It must have come as a nasty surprise to them, therefore, to find a large army consisting of both Mercian and West Saxon forces barring their route home at Tettenhall. This combined force was probably once again under the overall command of Lord Aethelred. There is no mention of King Edward's presence but only that he sent some of his West Saxon army to join the Mercians. The subsequent battle, on 5 August 910, ended in a decisive victory for the English. Many of the Danes were killed, including their kings Eowils and Halfdan and no less than ten of their leading commanders.[41]

This stunning victory stands as a worthy match to that won by King Edward against the Danes of East Anglia at Holme eight years previously. It had been achieved largely by Mercian forces under Lord Aethelred although with some West Saxon assistance. It is often ignored by historians but it represented a major setback for Danish power in Northumbria and may have contributed to making their rule vulnerable to subsequent predation by the Mercians and by the Dublin Vikings. In a little over four years Ragnall of Dublin would make his first moves in an ultimately successful campaign aimed at the conquest of York. It may also have contributed to the later decision by the English leaders to switch from a defensive strategy to an offensive one. The major defeats inflicted on Danish East Anglia in 902 and Danish York in 910 had left them incapable of offensive action against the English. Instead, they were forced to act defensively and wait for the tide to turn against them.

The new offensive strategy adopted by the English after this date would be aimed at the recovery of territory in eastern England previously lost to Danish occupation. It is true that a number of earlier raids had taken place, like those of 894, 902 and 909, but these had been probing attacks aimed at the weak boundary region between the spheres of authority of the Danes of Northumbria and East Anglia. They had perhaps been a harbinger of what was to come but remained raids rather than attempts to recover territory. The English leaders could now consider measures that would bring about a more permanent change in the political map of England.

It was later in the same year as the great victory at Tettenhall that Lady Aethelflaed, Lord Aethelred's wife, according to the Mercian Register, built a *burh* at *Bremesbyrig*, an as yet unidentified site. It has been suggested that it may have been either Bromsberrow in Gloucestershire or Bromesberrow near Ledbury in Herefordshire. The former is perhaps the most promising since it lies close to the Roman road linking Gloucester and Hereford. However, it seems likely that only future excavation will finally settle the matter.[42]

This first appearance of Lady Aethelflaed acting in a ruling capacity would seem to indicate that Aethelred himself was somehow unavailable. It would be very unusual for a woman at this time to assume such a male role other than in a capacity in which she deputised for her husband. It is just possible that Aethelred was occupied elsewhere in the aftermath of his victory but it would be unusual for him not to be identified with an action he had initiated even when not present. One Irish source, admittedly a much later one, informs us that he had fallen seriously ill and as a result his wife had been compelled to step into his shoes. This seems a much more plausible reason for the appearance of Aethelflaed in such a context. If this source is correct, it is possible that Aethelred had been wounded at Tettenhall and was thereafter incapacitated. It is often assumed by historians that Aethelred had been seriously ill for many years but the sources provide no real evidence to support this. The chronological details of the much later Irish source recording his illness should not be relied on in this context as it contains many of the aspects of a legend. If Aethelflaed had deputised for her husband on earlier occasions the Mercian Register would almost certainly have recorded this as otherwise it records her actions in considerable detail. The death of Aethelred in the following year seems to make the possibility of a case of illness or wounds received during the Tettenhall campaign more likely.

In 911 the Mercian Register and the Chronicle both record the death of Lord Aethelred, the ruler of Mercia. Unfortunately, they provide no further details about

Detail from sarcophagus cover, St Mary's Church, Wirksworth, Derbyshire. (Photograph by W. Walker)

the cause of his death or about Aethelred himself. The later chronicler Aethelweard adds only that he was 'buried in peace in the fortress of Gloucester', which had been the seat of his power. It is almost certain that this burial took place in Aethelred's own new foundation of St Peter's, soon to be renamed St Oswald's, in Gloucester. What can we say about this man and about his period of rule in Mercia?[43]

In the darkest days of Mercian history, Lord Aethelred stepped into the power vacuum left by Viking conquest and the collapse of the old kingdom. He sought out a firm alliance with Wessex to bolster his position against the Vikings and potential rivals and slowly gathered the other Mercian nobles under his wing. He commenced the process of building *burhs* across Mercia to assist the defence of the kingdom. He presided over a reform of the army, detailed in Chapter 7, which gradually transformed it into a force that could face up to the Vikings. He led a series of military campaigns with West Saxon support that built up the experience and confidence of the Mercian troops. He secured a number of significant successes over Viking forces and began the process of striking back against their bases. This military success culminated in, what should perhaps be seen as his crowning achievement, the stunning victory over the Northumbrian Danes at Tettenhall. He bequeathed to his widow and successor a strong and confident kingdom which she would be able to lead in an offensive aimed at the recovery of those lands lost to the Danes. In short, Aethelred saved part of Mercia from the wreckage of Viking assault and built the solid foundation from which a bid to restore the whole kingdom could be launched.

CHAPTER 5

Lady of the Mercians

In 911 Aethelred, Lord of Mercia, died, either of an unknown illness or possibly of wounds received at Tettenhall, leaving no male heir. In one of the most unique events in early medieval history, he was succeeded as ruler of Mercia by his wife, Aethelflaed. This is the only example from the entire Anglo-Saxon period of a female ruler of one of the kingdoms. In this period military leadership and ability was a highly prized and almost essential pre-requisite for political leadership and therefore adult males naturally monopolised such positions. Male minors rarely succeeded to positions of rule, and women had never done so. There does exist one recorded instance of a female regency for a male minor, but none of direct female rule. The succession of Aethelflaed was clearly an unprecedented occurrence and, as such, it needs an explanation.[1]

In Mercia at this time the political circumstances were rather unusual. Lord Aethelred had died leaving no known close male relatives who could succeed him. In addition, the earlier rival dynasties of Mercia appear to have been effectively removed from consideration either by their earlier extermination or by the taint of association with the heathen Vikings. This situation clearly presented a problem for a land that, in spite of recent successes, was still very much under threat from its Viking neighbours. The kingdom desperately needed a period of stability and security from Viking assault in order to complete its recent recovery. This could best be ensured by the maintenance of the vital alliance with Wessex and this alliance was now represented in the persons of Aethelred's wife, Aethelflaed, and their daughter Aelfwynn, respectively sister and niece of King Edward of Wessex. It was probably therefore pragmatic reasons of political advantage that led the Mercians to support Aethelflaed in succession to her husband, rather than any sentimental attachment to his new dynasty. They wanted to preserve the vital alliance with Wessex and she and her daughter were the living bonds of that alliance.

However, this is not to deny that there was probably also a strong element of loyalty, perhaps almost nostalgia, towards old Mercia in their support for Aethelflaed. She was herself part-Mercian through her mother, Ealhswith, the daughter of *Ealdorman* Aethelred Mucil of the *Gainas* and Eadburh, a lady who, according to

Asser, came from 'the royal stock of the Mercians'. However, more than this Aethelflaed represented an opportunity for Mercia to continue to maintain its distinct identity. The Mercians did not choose, as they might have done, to secure the backing of Wessex by submitting to the direct rule of King Edward himself. Instead, they chose to maintain the independence of Mercia and its traditions by supporting Aethelflaed, who could rule until her daughter became of age to marry. Thereafter, the old kingdom could still be preserved and later restored by the man who married Aelfwynn and would therefore succeed to the rule of the kingdom.[2]

In making this choice, the Mercian nobles clearly ran a number of risks. A female ruler might be viewed by potential rivals, whether Viking, Welsh or even West Saxon, as a weakness providing them with an invitation to attack Mercia. As we have seen, the Vikings particularly had shown themselves adept at detecting and exploiting such political weakness in the past. A female ruler might also prove unable to provide effective personal military leadership while any deputies fulfilling this role on her behalf might be tempted to assume direct rule themselves. A number of Mercian kings had found themselves subject to challenge following military defeats, for example, Beornwulf and Wiglaf. A female ruler might also present an opportunity for competition among rival nobles within Mercia itself, who might seek to secure her rights to the kingdom for themselves by marrying her. The fact that none of these risks became a reality would provide ample justification for their decision.

In their search for a stable and secure but distinct future for their homeland the Mercian nobles made the unusual but ultimately well-informed decision to support the Lady Aethelflaed as their ruler. The fact that she fulfilled this role very effectively was in part due to her own formidable character and in part to her close alliance with her brother King Edward of Wessex.

The Lady Aethelflaed appears to have inherited many of the qualities of character demonstrated by her father, King Alfred of Wessex and would reveal these during her personal rule. In addition, during her early years at her father's court in Wessex and subsequently as the consort of Lord Aethelred of Mercia, Aethelflaed had undoubtedly observed both of these able rulers very closely and learnt much about the exercise of political and military power. She appears as the joint grantor with Aethelred in a significant number of Mercian charters. Indeed, during the period prior to Aethelred's death she appears in effect to have ruled on his behalf while he was indisposed, either through illness or wounds. Thus, in 910, soon after the great victory at Tettenhall, the Mercian Register records that she had a *burh* constructed at an as yet unlocated site called *Bremesbyrig*. This was almost certainly one such occasion when she acted in place of her husband. In addition, an admittedly much later fragment of saga material from Ireland informs us that Aethelflaed operated as deputy for her sick husband and shows that this fact was widely known and remembered.[3]

Statue of Lady Aethelflaed, Tamworth, Staffordshire. (Photograph by W. Walker)

A key factor in her success was the fact that she represented in her own person the physical embodiment of the alliance with Wessex. It was her marriage to Aethelred that had cemented this original alliance between King Alfred and Aethelred of Mercia. This ceremonial union between Aethelred and Aethelflaed represented the concrete bond between the two families that mirrored and at the same time reinforced their political alliance. In the absence of Aethelred, his widow Aethelflaed and their daughter were now all that remained of this alliance. If the Mercians wished to retain this alliance, which was the essential assurance for their future existence, they had to maintain Aethelflaed in power. This made the alternative possibility of selecting a new ruler from among the ranks of the *ealdormen* an extremely unattractive prospect. It would carry not only the risk of internal dispute and civil war but also the prospect of abandonment by Wessex to face the Vikings alone – a dismal prospect for those who had lived through the crises following the fall of Burgred in 874 and the carving-up of Mercia in 877.

An important factor in Aethelflaed's personal rule was the fact that she remained a widow and did not remarry. This effectively ensured her own position by removing the possibility of any second husband assuming military and hence political control of Mercia in her place. It prevented the development of any rivalries for her hand among the nobles within Mercia itself. It excluded the possibility of a foreign marriage that might undermine or even break the West Saxon alliance. It also ensured that no alternative heir would be born to challenge the position of Aelfwynn, her daughter by Aethelred. In these circumstances, Aethelflaed's brother King Edward and many members of the Mercian nobility clearly had an interest in her remaining a chaste widow. It is impossible to be certain whether her status was the result of a personal choice or whether it was a condition imposed on her by her male relations or her own nobles. However, in light of what the sources tell us about Lady Aethelflaed it seems likely that this was her own choice informed by her realisation of the political risks. She chose to remain a widow to preserve her own power and to safeguard the future of her daughter.[4]

As a result of this background, Aethelflaed was to prove herself a formidable ruler and every inch a match for those contemporary male rulers, opponents and allies alike, who surrounded her. In 911 she succeeded her husband as sole ruler of the Mercian kingdom. This transition was undoubtedly eased for both Aethelflaed and her subjects by her activities as Aethelred's deputy during his periods of illness. She began her personal rule well by following the policies instigated by her husband in Mercia and by her brother in neighbouring Wessex, in emulation of King Alfred. However, she also took a groundbreaking initiative that, although probably controversial at the time, would contribute significantly to the future achievements of both Mercia and Wessex. Lady Aethelflaed showed by this move that she was prepared to offer a sacrifice to preserve the West Saxon alliance and secure her own power in Mercia. In 911, according to the Chronicle, Aethelflaed surrendered 'London and Oxford and all the lands which belonged to them' to her brother King Edward of Wessex. This transfer of valuable territory undoubtedly provided an enormous boost to West Saxon power in terms of land and the wealth that derived from it. Lady Aethelflaed probably made this concession in return for recognition of her authority by King Edward, who might otherwise have been tempted to try to take control of Mercia himself.[5]

It is more difficult to see how this surrender benefited the Mercians. Why did the nobles of Mercia permit this huge surrender of territory? The reason would appear to be that this concession was accepted as offering a number of worthwhile advantages. Most importantly it guaranteed the continuation of the essential alliance with Wessex without which Mercia might find itself facing the Vikings alone. It was a concession that allowed the rest of Mercia to retain its continued independence from West Saxon control. It also effectively released the Mercians from any obligation to defend this territory which stood exposed to attack from Danish East Anglia and the occupied East Midlands but distant from the new centres of Mercian power around Gloucester and Worcester in the far west. It is perhaps significant in this respect that *Ealdorman* Aethelfrith, the Mercian responsible for this region, had already been associating himself with King Edward. In 904 he sought endorsement of his renewed charters from Edward as well as Lord Aethelred. This seems to confirm West Saxon interest in this region and perhaps indicates that Aethelfrith would have found this arrangement personally acceptable, thus helping make it work. Another important point to make about this territorial arrangement is that it did not effect the future status of this area as Mercian territory. In subsequent years, the border between Mercia and Wessex would continue to be recognised as running along the Thames and all of the lands to the north of the river would be seen as part of Mercia. The arrangement was therefore a temporary expedient which allowed for more effective military and political control of this region.

In the future, this new division of political responsibility between Lady Aethelflaed and her brother King Edward would also guide their strategic interests during the process of reconquest of the Danish-occupied areas. They each directed their campaigns against different Danish kingdoms, so avoiding any possibility of conflict between their own forces. Lady Aethelflaed would direct her forces against those Danes subject to the kings of York in the area north of the boundary line that ran along the River Welland. King Edward of Wessex would set his forces against those Danes subject to the kings of East Anglia south of this boundary. There were, in fact, no truly joint campaigns between these rulers, although their individual activities almost inevitably impinged on each other from time to time, but rather two distinct but well directed ones. This clear and sensible division of responsibilities prevented any possible confusion and tension between the two kingdoms and their armies. Indeed, it proved so effective that it remained in effect right up to the death of Lady Aethelflaed when the whole political situation was reviewed. King Edward, was now faced with the task of defending this region from the Danes. Within a year, he would move to secure the new territory built around the existing Mercian *burhs* at Oxford and London. This left the Mercians free to concentrate on the defence and stabilisation of their new core territory in the west.

In 912 Lady Aethelflaed directed her first fully independent military operation within Mercia when she had fortified *burhs* constructed at *Scergeat* and Bridgnorth. The first of these was built on 2 May at an as yet unlocated site. No particularly suitable possibilities have been offered for the location of this site, but this may change in time. The second was built close to a vital strategic bridge over the Severn which had already been used by marauding Viking armies in 895 and 910. Indeed, the Mercian *burh* may have made use of an earlier Viking fortress built on this site in 895 to provide the Viking raiders of that year with a secure winter base. The securing of this vital crossing of the Severn meant that the previous free movement of Viking marauders through Mercian territory could either be inhibited or prevented altogether in the future. These measures continued the process of consolidation of the remaining Mercian controlled territory by the building of *burhs*, which had begun under Aethelred with those at Gloucester, Worcester, Hereford and, probably, Shrewsbury. This process would be completed and subsequently developed into one of expansion initially into debateable land and then into Danish controlled areas.[6]

In that same year, 912, King Edward proceeded to direct his own West Saxon forces to secure the area of Mercia ceded to him by his sister the year before. In the spring he led a West Saxon army northwards across the Thames to the borders of Danish-occupied territory. There, he built a *burh* on the north bank of the River Lea at Hertford to cover the crossing of the former Roman road, Ermine Street, and block any passage up the river Lea as in 894. This new *burh* also provided a bulwark against the Danes to the north of London. In the summer he followed this up by constructing a *burh* between 18 May and 24 June at Witham near Maldon in Essex to control the Blackwater Estuary and the approach to London from Colchester and Ipswich in Danish East Anglia. This *burh* was probably also intended to inhibit or prevent the possibility of future Viking activity along the Essex coast around their old haunts at Benfleet, Shoeburyness and Mersea Island. He sent another force to Hertford to build a second *burh* there on the south bank of the river Lea. This fortress was designed to reinforce his protective measures on the approach to London from East Anglia to the north. It possibly replaced or more likely reinforced that constructed earlier in the year.[7]

In the following year, 913, King Edward was unable to undertake any offensive action but instead found himself on the defensive against Danish attacks. The Danish armies based on Northampton and Leicester combined after Easter to invade his newly ceded Mercian territories. They perhaps hoped to exploit any weakness in his control over this area and to eliminate his advanced *burhs* at Hertford. One unit of their force advanced as far as Hook Norton in Oxfordshire, while another attacked Luton in Bedfordshire. They raided the surrounding areas and collected a great deal of plunder. However, while on their way home the raiders were challenged by local, and hence Mercian, forces near Luton and completely defeated. They were put to flight, abandoning their plunder and losing many of their horses and weapons. Although this Danish counterthrust failed it did indicate that they were still capable of acting in defence of their new settlements as Lady Aethelflaed herself would soon discover.[8]

In 913 Aethelflaed made a significant advance, extending the protective screen of *burhs* around West Mercia. In early summer of that year she directed a major military campaign deep into the heart of the old Mercian kingdom at Tamworth on the river Tame. This lay on the fringes of Danish-occupied territory centred around their fortresses at Leicester and Derby and hence vulnerable to attack. There she had a *burh* built on the site of King Offa's former capital. This fortification was ideally placed to offer protection to the site of the still functioning bishopric at nearby Lichfield. It directly guarded the crossing of the River Tame and could also cover the nearby junction of two Roman roads, Watling Street and Ryknild Street. The construction of a *burh* at this vital choke point on several routes further indicates the military importance of *burhs* as checks and barriers against potential Danish invasion. It may also have been in response to the earlier Danish attacks on her brother's territory in former south-east Mercia. This site may also have been selected for symbolic reasons: as the former royal capital of King Offa, it held powerful associations for all Mercians and the restoration of Mercian control there would demonstrate to all Aethelflaed's intention to restore the wider kingdom itself.[9]

In the late summer of this same year, Aethelflaed moved the focus of her campaign north and west from Tamworth to Stafford in the valley of the river Trent. There she had another *burh* constructed before 1 August which could guard the approach route to the crossing of the river Severn at Bridgnorth and so provide a forward defence for the probably already existing *burh* at Shrewsbury. This fortress and that at Tamworth also helped to screen the cities of Worcester and Gloucester to the north-west and to provide additional security to the heart of West Mercia. They signified more than this, however, representing the first steps towards a forward policy of consolidating under Mercian protection disputed areas near the margins of Danish-occupied territories. This policy would ultimately merge into one of moving offensively into areas actually occupied by the Danes.

In the following year, 914, Lady Aethelflaed once again directed a military operation designed to extend the screen of *burhs* on the margins of Mercian territory. In the early summer the Mercian army moved north into later Cheshire and built a new *burh* at Eddisbury Hill to the north-west of Aethelred's existing *burh* at Chester. This site was well placed on the line of the Roman road from Manchester to Chester to interdict the movements of any Danish army coming south from Northumbria. It also provided an effective flank guard for the *burh* at Chester itself.[10]

Until this point, Aethelflaed's military expeditions had been relatively unhindered by any reaction from her Danish opponents. Since none of the Mercian campaigns had yet ventured much beyond Mercian territory the local Danish rulers of Northampton, Leicester or Derby in the East Midlands may not have perceived them as a threat. They were perhaps more concerned about the West Saxon moves being directed against Bedford. They may also have felt unable to act without the support of their Northumbrian overlords, who were increasingly distracted by the contemporary struggle for control of York between the local Danish and Dublin-based Norse factions. Whatever the reason, it is apparent that they had offered no significant opposition to these Mercian fortress building activities. In 914 this situation changed. However, surprisingly, it was not the Danish rulers of the East Midland fortresses who provided the opposition for Aethelflaed but a new group of Vikings who had arrived unexpectedly from the Continent. They would land from the sea in the Severn Estuary while the main Mercian army was absent on their campaign around Chester in the far north, and would pose a deadly threat to the exposed heartland of West Mercia in the Severn Valley.[11]

This Viking naval force under *Jarls* Ottar and Harold, which had been raiding in Brittany, had crossed the Channel, sailed around Cornwall and entered the Severn Estuary. It raided extensively in South Wales capturing Cyfeilliog, the Bishop of Ergyng. Buoyed up by their success, these forces proceeded to attempt to invade Mercian territory around Hereford. Unfortunately for them, their earlier activities in South Wales had alerted the Mercian defences and they were prepared. The main Chronicle records how:

. . . the men from Hereford and Gloucester and from the nearest *burhs* met them and fought against them and put them to flight and killed earl Harold . . . and a great part of the army and drove them into an enclosure and besieged them there until they gave them hostages (promising) that they would leave the king's dominion.[12]

This Viking invasion had represented a very real threat to Mercia coming at a time when the main Mercian forces were already occupied in the North. The Viking *jarls* probably thought that the heartland of West Mercia would lie open and undefended before them. Instead, they met determined opposition from troops raised from those earmarked for the garrisons of Hereford, Gloucester and other *burhs* in West Mercia,

Ruins of St Oswald's Minster, Gloucester. (Copyright *The Citizen*)

including perhaps Worcester and *Bremesbyrig*. These men formed an obviously well-organised and well-led unit, able to operate flexibly and in a variety of roles. They fought a positional battle in the open, followed this up with a mobile pursuit of the retreating enemy and then carried out a successful siege of the trapped enemy in a fortified position. This incident reflects the ability of the new Mercian lordship to organise defence in depth. They were able to maintain a large fully trained and equipped army in the field but retained sufficient well-trained and equipped reserves to respond very effectively to a major attack elsewhere. This was clearly a result of the reform and reorganisation of the Mercian armies by Aethelred.

The Chronicle version of these events does allow for the possibility that the Mercians received some West Saxon aid on this occasion, although this cannot be certain. The Chronicle account, however, appears to go further and suggests that the whole defence against the Viking force was organised by the West Saxon king. He is correctly named as the leader, who stationed men along the south coast of the Severn Estuary in Wessex to repulse the enemy attacks. However, it was not, in fact, from his 'dominion' that the Viking force was repulsed by the men of Hereford and Gloucester, but from that of Lady Aethelflaed of Mercia. It seems more likely that the successful defence of the Severn Estuary was, on this occasion as often before, a joint effort by West Saxon and Mercian forces and one in which the Mercians perhaps played the larger role.

The successful local defence of West Mercia in 914 allowed Lady Aethelflaed to continue her planned campaign of fortress construction without interruption. In a second campaign in the early autumn, she sent the Mercian army westwards to Warwick on the river Avon. There, another *burh* was erected to monitor the Avon river crossing and to cover the western approaches to Worcester and Gloucester. The construction of this *burh* was particularly important in light of the raids undertaken the previous year by Danish armies from Northampton and Leicester into neighbouring West Saxon-administered territory in what was to become Bedfordshire and Oxfordshire. It is possible that its construction was intended to assist Aethelflaed's brother Edward in his campaign against Bedford, but it was just as important as part of the process of extending the defences of West Mercia in this area.[13]

In November of this same year, 914, King Edward of Wessex may have followed up his sister's securing of Warwick, perhaps as part of a co-ordinated effort to protect their now common frontier. He advanced on Buckingham and remained there for some four weeks, building two *burhs* at the crossing of the Great Ouse. These provided a solid point of defence on the Roman road north, which connected Oxford with Watling Street. This advance, following that on Hertford the year before, provided the second prong of a pincer movement aimed against the Danish fortress of Bedford. The threat of being surrounded in this manner quickly caused *Jarl* Thurketel, the Danish commander of the army based at Bedford, to submit to Edward along with all his followers. A number of those subject to the authority of the Northampton Danes also chose to submit at this time according to the Chronicle account.[14]

In 915 Lady Aethelflaed once again ordered the Mercian army into the field, this time on the Welsh border near Montgomery where it built a *burh* at Chirbury. The structure lay close to the line of Offa's Dyke, that monument to Mercian power constructed by Aethelflaed's great predecessor to mark the frontier with Wales. The location suggests that this *burh* was intended to guard the border with Wales but this route had also been used by Viking raiders in 893. In fact, this *burh* may have been a reconstruction or extension of one of the temporary fortresses erected back in 893 by the English forces as a base during their successful siege of the Viking fortified camp at nearby Buttington.[15]

In this same year of 915, Lady Aethelflaed went on to build a second *burh*, this time at *Weardbyrig*, another as yet unidentified location. A recent article by Coates argues fairly persuasively that it may have been located at a place called Gwespyr near Llansa in Clwyd. This site would certainly provide a useful location for the defence of the mouth of the river Dee against further Viking incursions like that of Ingimund in 902. It might also be seen as complimentary to the *burh* built at Runcorn to defend the Mersey later in 915. In the absence of any archaeological evidence supporting this suggestion, it must remain speculative at this stage.[16]

It may have been while supervising the construction work on this *burh* that, on 9 September 915, Lady Aethelflaed granted to her *thegn* Eadric by charter ten hides of land at Farnborough, probably in Worcestershire. The text of the surviving copy of this grant is obviously corrupt but nevertheless contains some interesting information. The location of the grant is a place called *Weardburg*, surely the same as Aethelflaed's *burh*. The year date of this grant is usually given as 916 (for the clearly incorrect 878 of the text). However, the list of witnesses includes an Abbot Egbert, who was probably the one killed in June 916. Therefore, the date of this grant may in fact be 915, which would certainly fit with its issue at *Weardbyrig*. Aethelflaed apparently made this grant independently of her brother, Edward of Wessex. The grant was also witnessed by her daughter Aelfwynn, mistakenly listed as a bishop in the surviving corrupt version of the text which has reached us, and by a number of her bishops, *ealdormen* and *thegns*.[17]

On a general point, it is fairly clear that all of those Mercian *burhs*, including Hereford, Shrewsbury, Chirbury, the later *Rhuddlan* and possibly those at *Bremesbyrig* and *Weardbyrig*, sited in the area of the Welsh frontier were probably intended primarily to contribute to the defence of Mercia against the Danes. They were positioned in response to possible Danish threats as much as to any perceived threat from the Welsh themselves. Thus we have seen that Chirbury was on a route used by

The Lichfield Gospels Ms. 1, p. 218. (The Dean and Chapter of Lichfield Cathedral)

Viking raiders. The forts built at *Weardbyrig* and *Rhuddlan* in 921 were probably intended to control access up the rivers Dee and Clwyd respectively and so into north-west Mercia rather than to defend the Welsh border. The Mercians had already demonstrated their ability to deal with Welsh armies, which presented a much less menacing threat than did the Danes. The Welsh were almost certainly much more poorly equipped than contemporary English or Danish forces, no doubt in reflection of the comparative poverty of their society. They probably had fewer expensive swords, no great axes and made little or no use of chainmail. In comparison, English and Danish armies were lavishly equipped with all these items. As a result, the Mercians were usually able to defeat opposing Welsh forces in most circumstances without the need for the sort of advantage provided by the *burhs*. Indeed, even in the direst of straits the much weakened Mercian army could still inflict severe defeats on the Welsh. In 878 Rhodri *Mawr*, that great Welsh opponent of the Vikings, and his son Gwriad were killed by Mercian forces. This happened at a time when Mercia was almost completely under the heel of the Vikings, having just been partitioned at their hands.

Still in 915 Lady Aethelflaed and her Mercians managed to construct yet a third *burh*, this time at Runcorn in Cheshire. This fortress provided security for the mouth of the river Mersey against the passage of Viking warships from Ireland. It would also have the advantage of restricting possible communication routes between the major Viking bases at Dublin and York. The forging of increasingly strong links between these centres meant that they appeared to pose a particularly potent threat to the restoration of Mercian power. This made the need for defences in the northern area especially pressing as would be witnessed by subsequent phases of *burh* construction.[18]

In November 915, meanwhile, King Edward of Wessex had continued the process of consolidating his authority in the area north of the Thames. He advanced with his army to the still Danish-held fortress of Bedford and took direct control of it. Its ruler, *Jarl* Thurketel, had offered his submission the year before but Edward clearly wanted to ensure that his control was made effective in practice. He once again spent some four weeks in the area constructing his own *burh* on the south bank of the river to keep the Danish fortress under observation. Thus he confirmed his control over his new client, Thurketel, and ensured his allegiance by establishing a force of troops to monitor and enforce his obedience and that of his followers.[19]

In 916 Lady Aethelflaed finally had to interrupt her fortress campaigns in Mercia to deal with what was a direct snub to her authority among her Welsh clients in the West. There is evidence in the sources that she had assumed from her husband the traditional Mercian overlordship over a number of Welsh rulers, including Tewdr of Brycheiniog, Hywel and Clydog of Deheubarth and Idwal of Gwynedd. The Chronicle subsequently records the submission of the last three of these men to King Edward of Wessex, after his assumption of power in Mercia in 918, in a way that clearly implies that they had previously been under the overlordship of Lady Aethelflaed herself. The first of them would be the prime reason for her intervention in Wales at this time.[20]

On 16 June 916 a Mercian abbot named Egbert, who was travelling through part of Wales with his English retinue, was killed, presumably by a group of local Welshmen. The abbot had probably been travelling under the protection of Lady Aethelflaed, and the local ruler had therefore broken his obligations to her as his overlord by failing to protect the abbot or to punish his killers. As a result, Aethelflaed was obliged to bring him back into line and she did so in no uncertain terms. The Mercian Register records that: '3 days later Aethelflaed sent an army into Wales and destroyed *Brecenanmere* and captured the king's wife and 33 others.' This entry records the destruction of the royal crannog of Tewdr, King of Brycheiniog on Llangorse Lake in Brecon and the capture of his queen and members of his court.[21]

This account shows Aethelflaed enforcing her overlordship over the Welsh rulers in a very practical and emphatic fashion. This Welsh lord may have believed that a female ruler in Mercia was a sign of weakness, an invitation and opportunity to ignore or flout his obligations. If this was the case then he discovered to his cost that Aethelflaed was neither weak nor powerless. She was the ruler of a powerful lordship and one fully prepared to act ruthlessly to defend her subjects and her interests. Although Tewdr himself escaped this disaster, he probably made his submission to Aethelflaed soon afterwards since he is subsequently found among the witnesses of a charter of King Athelstan in 934. In addition, Aethelflaed's punitive action in this case seems to have had a salutary effect on her other Welsh clients who appear to have remained loyal to her thereafter. This attack, although in the nature of a punitive expedition against a satellite state, nevertheless, appears to be the first indication of a shift from a defensive to an offensive policy on the part of Aethelflaed. In the next year she would strike against the Danes themselves.[22]

In the summer of 916, meanwhile, King Edward and the West Saxon army were active against the Danes building a *burh* at Maldon in Essex. This was probably intended to reinforce or replace that built at Witham some four years earlier. He also permitted *Jarl* Thurketel of Bedford and his followers to leave England for the Continent. They may have chosen to go there in order to join in the Danish settlement of Normandy which was underway at this time. It is possible that Thurketel and his men had found West Saxon rule and the consequent obligations and tribute payments too onerous and considered that the atmosphere in Normandy would be more congenial. Perhaps the undoubted requirement Edward would have laid on them to convert to Christianity may have jarred with their own beliefs. Whatever the reason, they decided to leave England. Edward can only have been pleased to see them off. The elimination of this alien force could only strengthen and safeguard his own rule in Bedfordshire.[23]

In the following year, 917, King Edward built *burhs* before 13 April at Towcester in Northamptonshire and between 19 and 21 May at a place called *Wigingamere*, apparently located at Newport on the River Cam in north Essex. This further advance, coming on top of the solid progress made by Edward against the Danes of East Anglia since 912, had gradually eaten away at their territory. The exile of Thurketel and his men and the English occupation of Towcester, so close to Northampton, appear to have finally jolted the Danes out of their apathy. They set about organising a major counter-offensive against Edward involving the armies of East Anglia and a number of the Danish fortresses in the East Midlands. Unfortunately, this would consist of three separate strikes rather than one knock-out blow. An army drawn from Northampton, Leicester and areas to the north attacked the new *burh* at Towcester between 24 June and 1 August. At the same time, a second army drawn from Huntingdon and parts of East Anglia advanced to Tempsford where they constructed a new fortress from which they launched an attempt to recover Bedford. A third army drawn from East Anglia attempted to seize the new *burh* at Wigingamere in Essex. In a classic demonstration of the failure to apply concentration of force, the Danes were defeated in all three attacks. They lost a large number of men, particularly at Bedford where a sortie organised by the besieged English garrison inflicted a severe defeat and put their army to flight.[24]

In 917 Lady Aethelflaed launched her first offensive foray into Danish-occupied territory and selected as her target Derby, one of the key fortresses that formed the foundation of their control there. The construction of the *burhs* at Tamworth and Stafford in 913 provided the necessary springboard for this operation. The timing of the assault for July 917 may, however, have had a lot to do with events further east. It seems likely that Aethelflaed took advantage of the temporary weakness presented by the absence of those Danish forces involved in the attack on Towcester. This campaign certainly involved the Danish forces from

Grave slab excavated at St Oswald's Minster, Gloucester. (Gloucester City Museum and Art Gallery)

neighbouring Leicester but may also have included men from Derby itself. If this was the case, it presented a golden opportunity to strike at a weakened enemy. It is a sign of sound military judgement that Lady Aethelflaed seized it with both hands.

In summer 917 the attack on Derby was launched and the Mercian Register relates how:

> Aethelflaed, lady of the Mercians, with the help of God, before 1 August obtained the borough which is called Derby, with all that belongs to it; and, there also 4 of her *thegns*, who were dear to her, were killed within the gates.

This direct attack on one of the major centres of Danish power was a bold move even when directed against an isolated or weakened defence. It was the first direct attack on one of the major Danish fortifications by an English army, a difficult military operation at any time. The previous assault made by Aethelred on Benfleet in 893, also against a depleted garrison, had been on a more temporary fortress. The mention of the need for God's help in the venture and the losses suffered by the Mercians in the assault both suggest that the victory was dearly won.[25]

In the aftermath of the failure of the Danish counter-offensive, and perhaps in emulation of his own sister's success against Derby, King Edward of Wessex launched his own offensive. In contrast to the Danes' attack, he concentrated all of his forces against the new Danish fortress at Tempsford. The result was a second dramatic success with the fortress taken by storm and many Danes killed or captured. The former included an unnamed king, who must surely have been Guthrum II, the Danish ruler of East Anglia and successor to the Eric killed at Holme in 902, and two *jarls*. This victory was quickly exploited by Edward when he launched a second offensive that same autumn against the Danish fortress of Colchester in Essex. The result was a third success involving the fall of the fortress and the slaughter of its garrison. A Danish retaliatory strike against his own *burh* at Maldon was also defeated.

The year 917 had proved disastrous for the Danes, with the failure of their great counter-offensive and the loss of Derby, Tempsford and Colchester. They appeared to have lost their last opportunity to turn the tide against the English and after this were unable to mount any further counter-attacks without the assistance of the men of York. The year would end on a note of surrender and submission. The writing was now on the wall for the Danish Kingdom of East Anglia and for those Danish *burhs* still remaining in the East Midlands. *Jarl* Thurferth and the men of Northampton and Cambridge recognised the inevitable and chose to submit to King Edward rather than face an attack. The latter then proceeded to occupy the deserted fortress of Huntingdon and transform it into an English *burh*. The subsequent collapse of East Anglia was a natural result of these West Saxon successes and the loss of their king and many of their fighting men at Tempsford and Colchester. The Danes had staked everything on their counter-offensive and they had lost. The once powerful kingdom of Guthrum had been reduced to a rump, incorporating only Norfolk and Suffolk and which was compelled to recognise West Saxon overlordship.[26]

Early in the following year, 918, Lady Aethelflaed once again directed her forces into Danish territory, this time against the important fortress of Leicester. This was no easy option since it had been forces drawn from Leicester that had sought to dispute her brother Edward's control of Hertford in 913 and to reduce his *burh* at Towcester in 917. The Mercian army probably ravaged the country around the city but this time there was no need to storm the fortress which surrendered peacefully. It had already effectively been isolated in the previous year by the Mercian capture of Derby to the north and the West Saxon occupation of Northampton to the south. This isolation and the presence of a Mercian army raiding the land around it must have persuaded the Danish force based at Leicester that their best option was to surrender, and thus another major element of the Danish force occupying Eastern Mercia fell under Aethelflaed's control. Only a year after they had defied King Edward, the Danes of Leicester submitted to Aethelflaed without a fight. This major success would pave the way for King Edward's assault on Stamford, which got under way in late May 918.[27]

This English penetration into Danish-controlled territory finally caused the men of York themselves to ponder where their best interests lay. Accounts of the situation in York at this time are confused, but it seems that the local Danes, who had been converted to Christianity around 893, had been subjected to rule by a pagan, called Ragnall, from Dublin. The Danes had proved unable to maintain their own Christian kingdom after their disastrous defeat by Lord Aethelred at Tettenhall in 910. The resultant power vacuum had been filled by Ragnall, who, on the evidence of the coinage, appears to have first seized control of York in 911. Initially, he subdued York quite effectively but as a result of distractions elsewhere, including attempts to conquer English Northumbria beyond the Tyne, conflicts with the Scots and raiding activities in Ireland, he apparently loosened his grip. It is clear that a faction in York remained unreconciled to his rule and was seeking leadership. It is possible that the Danish Christians in York found rule by this pagan distasteful, or perhaps many simply resented him as an outsider. Whatever the reason, by 918 they had apparently had enough and were actively seeking a more agreeable alternative. It was in these circumstances that they approached Lady Aethelflaed in the summer of 918 and promised to submit to her overlordship, giving pledges and swearing oaths to that effect. The reason they sought to submit to her rather than her brother seems fairly clear. She had forces on the borders of their kingdom poised ready to intervene should Ragnall attempt to interfere with their submission. In contrast, King Edward, who was engaged in a siege of Stamford at this time, faced fortresses at Nottingham and Lincoln between him and York. If these proposals had come to fruition they would have provided a spectacular conclusion to Aethelflaed's role in the subjugation of the Danish-occupied areas.[28]

Unfortunately, it was shortly after these promises had been made and before the associated arrangements had been finalised that Lady Aethelflaed died on 12 June 918 at Tamworth in the heart of her renewed Mercian lordship. She died in the eighth year of her rule and her demise was widely recorded in Britain, being noted in the Welsh and Irish Annals and the West Saxon Chronicle as well as the Mercian Register. The clergy of St Peter's, the cathedral church of Worcester, would recite daily the *Laudate Dominum* and say a mass every Saturday for her soul. The Mercian Register describes her as: '. . . holding dominion over the Mercians . . . with lawful authority . . .' The *Annals of Ulster* refer to her as 'a very famous queen of the Saxons'. The Danes of York had promised to submit to her direction. She was clearly a widely respected and feared ruler in the British Isles. She was laid to rest beside her husband, Lord Aethelred, in the east chapel of St Oswald's Church in Gloucester, the centre of their power in Mercia. What would become of Mercia after her death?[29]

It had undoubtedly been Aethelflaed's intention that she be succeeded by her sole heir, Aelfwynn, her daughter by Lord Aethelred. This had been made clear in a charter of 904 to Worcester Cathedral which stated that: 'if Aelfwynn survives them it (the land granted) shall similarly remain uncontested as long as she lives'. Although this statement dealt with succession to private land, there seems no good reason to deny that it also carried the implication of what was recognised as the succession to rule of Mercia itself. This intention is surely confirmed by her presence as a witness to her mother Aethelflaed's charter to Eadric of 9 September 915 mentioned above. She also appears as witness to a charter issued jointly in 904 by

Annals of Ulster, entry recording the death of Lady Aethelflaed. (The Board of Trinity College, Dublin)

her uncle King Edward and both of her parents to *Ealdorman* Aethelfrith. The Mercian Register makes it clear that Aelfwynn, in fact, succeeded to the full authority previously held by her mother over Mercia.[30]

Immediately after Lady Aethelflaed's death, King Edward of Wessex came from Stamford, where he was on campaign, to Tamworth and took control of Mercia. This event is described in the West Saxon-inspired Chronicle as if it represented a submission by the men of Mercia to Edward and no reference whatever is made to Aelfwynn. This is clearly an account of the events which took place in December 918 rather than those of June of that year. It does not portray the facts as set out in the more detailed contemporary Mercian account. The reason for Edward's presence in Tamworth, in the summer of 918, was probably to secure Aelfwynn's succession. He was after all her closest male relative and as such had a direct personal interest in securing her rights. In addition, as King of Wessex, he also had an interest in preserving undisturbed the close relations which currently existed between his kingdom and Mercia. He probably realised that the best way to achieve this, at least in the short term, would be by securing the succession of his niece as ruler of Mercia. He probably did so by ensuring that the Mercian nobles, and perhaps those Welsh princes previously subject to Aethelflaed, submitted to Aelfwynn's authority.[31]

Once King Edward had achieved this objective, he proceeded to assault and capture the Danish fortress of Nottingham, something which Aethelflaed may already have planned before her death. It would certainly have made an appropriate target to follow on from the capture of Derby in 917 and the surrender of Leicester early in 918. The capture of Nottingham was probably achieved by a joint force of Mercians and West Saxons since in the following summer Edward would be found directing Mercian troops. The Danish fortress there was subsequently repaired and garrisoned as an English *burh*. There is no mention in any of our sources of the fate of the Danish fortress at Lincoln but it seems likely that it also surrendered at this time. It seems certain that Aelfwynn did not direct this expedition because she was still considered too young and inexperienced to do so and that Edward had therefore stepped in to perform this role for his niece.

It was probably immediately after this campaign using Mercian troops that King Edward returned to Tamworth, to resolve the issues arising from the new political situation in Mercia. He had reached a momentous decision and, as a result, three weeks before Christmas 918 he deprived his niece Aelfwynn of all authority in Mercia and took her into Wessex. It seems clear that the need for strong military leadership in Mercia had proved decisive in causing Edward to abandon his earlier plans to support his niece. It is not surprising that Edward chose to assume direct control over Mercia but what is surprising is that the Mercian nobles allowed him to do so. We will consider what had finally caused them to abandon their old hostility to Wessex and accept the rule of a West Saxon king further in the next chapter. The fate of Aelfwynn, Aethelflaed's daughter, thereafter is unknown but it seems likely that she was placed in seclusion in a nunnery. This was the customary fate of royal widows, unmarried princesses and other noble women who had been deprived of the protection of male relations but who needed to be kept safe and secure. It had been the fate of her own aunt, Aethelgifu, the daughter of King Alfred, who became the first abbess of the latter's new foundation at Shaftesbury in Dorset. A royal nunnery was the ideal place to hold someone like Aelfwynn, a royal princess, who could not be permitted to marry. It might have been the fate of her mother in 911 too had she not demonstrated remarkable personal, political and military abilities.[32]

The records provide us with no clues to the exact location of Aelfwynn's exile but a suggestion may be offered on the basis of what is known. The Mercian Register makes it clear that Aelfwynn was taken out of Mercia and into Wessex. The most likely religious houses for her to be sent to there were those closely connected to the West Saxon royal dynasty. Shaftesbury and Wilton were recent royal foundations of King Alfred and indeed the former had particularly close connections, as we have seen, being ruled by Aethelgifu, Alfred's daughter. It was described by Asser as holding 'many other noble nuns' and there could surely have been few more suitable venues for Aelfwynn's confinement. This would seem an ideal place to hold this royal princess, who could not be allowed to marry and transmit her claim to rule in Mercia to any husband. She was, in effect, imprisoned, an exile from her own land of Mercia, although her imprisonment in her aunt's custody may have been relatively comfortable.

The deposition of Aelfwynn finally brought an end to a brief interlude unique in the Anglo-Saxon period. This was the short span of some seven years when the Mercians were ruled by female rulers. It is worth stressing this fact. The early medieval English kingdoms, like those elsewhere in Europe, were dominated by warfare and the needs of warfare. This consisted of warfare in defence of ones own resources and warfare in predation on the resources of others. In turn, all of this warfare was controlled and directed by rulers in person. The physical strength of men was considered essential to wield the heavy iron weapons and bear the armour required and to undertake the immense physical effort involved in warfare during this period. In such circumstances, how could a woman possibly rule a kingdom when warfare and the threat of it were ever present. The reason may lie at least in part in the relatively higher status which seems to have been accorded to the ruler's wife in Mercian society.[33]

In ninth- and tenth-century Mercia, the position of queen appears to have carried a higher status than in neighbouring Wessex and also involved a more prominent role in government. The wives of Mercian kings had regularly borne the unambiguous Latin title *regina* in charters since the reign of King Offa. Mercian queens also appeared regularly as witnesses in official documents, usually immediately after the

Silver penny of Queen Cynethryth; the obverse shows a stylised portrait and the reverse her name. (Ashmolean Museum, Oxford)

king. Indeed, a number of them fairly consistently witness the charters of their royal husbands, including Cynethryth, wife of Offa, Cynethryth, wife of Wiglaf, Saethryth, wife of Beorhtwulf, Aethelswith, wife of Burgred, and, of course, Lady Aethelflaed herself. Indeed, as noted in Chapter 1, Queen Cynethryth, wife of Offa, even features uniquely on the Mercian coinage itself. This was in marked contrast to Wessex where the king's wife appeared much more rarely in official documents and was apparently less frequently endowed with the full royal title.[34]

The reasons for the relative prominence of these Mercian queens, compared to their West Saxon counterparts, are not entirely clear. It seems likely, however, that it was connected to the rather different succession arrangements that applied in Mercia at this period. The kingship rarely passed from father to son but was frequently the subject of competition between rival dynasties. The successive changes of dynasty and lack of continuity in the kingship made the securing of sufficient support from among the senior nobility for each rival candidate essential. In this context the marriage of each king or prospective king provided an important opportunity either to recruit new supporters or to bind existing supporters more closely by means of a marriage alliance. This would give the latter a direct investment in the future of this dynasty through the children of such a marriage. In turn, this meant that those wives who successfully became queen were important and consequently treated with more respect and rewarded with greater influence in the royal household and administration than other royal wives. There is no firm evidence in our surviving sources which would confirm or refute this theory but it does seem likely.

This is not to say that all the wives of Mercian rulers were accorded such high status. The charters of Ceolwulf I, Beornwulf and Ceolwulf II offer no evidence of their consorts, although the latter two at least may simply have been unmarried. In 797 Alcuin wrote to a Mercian *ealdorman* named Osberht to express concern that King Cenwulf had put aside one wife in favour of another. This clearly shows that in some cases Mercian rulers were prepared, like those elsewhere, to replace a wife where necessary, for example, to provide a male heir or to secure noble support. The latter was probably the case with Cenwulf. In 797 Cenwulf was a newly consecrated king probably seeking to consolidate his own hold on power through a marriage alliance with a powerful noble family. He therefore may have put aside a previous wife in order to arrange a politically advantageous match with a more well-connected woman. A politically motivated action such as this was not something which would have met with Alcuin's approval.[35]

This ninth-century tradition of the prominence of Mercian queens in activities associated with government and administration was one followed by Lady Aethelflaed after her marriage to Aethelred. She regularly features as a witness to his charters and in many cases also fulfils a joint role in the business being transacted in these documents. This already prominent and active role prepared her to deputise for her husband during his period of illness or incapacity after 910. In turn this must have made it that much easier for Aethelflaed to take the next logical step and assume direct control of government after her husband's death. It seems very unlikely that she would have been able to do the same in Wessex.

This does not mean, however, that Aethelflaed's succession to direct rule over Mercia was inevitable. She could have been ousted in the same fashion as her daughter, Aelfwynn, would be after her own death. It was a combination of factors which made it possible. The first and arguably most important was her own strength of character. Lady Aethelflaed was clearly a woman well able to wield power and to command respect in a male environment. This was demonstrated by her ability to direct her own armies in a series of very effective military operations. It is equally obvious from the respect shown to her by those of her enemies who were willing to offer their surrender and their tribute to her, including many of the Welsh rulers and the Danish lords of York and Leicester. The second factor which ensured Aethelflaed's direct rule was the lack of any serious male rival for the leadership. The English of this period consistently demonstrated a preference for male leadership even where this meant accepting an entirely new dynasty without any close royal antecedents. In Mercia, after the death of Beorhtsige at the Battle of Holme in 902, no remaining rival native candidate for rule appears to have survived. The third factor in Aethelflaed's favour was the desire of the Mercian nobility to preserve as much of their independence as possible. This appears to have effectively prevented the majority of them from considering switching their allegiance to Edward of Wessex in 911.

Unfortunately, in 918 these very same factors militated against her daughter Aelfwynn. It was the absence of signs of any similar strength of character and a lack of experience of rule in this young woman that told against her. In 918 she was apparently still quite young and inexperienced. She had witnessed at least one of her mother's charters in 915 but is not known to have been involved with any military activities. She could not therefore command the same level of respect that her mother had earned. This difficulty had been overcome in the short term by the intervention of King Edward of Wessex. He had been able to undertake the military expedition on her behalf against Nottingham. However, this temporary expedient was ultimately

End of the text of the Mercian Register from the 'C' version of the Chronicle. (BL Cotton Tiberius B I, f. 140v) considered unsatisfactory for the longer term and instead Edward took direct control of Mercia. The Mercian desire for continued independence, which this action threatened, was recognised and safeguarded through concessions which will be detailed in the next chapter. This was the reason for the different fate which befell Aelfwynn.

At the end of 918, with the removal of her daughter Aelfwynn from power, Aethelflaed, Lady of the Mercians, seemed to have passed into history. However, in spite of determined attempts by the West Saxon historians of this period to completely ignore her and her key role in events she would not be forgotten. Instead, her memory would be preserved until the present day by a combination of two important factors.

The first was the compilation and subsequent preservation of the text of the Mercian Register, a brief contemporary annalistic record of the activities of Lady Aethelflaed as ruler of Mercia. The narrow focus of this record makes it fairly clear that it was compiled by someone with a strong interest in recording the deeds of Aethelflaed specifically rather than Mercian history more generally. It has almost nothing to say, for example, about her husband Aethelred apart from recording his death in 911. It is even possible that Aethelflaed commissioned this text herself. It would surely come as no surprise to find the daughter of King Alfred, who commissioned the main Chronicle itself, instigating her own version. She may have followed her father in this as in many other things. The text of the Register proper begins with entries recording the death of her mother, Queen Ealhswith, and the battle of Holme where her only rival to the rule over Mercia was killed. It proceeds to record the transfer of the relics of St Oswald to Gloucester in 909 to the new minster which she had founded with her husband and where she would later be buried. Thereafter, it records the actions of Aethelflaed herself until her own death and, after recording the deposition of her daughter by Edward of Wessex in 918, it rapidly loses interest in any further events. The exception is the sequential succession of King Athelstan first to the rule of Mercia and thereafter to that of Wessex in 924, an event of significant interest to the Mercians.[36]

The compiler of this source appears to have been a Mercian cleric. This is likely not merely on the grounds that most literate men were clerics and most records were produced by them. A clerical background is suggested by a number of features of the text itself: the use of what was probably a form of Easter Table for inserting the original entries, as suggested by the initial unrelated entries on a comet and an eclipse; the references to God and his influence in events; and the reference to the rather obscure festival of St Ciricus in the entry for 916. The emphasis on Aethelflaed's position and status as Lady of the Mercians and the tone of the account of the deposition of her daughter Aelfwynn in 918 reveal his strong Mercian sympathies. He was probably not linked to the Abbot Egbert recorded in his text since he makes no effort to identify this man's monastery. It is unlikely that we will discover enough information to identify him further but we can, nevertheless, be grateful to him for preserving his unique record of Mercian history and of a unique individual.

The anonymous author of the Register was clearly not alone in his wish to preserve the memory of his heroine or patron. The evidence of this comes from the fact that the text of his Register would subsequently be preserved in a number of versions of the main Chronicle, all of them associated with Mercia in some way. The earliest surviving text of the Register is that inserted, as a discrete unit, into the text of the tenth-century MS 'B' of the Chronicle between the annals for 915 and 934. It is not integrated into the main text but stands alone as a series of independent entries dated from 901 to 924 and sometimes duplicates information found in the main text. A closely related but perhaps independent text of the Register can be found in the eleventh-century MS 'C' of the Chronicle. This version has been inserted in the same place and in the same way as in MS 'B' but it has an additional entry for 921 not found in the latter. The text of the Register was also used by the compilers of the eleventh-century MS 'D' of the Chronicle. They appear to have had access to the same version as used in MS 'C' since it incorporates the entry for 921. However, rather than insert the text in a block entry, they attempted, rather unsuccessfully, to integrate it into their main text under appropriate dates. The twelfth-century *Chronicle of John of Worcester* used a text of the Chronicle similar to MS. 'D' in that it incorporates the Register entries within the main text. However, it is unlikely that it was MS 'D' itself since it does not have the entry for 921 present in 'D' and uses different spellings for a number of key place-names. The twelfth-century writer Henry of Huntingdon uses a version of the Chronicle related to MS 'C'. He features the Register as a block of independent entries inserted into the main text between 915 and 924, includes the entry for 921 and retains the same spellings of a number of key place-names as are found in MS 'C'.

The second factor in preserving the memory of Aethelflaed for the future was her place in the consciousness and affections of the Mercian people, where the impression made by her deeds and character clearly lived on. The most obvious indication of this otherwise ephemeral fact is the popularity of her name among the Mercian nobility in the century after her death. If we look through the names used by the leading Mercian noble families in this period we find a significant number of women named Aethelflaed, most probably in her honour. They included two future queens of England; Aethelflaed of Damerham, daughter of *Ealdorman* Aelfgar of Essex and second wife of King Edmund I, and Aethelflaed *Eneda*, daughter of Ordmaer and wife of King Edgar. There were also a number of noble ladies called Aethelflaed among the families of the *ealdormen*. There was Aethelflaed, daughter of *Ealdorman* Ealhhelm of Mercia, himself a descendant of Lady Aethelflaed's own *ealdorman* of that name, who later married Aelfric *Cild* and secured him the succession to her father's authority. There was also Aethelflaed, daughter of *Ealdorman* Aethelmaer, who later married *Ealdorman* Aethelweard of Hampshire. In addition, the wives of *Ealdorman* Aethelwine

Poem on Lady Aethelflaed, from the Chronicle of Henry of Huntingdon. (National Library of Scotland, Adv. Ms. 33.5.4, f. 58v)

of East Anglia and *Ealdorman* Aethelweard the Chronicler were both named Aethelflaed, although their antecedents are unknown. It would be interesting to be able to confirm whether Aethelweard's wife was indeed of Mercian origin since she could have been the source of the unique Mercian information included in his Chronicle. The will of a lady called Wynflaed, who may have been of Mercian origin, records no less than three separate Aethelflaeds including her own daughter, a woman called Aethelflaed the White and the Aethelflaed, daughter of Ealhhelm, already noted. It is undoubtedly significant that many of these noble ladies were from Mercian families. It is therefore more than likely that their naming involved an element of pride in an independent Mercia as well as a desire to preserve the memory of this great individual. Whatever the case Aethelflaed was certainly well remembered among her former subjects.[37]

Perhaps one of the most interesting aspects of Lady Aethelflaed's remarkable career is how it was described by her male contemporaries and later historians. The records of her time were compiled overwhelmingly by men and these men were almost without exception clerics. In this context, one might expect her career in an almost wholly male environment to be viewed as exceptional and in need of some explanation. In spite of this, the most remarkable aspect of the account in the Mercian Register is the lack of recognition of how exceptional these events were. The account demonstrates a great deal of quiet pride but provides no hint of wonder or even surprise at her role in events. It is all very matter of fact and unaccompanied by any misogynist commentary. The compiler appears to find no discomfort in the fact that she performs a male role. This, of course, may simply be a result of the very brevity of the entries themselves. However, the fact that others felt compelled to add their own comments to their equally brief accounts of her career perhaps suggests otherwise.[38]

The works of later twelfth-century male historians provide a sharp contrast to this picture of apparently relaxed acceptance. They appear to have felt a strong need to justify the male role adopted by this remarkable woman by describing her using specifically male terminology. John of Worcester, who gives a spare annalistic account of her career largely based on the Mercian Register, still feels compelled to add the term 'vigorous' to his description of her on no less than two separate occasions. Other writers like William of Malmesbury and Henry of Huntingdon seem to have felt even more this need to justify her actions by employing male terminology. The former describes her as a woman with 'an enlarged [and hence male] soul' and a woman 'able to protect men at home and intimidate them abroad'. The latter describes her as a 'king' and speaks of her 'surpassing all men in valour' before launching into a colourful flight of verse, which conveys sentiments that may seem rather jarring to a modern reader:

> O mighty Aethelflaed! O virgin, the dread of men, conqueror of nature, worthy of a man's name! Nature made you a girl, so you would be more illustrious; your prowess made you acquire the name of man. For you alone it is right to change the name of your sex: you were a mighty queen and a king who won victories. Even Caesar's triumphs did not bring such great rewards Virgin heroine, more illustrious than Caesar, farewell. [By permission of Oxford University Press]

In short, these writers clearly felt a strong need to classify this woman in a male context by using acceptable male terminology. She performed the role of a man and must therefore have been 'a man' in some way, whether by an enlarged soul or greater virility.[39]

In December 918 this unique example of female rule during the Anglo-Saxon period came to an end. It had come about due to the coincidence of a unique set of circumstances in 911 and it ended seven years later when those circumstances altered. It would never be repeated during this period. In spite of this, it proved to be remarkably successful and Mercia had prospered under the guidance of this female rule. It had been successfully defended against outside aggression while equally successfully imposing its own authority abroad on the Welsh and on the Danes. That such a positive outcome had been achieved was in no small measure due to the character of the woman concerned, Lady Aethelflaed. She had certainly inherited many of her father's abilities and learned much from a period of rule alongside her husband but it was most of all her own qualities of strength and wisdom that ensured her success. She had ruled the land, imposed her authority, dispensed justice and patronage and directed armies with as much, if not more, skill than her male contemporaries. She had upheld her own position in face of their rivalry and had gained their respect. She had been offered a unique opportunity and she had exploited it to the full to the benefit of the whole of Mercia and to the benefit of the wider England that would later emerge. No other Englishwoman of this period achieved so much.

CHAPTER 6

Mercia into England

In the period before Christmas 918 King Edward of Wessex assumed rule over the kingdom of Mercia and most historians consider this as the moment when the independent existence of both Mercia and Wessex ended and the new kingdom of England officially began. However, the evidence of the contemporary record does not entirely support this view. What appears to have occurred was a temporary assumption of control over Mercia by Edward brought about by the specific circumstances of that year.[1]

It was the death of the Lady Aethelflaed in the summer of that year, leaving as her sole heir her young daughter Aelfwynn, that caused Edward to intervene. In normal circumstances such a young girl would have been considered unsuitable on grounds of both her sex and her age to assume the political and military functions of lordship. However, seven years previously similar doubts, at least in terms of her sex, about the suitability of her mother, Aethelflaed, had been set aside since the circumstances of the time were not normal. In a sense, the December crisis of 918 was a repeat of that earlier one and many of the same arguments were undoubtedly rehearsed.[2]

Initially, the Mercian nobles had once again decided to go against custom and convention and support Aelfwynn as their ruler and no doubt for the same reasons. The Mercians appear to have retained their desire for a separate kingdom but remained fully alive to the necessity for the alliance with Wessex. A decision in favour of Aelfwynn allowed them to maintain the physical independence of their kingdom from Wessex while still retaining the family ties and the associated alliance with Wessex which provided the foundation for Mercian security. After all, Aelfwynn was the niece of King Edward of Wessex and he could therefore be expected to support her. Thus Aelfwynn became the Lady of the Mercians in succession to her mother in yet another unique example of succession practice for the Anglo-Saxon period.

The main reason that Aelfwynn subsequently proved unable to maintain her personal rule, in contrast to her mother before her, seems to have been that, although circumstances were similar to those of the year 911, they were not the same. The rule of Aelfwynn suffered from more disadvantages or risks than that of her mother and it had fewer of the compensating advantages or benefits. Aethelflaed had been an adult woman with a strong character and considerable experience of rule. In contrast, Aelfwynn was a young girl with little experience whose character remained untried.

It was these different circumstances that brought King Edward of Wessex to Tamworth in late 918. The Mercian alliance and Mercian military support were as important for Wessex as they were to Mercia. King Edward could not afford any unrest or instability to arise in Mercia as a result of the inexperience of his young niece. In spite of the progress made by both kingdoms in their conquest of Danish-occupied territory, the Danes remained a very real threat. Edward was all too aware of this situation and in order to resolve it he decided to secure direct control of Mercia. This explains Edward's actions in this year but why did the Mercians, who had initially supported Aelfwynn as their ruler, now decide to allow her to be put aside? They had clearly wished to maintain an independent Mercia in preference to direct West Saxon rule and had accepted the succession of Aelfwynn in June 918 largely on this basis. However, less than six months later, in early December, these same Mercian nobles allowed Edward of Wessex to depose Aelfwynn and impose his own authority on Mercia directly.

The reasons for this apparent contradiction would appear to be that the Mercian nobles were faced with a much more difficult situation now than seven years previously. The Danish threat remained as real in 918 as ever and the Mercians therefore still needed strong political and military leadership and they needed the alliance with Wessex. It seems likely that they had realised now, after six months, that Aelfwynn, unlike her mother, would be unable to provide the leadership required. In the short time that she had ruled, her youth and inexperience may already have revealed itself. There existed no alternative Mercian candidates for the throne who could guarantee the continuance of the alliance with Wessex. The only alternative was to seek to come to some arrangement with Edward which would secure West Saxon support but preserve the independent status of Mercia in some way. In this situation, and at the end of the day, they were persuaded, by a combination of hard facts and some concessions, to change their minds.

It seems that such an arrangement was reached and that it involved the temporary assumption by Edward of direct rule in Mercia. Indeed, the fact that the deposition of Aelfwynn occurred near the Christmas festival suggests that it was probably accompanied by a meeting of the Mercian *witan*. There is also reason to think that the sensitivities of the Mercians proved able to accept this new situation now because of the long period of co-operation between the formerly rival kingdoms. This co-operation had begun as far back as 853 when Burgred entered into his alliance with King Aethelwulf of Wessex but had become increasingly close in the time of Aethelred and Alfred and their children. During this period, the nobles of the two kingdoms had faced the same opponents, followed similar policies, fought in joint campaigns and very probably inter-married. This closeness of the nobility of the two kingdoms must have made the acceptance of Edward in Mercia much easier. However, it seems likely that some concessions were also necessary to accommodate Mercia's independence and traditions. What might these concessions have been?

In the admittedly much later account of this period by William of Malmesbury, there is reference to a tradition that Athelstan, son of Edward, had been raised in Mercia. The reason for this arrangement remains unexplained by William. However, in 924, on the death of Edward, the Mercian Register records that Athelstan succeeded to the throne of Mercia while his half-brother Aelfweard succeeded to that of Wessex. This evidence taken together suggests that Edward may have conceded the future independence of Mercia as part of the arrangements which ensured his temporary assumption of power there in 918. In this context, the reference to Athelstan's upbringing in Mercia would make sense as part of a process of preparing him to be the future ruler of Mercia. In effect, King Edward undertook to make detailed succession arrangements for the two kingdoms which would result in the restoration of a separate Mercian kingdom after his death. Such an undertaking would certainly have made his assumption of power in Mercia more acceptable to those Mercian nobles who wished to maintain the separate identity of the kingdom. This arrangement should not surprise us since it was one frequently used by the Frankish kings who so often provided a model for English rulers.[3]

Thus Edward almost certainly assumed power in Mercia on the understanding that he would pass his authority over that kingdom to Athelstan, while Aelfweard would succeed him in Wessex. In effect King Edward was not the first king of a united England but rather the joint ruler of two individual kingdoms, being King of Mercia in addition to being King of Wessex. This scenario may derive some support from the survival of the text of a charter relating to lands in Mercia which names Edward as King of the Mercians. It is true that this text is generally considered spurious but the fact that a later forger considered this title credible is perhaps significant in this context. The fact that the succession did not actually take place as originally planned by Edward but that instead Mercia and Wessex were combined under the rule of one man was entirely due to an accident of fate.[4]

Silver penny of King Edward the Elder (reverse), showing a tower perhaps reflecting his construction of fortifications in the Danish occupied lands. (Ashmolean Museum, Oxford)

Whatever concessions were made, the securing of his rule over Mercia undoubtedly brought

King Edward a tremendous increase in his power. Indeed, the lands subject to his rule and the wealth and manpower they brought with them had virtually doubled in size. This was recognised by his neighbours, who swiftly made their acknowledgement of the new superiority conferred by his greatly increased power by submitting to his overlordship. In this way, they sought to avoid any warlike attention from the new ruler of most of southern Britain. The first to do so, early in 919, were those Welsh kings who had previously acknowledged the overlordship of Lady Aethelflaed. They would soon be followed, in 920, by the rulers of northern Britain: Ragnall, King of York, Eadwulf, *Ealdorman* of Bamburgh, Owen, King of Strathclyde and Constantine II, King of Scots.[5]

In the autumn of 919 King Edward began his rule of Mercia by leading a Mercian army to Thelwall in Cheshire, where he ordered them to construct a *burh*. He remained there with this force but sent a second Mercian army further north to occupy Manchester in Northumbria and repair its old Roman walls and garrison it. These actions advanced Mercian control northwards into Northumbrian territory and secured the northern frontier against the dangerous kings of York. This was an important action for Edward to undertake to demonstrate his value as a leader of Mercian military forces and a ruler. It allowed him to form bonds with the Mercian *ealdormen* and the many important royal *thegns* who had previously supported his sister and who must have accompanied him during this campaign. It may also have had the advantage of removing some Mercian leaders and their forces from the centres of Mercian power, who might otherwise have fostered discontent against his rule. It was perhaps during the course of this campaign that he finally secured support or, at least, acquiescence for his deposition of Aelfwynn.[6]

In the summer of 920 King Edward sought to further secure his two kingdoms by leading what was probably a combined army to Nottingham. There he constructed a *burh* on the south bank of the river Trent opposite the existing Danish fortress, and a bridge across the river between the fortresses. He then proceeded northwards to Bakewell in the Peak District of Derbyshire and ordered the building and garrisoning of a *burh* there. This further advance reinforced his control over Mercia and increased its security in the face of Ragnall Guthfrithson, the new ruler of York. The campaign apparently had the desired effect on this ruler, who submitted to Edward to avoid any further encroachment on his newly won domain. He was followed in this by a number of other northern rulers, according to the Chronicle record noted above. It is almost certain that Edward's greatly augmented authority as ruler of both Mercia and Wessex must have caused many in the north to consider him worth courting. The Welsh kings had already recognised his overlordship. The Scots, the survivors of English Northumbria and the men of Strathclyde all had good reason to seek his alliance against the threat presented by Ragnall of York.[7]

Tower of All Saints' Church, Earl's Barton, Northamptonshire, similar to that shown on Edward's coins. (Copyright English Heritage)

In the following year of 921 King Edward built a *burh* at Rhuddlan on the coast of North Wales to further secure his northern frontier. This fortification could support his dominance over the Welsh but more importantly it helped defend these coastlands near Chester against assault by Irish Sea Vikings. This was particularly important in view of the recent recovery of control in York by Ragnall Guthfrithson from Dublin. He had resumed the process of consolidating his power there following a successful battle against the Scots at Corbridge in 919.[8]

It was while in the process of securing the northern frontier of Mercia that King Edward of Wessex died at Farndon in Mercia on 17 July 924. It is not known for certain whether this was the Farndon in Cheshire or in Nottinghamshire, but either would reflect his continued concern with the northern frontiers. The possibility of an invasion by the new ruler of York and his allies from Dublin was clearly the single most important threat facing the joint English kingdoms at this time.[9]

On his death, Edward left a total of five surviving sons by three wives. By 924 three of those sons were adults: Athelstan, son of Ecgwynn, and Aelfweard and Edwin, both sons of Aelfflaed. The younger sons - still infants – were Edmund and Eadred, sons of Eadgifu. It seems likely that Edward had made arrangements for the succession to his two separate kingdoms as early as 918. In that year, he had almost certainly entered into an agreement that Athelstan would succeed to the throne of Mercia. He had probably also decided that Aelfweard, his eldest son by Aelfflaed, would succeed to the throne of Wessex. This settlement would fulfil the obligations he had given to the Mercian nobles at Christmas 918 by effectively restoring the independent existence of the Mercian kingdom. What benefits did the settlement hold for Wessex? The restoration of Mercian independence would allow Wessex to regain the full attention of its king. As we have seen above, after his seizure of Mercia in 918, King Edward had spent a great deal of his time in Mercia consolidating his rule there and ensuring the security of his new domain. This left Wessex without a personal royal presence for much of the time. This could only undermine the effectiveness of the processes of direct rule including personal service and reward on which government relied at this time.

The division of his two kingdoms between his two families, in the person of Athelstan and Aelfweard, also allowed Edward to reward both families. This prevented the usual tensions, which would inevitably have resulted from the inheritance of both kingdoms by only one son and the exclusion of all the others. It was no doubt hoped that the two royal half-brothers, their ambitions satisfied, would be able to continue to co-operate with each other against their adversaries. However, this solution also carried some risks. It effectively ignored the sons of Edward's third wife, who were too young to inherit at present. It relied on the goodwill of the half-brothers, Athelstan and Aelfweard, to ensure the preservation of the alliance between Mercia and Wessex. It also carried the potential for future conflict between the two kingdoms as the currently close family relationships and the policies of the kingdoms diverged over time. It might ultimately result in a return to the rivalry of the old days. It was a solution to the problem of how to rule over wide regions of different peoples which had often been adopted by the Franks with similar risks and advantages.

However, in the event, none of these possibilities was to be put to the test since Edward's elaborate plan came to grief only sixteen days after his own death. On that day, 4 August 924, Aelfweard, the new king of Wessex, died unconsecrated at Oxford. In the wake of this unexpected disaster, King Athelstan of Mercia managed to assume direct control of Wessex. The complex details of this process are, perhaps not surprisingly, recorded in the Mercian Register and not in the main Chronicle itself. The former, unlike its West Saxon counterpart, had an immense interest in what was effectively the succession of a Mercian ruler to the throne of Wessex. This take-over was not completed overnight but appears to have taken Athelstan over a year to accomplish. This perhaps reflects the delay caused by active opposition from Aelfweard's younger brother, *Atheling* Edwin, and his supporters. This would not be surprising since Edwin must have anticipated succeeding his elder brother in Wessex. The struggle was longer and so perhaps harder than that put up by *Atheling* Aethelwold in 900. It was to be more than a year before Athelstan was finally crowned King of Wessex at Kingston-on-Thames on 4 September 925. King Athelstan was now effectively ruler of both Mercia and Wessex.[10]

This new joint rule of Mercia and Wessex by one king appears to have proved acceptable to the Mercian nobility. There are no signs of any significant discontent among Athelstan's Mercian subjects during his reign. This was probably the result of the succession of a 'Mercian' king to Wessex rather than vice versa. In this context and in view of his probable Mercian upbringing he was apparently seen, somewhat ironically, by the Mercians as one of their own who had made good by taking control of Wessex rather than as an outsider imposed on them. This is apparent, as we have seen, from a reading of the account contained in the Mercian Register. The West Saxons for their own part appear to have accepted Athelstan as their king on the basis that he was a son of their own King Edward. This does not mean that there was no opposition to Athelstan's rule of both kingdoms, since *Atheling* Edwin continued to provide a focus for this. It may be suggested, however, that in this struggle Athelstan, as king of the Mercians, might anticipate fairly solid support from his Mercian followers.[11]

The distinct phases of Athelstan's succession to the thrones of his two separate kingdoms, are reflected in his joint rule thereafter. In the Chronicle, the status of West Saxons and Mercians as separate peoples is preserved in the text of the poem on the Battle of *Brunanburh* in 937. In this the allied but still distinct contributions of the Mercians and West Saxons to Athelstan's victory over the great coalition of Norse and Celtic powers is emphasised. It is true that the narrative sources for this reign are very sparse but we are fortunate in that a number of surviving diplomas include dates and places of their issue. This is a relatively rare feature for this early period and provides us with precious information on the king's itinerary. They provide evidence that Athelstan was accepted as king of both Mercia and Wessex, with surviving examples issued in Mercia itself, in contrast to his predecessors, Alfred and Edward.[12]

The succession of Athelstan to the rule of both kingdoms, once accepted, brought him the same increase in power that it had brought his father. However, this power would enable Athelstan to achieve much more than his father had ever done. This may be a result of the fact that, as one who had been specifically groomed for the Mercian throne, his rule proved more acceptable and therefore secure there. Equally, it may be that Edward's brief four-year rule of the combined kingdoms was a necessary period of consolidation, which was vital to the process of commencing the integration of Mercia and Wessex, without which Athelstan's subsequent achievements would have been impossible. In either case, Athelstan would use his increased power to good effect in imposing his authority on his northern and western neighbours.

The Norse kingdom of York, which had remained such an ominous threat to his father's rule in Mercia, was the problem that Athelstan tackled first. He chose to do so by arranging a marriage alliance between Sihtric, King of York, and his sister Eadgyth. The wedding notably took place at Tamworth, at the centre of Mercia, on 30 January 926. It may have been the first great royal occasion to have taken place in Mercia for many years. This alliance was intended to bring York into the orbit of Athelstan's overlordship and to prevent any further attacks on Mercia from this source. It therefore included the conversion of Sihtric to Christianity as a recognition of the superiority of Athelstan's religion and as a way of tempering the vehemence of his aggression. It has been suggested that this alliance was made in anticipation of the incorporation of York into Athelstan's expanded kingdom. At this point in time, however, such an eventuality was by no means inevitable.[13]

It is important to remember here that, as already noted with regard to the unification of Mercia and Wessex into a new English kingdom, there was nothing inevitable about the outcome of events. There was no certainty that a new kingdom of England would incorporate the kingdom of York. The latter could have developed into an independent kingdom on the model of the old Northumbria, perhaps incorporating the remnants of English Northumbria around Bamburgh and possibly linked with Dublin in Ireland. Indeed, King Ragnall of York had already attempted to seize control of English Northumbria in 914 and 919. Alternatively, it could have been absorbed by the expanding young Scottish kingdom under Constantine II. It was the Scottish king who had earlier disputed control of Strathclyde and English Northumbria with Ragnall of York in 914 and 919. In this situation, there can be no doubt that a unified kingdom of Mercia and Wessex had an immense advantage over its potential rivals. It encompassed a much greater and agriculturally much richer area of land and hence could bring much greater resources to bear on this contest. However, this enormous advantage could always be undermined by political weakness and, in particular, by any divisions between the Mercians and West Saxons. It is as well to keep in mind the possibility of a range of various outcomes when discussing this three-cornered struggle for Northumbria rather than assume the inevitable triumph of the West Saxon dynasty.

The kingdom of York itself was going through a very unstable period at this point with a series of rulers replacing one another in rapid succession. The last Danish kings of York, Halfdan and Eowils, had been killed at the Battle of Tettenhall in 910. Shortly after this, and certainly before 914, the Norseman Ragnall had come from Dublin to seize control of the city. However, he found it difficult to retain the loyalty of York while preoccupied with campaigns elsewhere and Lady Aethelflaed had sought to exploit this situation in 918. Unfortunately, the latter's early death in that very same year, had allowed Ragnall to restore his authority there. When Ragnall himself died in 920 he was replaced by his brother Sihtric, also from Dublin. The latter would himself die in 927, less than a year after his marriage to Athelstan's sister, being succeeded in his turn by yet another brother from Dublin, Guthfrith. This rapid turnover of rulers can only have served to undermine their authority by loosening the personal ties of loyalty between them and their nobles.[14]

The death of his brother-in-law Sihtric and the succession of Guthfrith would have brought with it an immediate loss of influence for Athelstan. As a result, he appears to have decided to assume direct control of this northern kingdom. In 927 he invaded the territory of the kingdom of York, seized control of the city itself and expelled King Guthfrith. In a curious passage, Simeon of Durham states that Guthfrith was driven from 'the kingdom of the Britons'. This perhaps indicates that the Britons of Strathclyde may have exploited the recent weakness of York to occupy Cumbria and that Guthfrith now sought refuge from Athelstan there. King Athelstan could now be considered as the first king to rule all the English lands if we include the submission of English Northumbria. However, this first attempt by Athelstan to directly absorb the Kingdom of York would prove in vain. It would turn out to be a much more difficult process than the initial unification of Mercia and Wessex under his leadership. The contrast between these processes offers an opportunity to highlight some important differences.[15]

The unification of Mercia and Wessex had come about in a context that made it acceptable to a majority of leading men in both kingdoms. These two kingdoms had enjoyed a long and successful period of peaceful co-operation against a common enemy. The leading men of both had worked together during this period towards common goals. The two kingdoms had already experienced a period of joint rule under King Edward. The kingdoms were now ruled by a king, Athelstan, whom the leading men of both could accept as their legitimate ruler.

An important feature of the building up of this legitimacy would be the increasing trust placed in the leading men of Mercia by Athelstan. This was something that was to some extent forced on Athelstan and his successors by their physical absence from Mercia for prolonged periods. In spite of his Mercian background, Athelstan found himself on his succession to the West Saxon throne having to spend a significant amount of his time in Wessex. This was probably an inevitable result of the need to foster contacts and loyalty among the leading men of what was to Athelstan a new kingdom. It may also have been due partly to the need to be present in Wessex to monitor the activities of his sidelined rival *Atheling* Edwin. The latter would pose a constant threat to the security of Athelstan's rule until his death by drowning in 933. In these circumstances Athelstan had largely to rely on local men to rule Mercia in his absence. The men chosen were probably those he had known and learned to trust during his upbringing in Mercia. Unfortunately we have little evidence until later periods to allow us to identify these men clearly.

One of them who has been identified is Athelstan 'Half-king', son of that Mercian *ealdorman* named Aethelfrith, who had witnessed a number of charters of Aethelred and Aethelflaed. This Athelstan first appears with the title *ealdorman* as a witness in the charters of his royal namesake in 932. He continues to do so thereafter and always in prominent positions until the end of the reign. He appears to have held authority over his father's area of south-east Mercia, probably the same area transferred by Lady Aethelflaed to the control of her brother, King Edward in 911. This area of authority was subsequently extended either by Edward or more probably by Athelstan himself to encompass the newly restored area of Danish East Anglia. This extensive command apparently included not only Norfolk and Suffolk but also the shires of Cambridge, Huntingdon and Northampton. This was all in addition to his father's former command of Oxford, Buckingham, Middlesex, Hertford and Bedford. This Athelstan was clearly a trusted supporter of the king who fully deserved his nickname of 'Half-king'. It seems likely that he played a key role in supporting the king against his rival *Atheling* Edwin and in controlling the newly conquered Danish kingdom of East Anglia.[16]

In contrast to the situation with Mercia and Wessex, the absorption of the strongly Scandinavian York into Athelstan's kingdom came about largely by conquest. There had been a long period of hostility between this kingdom and its new English ruler. There was little common interest between the leading men of York and those of the English kingdoms. The English king was not viewed as a legitimate ruler by these leading men. These factors would prove to be the undoing of Athelstan's deceptively easy conquest and would continue to undermine and delay the final absorption of York for many years to come.

The dramatic action taken by Athelstan against Guthfrith of York initially encouraged the other rulers of northern and western Britain to move swiftly to acknowledge his overlordship. On 12 July 927, at Eamont Bridge in Cumbria, the Chronicle records the submission to King Athelstan of the Scottish king Constantine II and the *ealdorman* of Bamburgh, Ealdred son of Eadwulf. It seems likely that the Welsh kings Hywel *Dda* of Deheubarth and Owain of Gwent, who are also mentioned, had probably submitted to King Athelstan already and were present at Eamont Bridge as part of the forces he had brought north to subdue Northumbria. This possibility is suggested by the otherwise well-recorded presence of Welsh kings both at the English court and on other similar military expeditions.[17]

Another indication of the enhanced power and prestige of Edward and his son Athelstan, as rulers of both Mercia and Wessex, was the willingness of important Continental rulers to seek marriage alliances with them. Already, at some point between 917 and 920, perhaps shortly after his succession to rule over Mercia in 918, Edward had married his daughter Eadgifu to Charles the Simple, King of the Franks. The couple had a son called Louis, who was subsequently forced to flee with his mother to England in 923 after his father had been deposed. In 926 Athelstan was approached by Hugh the Great, a rival of Louis, who subsequently made arrangements to marry his half-sister Eadhild perhaps in an effort to prevent Athelstan supporting the exiled Louis. In 930 Henry the Fowler, King of Germany, successfully requested another of Athelstan's half-sisters, Edith, as a bride for his son and heir Otto. Another half-sister apparently married Conrad, King of Burgundy. All of these men were seeking to secure powerful allies in an effort to bolster their own dynasties, whether declining or rising, and they all turned to the new power across the Channel. In the same sense Edward and Athelstan as rulers of their own new polity were seeking to enhance their prestige and extend their own Continental contacts through these marriages.[18]

In 933 the Chronicle records that *Atheling* Edwin, the full brother of Aelfweard and half-brother of Athelstan, drowned. A contemporary account by Folcwin, Deacon of St Bertin's in Flanders, suggests that there was more to this death than meets the eye. He writes that Edwin, whom he describes as a 'king', as a result of 'some disturbance in his kingdom' was forced to flee abroad. On route to refuge in Flanders, which was then ruled by his cousin Count Adelolf, he was apparently caught in a storm and drowned. Subsequently, the body of the dead *atheling* was recovered by Count Adelolf and buried at St Bertin's monastery. This story may suggest that Edwin had made some sort of attempt to seize the West Saxon throne, hence the use of the royal title. This throne had, after all, been held by his brother, Aelfweard, however briefly, before the latter's early death and he must have considered it his own rightful inheritance. It may be no coincidence that, according to a surviving charter, Athelstan was at the site of West Saxon royal consecrations at Kingston-on-Thames on 16 December 933, perhaps to prevent Edwin being consecrated or simply to emphasise his own royal dignity after an attempt to call it into question. Presumably Athelstan, who had seized the kingdom on Aelfweard's death and, effectively, excluded Edwin, opposed the latter's attempt to recover it and caused him to flee and so meet his death. Indeed, version 'A' of the Chronicle goes as far as to accuse Athelstan of ordering Edwin's death. This is obviously untrue since Athelstan, however great a king, had no control over the weather. However, the fact that Athelstan later sent gifts to St Bertin's suggests that he felt responsible, at least, for driving his half-brother into exile. This incident is interesting since it reveals continuing tensions within the dynasty and the inherent possibility of the break-up of Athelstan's union of Mercia and Wessex.[19]

In 934 King Athelstan invaded distant Scotland by land and sea in a lightning campaign which was a first for a southern English ruler. The evidence from charter dates reveals some of the background to this extraordinary and unprecedented campaign. The place and date of one charter shows that Athelstan must have set out from Winchester in the heart of Wessex sometime after 28 May following a meeting of his *witan* which was probably held in order to take advantage of the presence of the nobles who were forming his army. Another charter proves that he was already at Nottingham in Mercia by 7 June on his way north, where he was probably joined by Mercian and Welsh forces. In this text he confirmed a grant of lands in Amounderness to Archbishop Wulfstan of York no doubt as part of the process of assuring his support and co-operation. The witness list of this charter also reveals the

The *Life of St Cuthbert*; the frontispiece showing King Athelstan presenting a copy to this Northumbrian saint. (Master and Fellows of Corpus Christi College, Cambridge, Ms. 183, f. 1b)

presence of a number of Welsh kings with the royal army, including Hywel *Dda* of Deheubarth, Morgan of Gwent and Idwal of Gwynedd. The presence of these men reflects a pattern we will see repeated of the apparent use of Welsh troops in northern campaigns, where their familiarity with upland warfare must have made them very useful. Athelstan proceeded as far north as Dunnottar and *Wertermorum* with his army while his fleet, probably drawn from York, sailed as far north as Caithness. He successfully secured the submission of King Constantine and the whole campaign must have been over before 12 September. On that date Athelstan appears back at Buckingham in Mercia accompanied by the King of Scots. The latter may have remained in England over the winter since he appears as witness in another charter dated to 935. The reasons for this important campaign are not entirely clear. It was undoubtedly an amazing feat and one not to be repeated until the days of King Edward I. It clearly reflects Athelstan's immense organisational and military abilities. It may have been mounted to demonstrate that Athelstan had assumed the mantle of his Northumbrian predecessors. In the same context, he called in at the shrine of St Cuthbert at Chester-le-street on his way north to present gifts to this great Northumbrian saint.[20]

The success of this major expedition appears to have encouraged King Athelstan to increase the range of his activities. In 936 he would instigate two major ventures across the Channel using the new naval power so much in evidence against the Scots. He first sponsored the return to Brittany of the exiled Alan *Barbetorte* or 'Twisted-beard' and his followers by supplying him with ships. Alan had originally been forced to flee from his homeland in 919 when it had been conquered by the Loire Vikings and his father had been expelled. Now he landed safely at Dol and, rallying local support, proceeded to defeat the Vikings in a series of campaigns before finally driving them out and restoring his own rule throughout Brittany by 939. In this way Athelstan had successfully removed a potential threat to his own kingdom and provided himself with a grateful ally on the Continent.[21]

In the same year, 936, the death of King Ralph had produced an interregnum in the Frankish kingdom. As a result, Hugh the Great invited the exiled prince, Louis *d'Outremer*, son of Charles the Simple and Eadgifu, to return from England to rule the kingdom. King Athelstan, as the main protector of his young nephew, played a major role in the negotiations leading to his restoration to his father's throne. He also provided him with ships to transport him to Boulogne and an escort to accompany him to Laon for his coronation on 19 June 936. The result of this process, at least in the short term, was to increase English prestige and influence across the Channel. This reveals Athelstan taking on the role formerly adopted by Charlemagne by providing refuge for exiles from across the sea and reveals how circumstances had changed over the last 130 years.[22]

An important aspect of Athelstan's campaigns in 934 and 936 was the significant use of naval power. This represented the recovery by the English kings of an ability to strike at their enemies across the sea. This would be an important factor in completing the process of turning the tide against their Viking opponents who had previously been free from such counter-attack. This development was probably a result of the conquest of the Danish-occupied areas of England and perhaps particularly York. After all, these Danes had a strong tradition of shipbuilding and seamanship and ready access to flexible and effective fleets. It was probably this that provided Athelstan with a naval superiority that his predecessors had so obviously lacked. It is notable that King Alfred's earlier naval experiments ultimately proved disastrous in spite of attempts by the Chronicle and later historians to view them as a success.[23]

The most compelling sign of the extent of King Athelstan's new status as a naval power is unfortunately recorded only in much later and less reliable sources. This is the story of his intervention in the succession to the rule of distant Norway itself. William of Malmesbury records that an embassy from King Harald Fairhair of Norway presented gifts to Athelstan at York, presumably after the latter's conquest of that city in 927. The connection apparently went further than this, at least if we are to believe the much later Norwegian traditions incorporated into the kings sagas composed by Snorri Sturlusson in the thirteenth century. In these, it is said that King Athelstan provided refuge for King Harald's exiled son Hakon, who subsequently became known as *Athalsteins fostri*, or 'Athelstan's foster-son'.[24]

The tradition goes on to state that Athelstan subsequently provided Hakon with ships to assist him in wresting control of the kingship of Norway from his brother Eric Bloodaxe. Unfortunately, there is no reliable indication of the precise timing of these particular events. They presumably occurred at some point between Athelstan's first occupation of York in 927 and his death in 939 and certainly before the subsequent appearance of Eric Bloodaxe in England in 947. However, such a remarkable display of the long reach of English sea power would certainly seem to fit most appropriately into this period of expansive English naval activity. This action installed a ruler who was indebted to King Athelstan in power in Norway and was probably intended to control Viking activity in one of its principle sources. Unfortunately, it also had the effect of setting loose on the northern seas a maverick, in the person of Eric Bloodaxe, with his own reason to hate the English, who would cause significant difficulties for Athelstan's successors.

These dramatic demonstrations of new power by King Athelstan must have stirred up much resentment against his rule among those on the receiving end. The campaign of 934 may have been intended to dissuade Constantine II, King of Scots, from attacking Athelstan's newly won domain around York or his new allies in English Northumbria. In fact, Constantine's close personal experience of the new

English power on his borders seems to have had exactly the opposite effect by arousing his hostility. It made him all the more susceptible to the blandishments of King Olaf of Dublin, the son of that King Guthfrith expelled from York in 927. The latter was eager to regain his own patrimony in York and was busy seeking allies to this end. He was able to persuade both Constantine and the men of Strathclyde to join him in an alliance against Athelstan. They all shared a common interest in restraining or reducing the power so recently demonstrated by the new English king. Olaf also tried to involve the Welsh kings, who had been compelled to pay heavy tribute to King Athelstan and to serve in his army against Scotland, in the conspiracy. The contemporary poem *Armes Prydain* was probably part of a propaganda campaign designed to encourage their participation. However, this part of the plan proved a dismal failure since the Welsh kings remained loyal to oaths to support Athelstan. It is possible that they were enjoying sharing in the profits of his victories or that they were simply glad not to be among his current targets. The time spent by King Olaf in negotiations to forge this wide alliance naturally meant that intelligence about it reached the ears of Athelstan. This early notice of the intentions of his enemies allowed him to collect his own forces to oppose them. He gathered armies from both Mercia and Wessex and brought them north. The English sources make no mention of Northumbrians in his force which perhaps suggests he had already lost control of this area before the battle or that he could not fully trust the natives there.[25]

In 937 King Olaf and his allies finally invaded the English kingdoms, while Athelstan responded to this threat by bringing north his combined force of Mercians and West Saxons. The opponents came face to face at a still unidentified place, called variously *Brunanburh*, *Brunefeld* or *Wendun*. It now seems established that it must have been located somewhere in the northern portion of Mercia but exactly where remains open to argument. It has been claimed that the site lies in the East Midlands largely, it would seem, on the basis of a reference in John of Worcester to Olaf having landed in the Humber. However, in view of the composition of the armies involved on each side, the arguments for a location in the north-west seem more convincing on the grounds that this offered them easier access. The debate remains open at present and other suggestions and perhaps an eventual conclusion offer some hope of clarifying more of the background to this battle in the future.[26]

What is beyond doubt is that this battle resulted in an important victory for Athelstan and the combined armies of Mercia and Wessex. This victory was recorded in a celebratory poem in Old English which was inserted into the Chronicle. This attributes a prominent role in the battle to the Mercians noting: 'The Mercians refused not hard conflict to any men who with Olaf had sought this land in the bosom of a ship over the tumult of waters coming doomed to the fight.'

It is important to note that this poem continues to recognise the West Saxons and Mercians as separate peoples who contributed their forces to the overall English victory. The battle was also recorded by the Welsh and Irish annals which naturally had a strong interest in the outcome. The latter record it as a 'horrible battle' which was 'cruelly fought' and in which 'several thousands' were killed.[27]

In 939, flushed with his recent victory at *Brunanburh* and secure in the north, King Athelstan once again intervened in Continental affairs. In that year his protégé King Louis IV was in difficulties with a number of prominent members of his nobility including Count Arnulf I of Flanders. According to annals compiled by Flodoard of Rheims, Athelstan sent an English fleet to support King Louis against his enemies. This fleet was directed against Arnulf of Flanders and it ravaged 'certain places near the coast

Part of the text of the poem on the Battle of *Brunanburh* from the 'A' version of the Chronicle. (Master and Fellows of Corpus Christi College, Cambridge, Ms. 173, f. 26v)

of Therouanne'. The results of this raiding were, however, inconclusive. It failed to improve the overall position of Louis while incurring increased hostility towards him on the part of Count Arnulf.[28]

On 27 October 939 King Athelstan died at the height of his power in Gloucester, the former power base of Lord Aethelred of Mercia. The Irish annals record his death by describing him as the 'pillar of the dignity of the Western world'. The succession to both Mercia and Wessex fell to his eighteen-year-old half-brother Edmund. The relatively long and stable reign of King Athelstan in Mercia was crucial to the development of an acceptance in Mercia that members of the West Saxon dynasty could also be rulers of Mercia. He had blazed the trail as the first member of that dynasty to be accepted as the full king of Mercia without conditions and this made it much easier for his brothers and nephews to follow him in that role. He had demonstrated that a West Saxon ruler, with appropriate Mercian support and involvement, could rule Mercia well even when faced with the additional responsibility of rule in Wessex. It was this that enabled Edmund to succeed to rule in both kingdoms, largely unchallenged. Although he lacked the specifically Mercian upbringing enjoyed by his older half-brother, Athelstan, he had fought with the Mercians at *Brunanburh*.[29]

It is notable that Edmund was able to succeed to both kingdoms on Athelstan's death and that there was no division as occurred in 924. This seems at first sight to suggest that the distinction between Mercia and Wessex was no longer important, and that Athelstan during his reign had in effect created a kingdom of England. This would probably be stretching the evidence too far since there was no other ruler available for Mercia at this point. In 940 Edmund's brother Eadred was perhaps only fourteen years old and hence too young to be entrusted with the rule of a kingdom of his own, particularly one as exposed as Mercia. He had not, for example, been involved in the 937 campaign. It should be remembered here that Edmund himself was only around eighteen years old. In these specific circumstances there could be no division of the joint kingdom even had this been desired or intended. This does not mean that such a division had become unlikely or impossible as the events of 955 would subsequently demonstrate.

The chronology of events following the death of King Athelstan becomes very confused in the Chronicle and it is necessary to try to reconstruct their sequence with reference to a number of other sources. In this context the annals preserved by Simeon of Durham and Roger of Wendover appear to offer considerable assistance by recording a sequence of events spread over the four-year period 940 to 943, which the Chronicle itself conflates under the single date 943. If we utilise this admittedly later evidence and consider the general political situation in this period we can reconstruct a probable sequence of events for these years.

It would appear likely that King Olaf Guthfrithson of Dublin, still smarting from his heavy defeat at *Brunanburh* in 937, quickly sought to test the strength of the new young king by invading York. According to the Chronicle, he was initially very successful, crossing with a large fleet and seizing control of the kingdom of York from the English ruler and expelling his agents probably before the end of 940. Archbishop Wulfstan appears to have abandoned his allegiance to Edmund and allied with his old Viking masters, as will be seen. Olaf had finally recovered the patrimony briefly held by his father Guthfrith before being lost to Athelstan some thirteen years earlier.[30]

In the following year, 941, Olaf undertook a major campaign against formerly Danish areas of Mercia. It seems to have been aimed at wresting control of this area from King Edmund and restoring the buffer zone that had once protected the Kingdom of York from invasion. He was apparently accompanied on this campaign by Archbishop Wulfstan. Initially, Olaf met with dramatic success, apparently occupying the five former Danish *burhs* of Lincoln, Leicester, Derby, Nottingham and Stamford with little difficulty. He may have been assisted in this by allies among the local

Danish leaders, who may have been feeling restless under English rule. They had, after all, lost their independent status only twenty years before. The ease with which he had occupied these *burhs* certainly suggests as much. Olaf would subsequently marry the daughter of a certain *Jarl* Orm, who was probably from this area and must at least have supported his rule even if he had not helped bring it about.[31]

However, King Olaf did not rest with this achievement but went on to push further into Mercia as far as Watling Street. He first attacked and besieged the *burh* of Northampton but it was stoutly defended and he failed to take it. Baulked of this prize, he turned back north-west and raided widely around Tamworth, the ancient capital of Mercia. He went on to storm the *burh* at Tamworth although his army appears to have suffered severe casualties in the process. He succeeded in capturing an immense amount of booty in the town and a very important captive, the Lady Wulfrun, who would later be ransomed at great cost. This campaign demonstrated the continued importance of the defended *burh* which had caused significant delay and disruption to Olaf's campaign. He had not found his progress easy in the face of the stoutly defended Mercian *burhs* at Northampton and Tamworth.

It was while returning from this now flagging campaign with his badly depleted forces that Olaf was overtaken by King Edmund at Leicester. He sought refuge in the *burh* there which was then closely besieged by Edmund. This siege was probably intended to bring about the capture of Olaf and Archbishop Wulfstan and the end of their campaign but they managed to escape with a small party from the *burh* under cover of night. The result was a stalemate with Edmund unable to abandon the siege of the army in Leicester to deal with Olaf, and the latter unable without troops to free his army from its encirclement. This stalemate was brought to an end by negotiations conducted between Archbishops Oda of Canterbury and Wulfstan of York. They managed to reconcile the two kings with a peace treaty which essentially recognised the status quo with Olaf holding the area around the five Danish *burhs* and Edmund retaining the rest of Mercia with the frontier between them close to Watling Street. This undoubtedly represented a major set-back for Edmund with a return almost to the political situation in the early years of his predecessor Lady Aethelflaed. This could only be viewed by him as a temporary solution and one badly in need of reversing. According to the account preserved by Roger of Wendover, it was about this time that an important marriage was celebrated. This was the marriage between King Olaf of York and the daughter of *Jarl* Orm, Danish ruler of one of five *burhs*, very possibly Leicester itself. This Orm had earlier appeared as a witness in the charters of King Athelstan. He may have assisted Olaf in his conquest of this region and the latter sought to cement his loyalty by means of this marriage alliance.[32]

It was probably late in 941 that King Olaf decided to round off his wide new domain in the north by subduing English Northumbria. The English *ealdormen* of

Bamburgh had remained bitter enemies of the Scandinavian rulers of York since the original Viking conquest of that city back in 867. They had sought, however tenuously at times, to maintain in existence a remnant of the ancient Northumbrian realm between the hostile attentions of the Scots and the men of York. In this situation they had increasingly looked to the southern rulers of Mercia and Wessex for aid. The current *ealdorman*, Oswulf of Bamburgh, had featured as a witness in a number of the charters of King Athelstan. King Olaf invaded the territory of *Ealdorman* Oswulf and ravaged as far north as Tyninghame in East Lothian. It was 'soon after' the destruction of the church of St Bealdhere there that Olaf met his death, apparently a victim of the saint's revenge. As a consequence, the men of York sought their own more secular revenge for Olaf's death by burning the church at Lindisfarne.

The intervention of St Bealdhere was to prove crucial to the recovery of King Edmund. The dead Olaf was succeeded as King of York by his cousin, another Olaf, nicknamed *Cuaran*. He appears to have been a very different man, an altogether less capable and less gifted one. He would quickly prove to be no match for Edmund and lose all that his cousin had gained. In addition, Olaf *Cuaran* probably lost the advantage of the support of *Jarl* Orm with the severance of the important marriage alliance enjoyed by his predecessor. Certainly, Orm appears to have returned to the fold, once more appearing among the witnesses in the later charters of Edmund's brother Eadred.[33]

It was to be 942 before King Edmund felt able to mount an offensive aimed at the complete recovery of Mercia from occupation by Olaf *Cuaran*. In this year the sources all agree that King Edmund conquered the five *burhs* of Lincoln, Leicester, Derby, Nottingham and Stamford. This, in fact, represented the recovery of the whole area of Mercia north of Watling Street ceded to King Olaf Guthfrithson the previous year. This success may have been significantly assisted by the defection of *Jarl* Orm, whose alliance with York had ended with the death of Olaf Guthfrithson in 941. What is certain is that *Jarl* Orm was sufficiently restored to royal favour to appear in a charter of Eadred dated 946. Nevertheless, it was a glorious achievement which the compilers of the Chronicle sought to record in heroic verse: 'In this year, King Edmund, lord of the English, protector of men, the beloved performer of mighty deeds, overran Mercia . . .'.[34]

In 943, no doubt as a reaction to this humiliating disaster, a faction of the men of York sought to drive out Olaf *Cuaran*. They summoned his cousin Ragnall Guthfrithson, brother of the deceased Olaf, from Dublin to rule in his stead. A struggle ensued between the supporters of these two rivals which produced no conclusive result. Olaf was able to retain some support and Ragnall was unable to oust him entirely. As a consequence the two kings ended up uneasily sharing the rule of York. This result satisfied no-one and provided plenty of scope for tension and disagreement which Edmund naturally stood ready to exploit. He did this so effectively that, in this same year, he imposed his authority on York, compelling the submission of both Olaf and Ragnall and sponsoring their baptism into the Christian Church. He had undoubtedly been assisted in this process by their dispute over the throne of York. This division among his enemies had made it easy for Edmund to subdue them both. The rivals remained in dispute over control of a technically independent kingdom of York but very much subject to their overlord King Edmund.[35]

In 944 King Edmund felt confident enough to initiate the final moves against the politically divided kingdom of York. He sent an army north which captured York and expelled both Olaf and Ragnall from the kingdom. According to the account preserved by *Ealdorman* Aethelweard, this task was carried out by Archbishop Wulfstan, who had once again changed sides to suit the prevailing situation, and 'the Mercian *ealdorman*'. The latter was probably Ealhhelm, who became *ealdorman* of part of Mercia under King Edmund in succession to his father of the same name, who had previously served Lord Aethelred and Lady Aethelflaed. He had first appeared as a witness to the charters of King Edmund in 940 and continues to appear in such lists thereafter until the close of King Eadred's reign in 950. This provides an example of the reliance of Edmund on the local nobility in ruling his enlarged kingdom. In 945 Edmund would present two large church bells to York, probably as a reward to Archbishop Wulfstan in recognition of the services he had rendered during the expulsion of the two kings Olaf and Ragnall.[36]

Silver penny of St Peter's, York, probably issued by the archbishop on behalf of his Danish masters. It features a sword and a small hammer of Thor. (Ashmolean Museum, Oxford)

In 945 Edmund sought to deal with a further threat to his new northern frontier on the Mersey and in North Yorkshire. He invaded and ravaged the kingdom of Strathclyde which then stretched from the Clyde Valley in present-day Scotland to the Mersey and the borders of Yorkshire. According to Roger of Wendover he performed this task with the aid of his ally, King Llwellyn of Dyfed in South Wales. This employment of Welsh troops looks very much like a case of setting a thief to catch a thief.

King Edmund was certainly successful in his aims, securing the submission of King Dyfnwal of Strathclyde but only after capturing and blinding his two sons.

Thereafter, somewhat surprisingly, he ceded the overlordship of this kingdom to Malcolm, King of Scots. This was an important action which aimed at providing an element of security for his rule in the north. He was well aware that his resources would be too overstretched by the process of absorbing the kingdom of York to permit him to hold Strathclyde permanently. He therefore surrendered it to the Scottish king as the price of securing his alliance against the Dublin kings. This was a complete reversal of the policy of Athelstan, who had tried to cow the Scots only to bring their enmity down on him at *Brunanburh*. Instead, King Edmund sought to provide Malcolm with a common interest in opposing the return of the Dublin kings to York.[37]

On 26 May 946 King Edmund was killed at Pucklechurch in Gloucestershire by a *thegn* named Leofa, and his brother Eadred succeeded him. He was the third King of Mercia and Wessex to die within Mercian territory, indicating how the focus of these rulers had shifted northwards into their new domains. He had begun his reign badly with the loss not only of York but of much of the Danish-settled area of Mercia. However, he had subsequently recovered well and, with the assistance of St Bealdhere in eliminating King Olaf, was able to restore his rule in both of these areas. King Edmund was survived by two infant sons, who were still too young to rule, and hence his brother Eadred was his sole heir. In these circumstances, there could be no division of the joint kingdom which remained once again in the hands of a single ruler.[38]

The new king, Eadred, was consecrated by Archbishop Oda of Canterbury at Kingston-on-Thames on 16 August 946 and in the very same year, perhaps even before his consecration, the Chronicle records that he had enforced his authority over York. A summer campaign in the north would have provided an ideal opportunity to prevent a defection by the men of York such as had occurred immediately after the death of Athelstan. Indeed, this may have been the reason for the fairly long delay between the death of his brother and his own consecration. King Eadred also renewed his brother's Scottish alliance in this same year. It seems that he also recognised that the Scots could provide a useful counterweight to the still restive Kingdom of York.

In spite of these arrangements, in the following year of 947, King Eadred found it necessary to bring an army north to Tanshelf in the South Riding of Yorkshire. There, Archbishop Wulfstan and the leading men of York once again submitted to his overlordship and gave pledges on oath to support him. This is a clear sign that the men of York remained unsettled and uncommitted to English rule. Indeed, the Chronicle admits as much by stating that 'they were false both to their pledges and their oaths'. However, the power of the joint kingdom of Mercia and Wessex remained too great for the much smaller kingdom of York to resist except in extraordinary circumstances, for example under the rule of someone like Olaf Guthfrithson or with outside assistance from Dublin or elsewhere.[39]

In 948 the Chronicle records that the men of York summoned the exiled Eric Bloodaxe of Norway to be their king. Once again they viewed the succession of a new king as an opportunity to throw off English domination. They clearly remained unreconciled to the possibility of English rule in spite of the conversion of their leaders to Christianity. This time, however, they appear to have been convinced that the Dublin dynasty could offer them little assistance. Indeed, the Dublin kings had conspicuously failed to maintain the independence of York in the period between 943 and 944 when their own internecine struggles had left the city open to attack by King Edmund. As a result, on this occasion they sought the aid of the exiled King Eric of Norway. The latter had been expelled from Norway by his brother Hakon some time before this, possibly between 934 and 939, with the aid of Athelstan. He therefore had his own personal reasons to intervene in this contest against those he considered to have been responsible for his exile.[40]

In response to this rebellion, King Eadred harried throughout Yorkshire and destroyed the famous church of St Wilfred at Ripon. This raid clearly inflicted a great deal of damage but it failed to subdue the natives entirely since on his return journey the men of York sortied from the city, ambushed the rearguard of the royal army at Castleford and almost completely destroyed it. In response, Eadred repeated his raiding for a second time that same year and completed the devastation of the kingdom. The men of York finally got the message and expelled King Eric in fear of further retaliation. They followed this up by placating King Eadred with gifts before submitting to his rule.

This was not the end of the matter, however, for in 949 Olaf *Cuaran* returned from Dublin and seized the throne of York. King Eadred must have wondered how he could ever achieve a settlement of this problem. Olaf apparently sought to placate Eadred by offering his immediate submission, but could hardly be viewed by the latter with equanimity. It may have been at this point that he began to consider ways of securing his rule over York in the longer term. It was probably this that led to the policy he would adopt after 954: that of appointing a series of local rulers as his representatives in York. The idea was that these men could provide the necessary local knowledge and support to be acceptable while still representing his authority.[41]

In 952 King Eadred made his first move in this new policy and it was directed against the man that he clearly considered the real cause of much of the Northumbrian unrest. He imprisoned Archbishop Wulfstan of York at an unidentified place called *Iudanbyrig*. He appears, with some justification, to have considered the archbishop as an unreliable figure liable to betray him and York to any prospective rival. There seems to have been no shortage of people advising the king to dispose of this man since the Chronicle states that 'he had frequently been accused to the king'.[42]

In the wake of this move by Eadred, the exiled Eric of Norway returned to reoccupy York and expel Olaf *Cuaran*. It is possible that he faced opposition on this occasion and that King Edmund's earlier efforts at rapprochement with the Scots were beginning to pay dividends. In 952 the Irish annals record a battle involving the 'foreigners' or Vikings on one side against the Scots, Strathclyde Britons and the 'Saxons' or English on the other. In this particular case the English referred to were probably those of English Northumbria from north of the river Tyne. This battle may therefore have represented an attempt by the northern allies of King Eadred to defend newly restored York against Eric Bloodaxe. In this instance they were clearly unsuccessful since Eric gained possession of the city, but this infant alliance would pay dividends in the not too distant future.[43]

In 954 King Eadred made what would prove to be his final moves in the campaign against York by once again expelling Eric of Norway. However, on this occasion he was not content to rule with Wulfstan's co-operation. Instead, he appointed

Crucifixion scene from one of the Sandbach Crosses, Sandbach, Cheshire. (Photograph by W. Walker)

Ealdorman Oswulf of Bamburgh to rule over York on his behalf. This Englishman had been prominent at King Eadred's court in 949 as revealed by his place at the head of the *ealdormen* in the witness lists to royal charters of that year. He had subsequently demonstrated his loyalty to the king through his role in the battle of 952 against Eric Bloodaxe, as recorded in the Irish annals. He could therefore be relied on in the long term, as an opponent of the Dublin dynasty, to enforce Eadred's rule. He also had the advantage of being able to call upon local support from north of the Tyne. According to Roger of Wendover, King Eric was subsequently treacherously slain by a certain *Jarl* Maccus on Stainmore not much later that same year. A great number of men died with Eric in this ambush, including his own son, Eric, and the son of Ragnall Guthfrithson, another former king of York. Roger adds that King Eric had been betrayed by *Ealdorman* Oswulf, suggesting that King Eadred and his new agent in the north had engineered these killings.[44]

This turned out to be the last attempt by the men of York to maintain their independence from rule by southern kings. In view of their previous reluctance to accept this rule, demonstrated by no less than four major rebellions in the last twenty-seven years, there must have been significant reasons for this change. One important factor was undoubtedly the elimination of a number of men who had been key figures in the long struggle. The ambush on Stainmore had not only eliminated Eric Bloodaxe and his son but also the son of Ragnall, the last surviving relative of Olaf Guthfrithson. On 16 December 956 came the death of Archbishop Wulfstan of York, that grey eminence who had been a key supporter of many of the kings of York and who had recently been imprisoned on suspicion of treason. The last hope of the men of York, Olaf *Cuaran* of Dublin, appears to have lost interest. He was fully absorbed in holding on to his own base in the kingdom of Dublin until his retirement to Iona in 980.[45]

Another important factor in the final settlement of York and English Northumbria may have been the provision of a local ruler for the area in the form of *Ealdorman* Oswulf. He could provide a local focus of loyalty and a source of patronage for the men of York, while remaining loyal to the southern kings. He was not a Scandinavian ruler but he did have local associations in English Northumbria. In a similar way, the appointment of Osketel, a descendant of Danish settlers from Leicestershire, to succeed Wulfstan as Archbishop of York provided a comparable local focus for the Church, who would nevertheless remain loyal to southern kings. In this way, the previous representatives of the community whose interests were linked to the independence of the area were replaced by men whose own loyalties lay with the kings who had appointed them.[46]

In 955, within a year of what would subsequently prove to be his final triumph over the men of York, King Eadred died. He was survived by no sons of his own but by the two sons of his elder brother Edmund. Initially, the joint kingdom of Mercia and Wessex that had been ruled successively by Athelstan, Edmund and Eadred passed to a single ruler, King Eadwig, the elder of Edmund's sons. It was only in 957, after a period of two years, that tensions apparently arose between King Eadwig and his younger brother Edgar. The cause of these tensions is unknown but probably related to a desire on Edgar's part for a share of power. The important point was that this internal family tension apparently found a resonance in a parallel tension between the old divisions of Mercia and Wessex. This is reflected in a clear division among the *ealdormen* evidenced by the witness lists of charters from 957 to 959 between those from Mercia who followed Edgar, and those from Wessex who continued to support Eadwig. It was probably as a result of this combination of factors that the long combined English kingdom found itself once again divided between two available heirs, as recorded in the Chronicle. The elder son, Eadwig, retained the rule in Wessex while the younger son, Edgar, took control of Mercia and Northumbria. Thus, in spite of the last thirty years of unified rule, Mercia and Wessex still remained distinct and separate kingdoms. There was apparently still no truly united England but three separate regions with their own viewpoints and a strong sense of their former identity as separate kingdoms.[47]

In 959 King Eadwig died unexpectedly, without heirs, and his brother Edgar succeeded him, adding the kingdom of Wessex to those of Mercia and Northumbria that he already held. Once again, as in 924, an accident of fate had resulted in the unification of the kingdoms of Wessex and Mercia. In other circumstances Mercia and Wessex might have developed over time into fully separate kingdoms once again. When King Edgar became king of the unified realm he did so, as had Athelstan in 924, as King of Mercia and so once again pulled Mercia into England. In fact, this proved to be the final appearance of an independent Mercia and it should perhaps be seen as the point at which England really began. This does not mean that Mercia disappeared overnight since it remained in existence at least until the Norman Conquest and arguably for longer. It did so, however, as an administrative and legal unit that was firmly part of England rather than as a kingdom.[48]

During a sixteen-year reign, Edgar would preside over the completion of the process of integration of these two former kingdoms. He introduced a standard national coinage and encouraged the reform of the Church, including the founding of monasteries across England. This was carried out under conditions of relative peace and tranquillity, free from external invasion. The virtual absence of a foreign threat, previously represented by the Vikings and then the Kingdom of York, allowed scope for the emergence of some internal tensions. However, these tensions remained below the surface and did not become apparent until Edgar's death when he left behind two sons of different mothers to succeed him. It might have been anticipated that, as in 957, these tensions would have focussed on the divisions between Mercia and Wessex. However, this was not to be the case, as the new divisions that emerged straddled the Thames and included both Mercians and West Saxons. In this context, the difference between Mercia and Wessex was obviously becoming less important as the members of the noble families of each former kingdom mixed socially and intermarried. This process had continued throughout the peaceful reign of King Edgar and it is probably in his time that we can see the emergence of a more identifiable English identity.

In 975 King Edgar, who was aptly described by the Chronicle as 'protector of the Mercians', died. On this occasion, however, there would be no division of the kingdom like that of 957 although, once again, two sons existed. Instead, the

Frontispiece of King Edgar's Charter to New Minster, showing the king presenting a copy to Christ. (BL Cotton Vespasian A viii, f. 2v)

supporters of the two young *athelings* Edward and Aethelred would embark on a struggle for control over the whole of Edgar's united kingdom. The factions involved in this struggle were no longer directly linked solely to Mercia or Wessex but represented interests and concerns that crossed the old boundaries and stretched across both kingdoms. The elder of the boys, Edward, was supported by Dunstan, Archbishop of Canterbury and Aethelwine, *Ealdorman* of East Anglia. The younger boy, Aethelred, was supported by his mother Aelfthryth, Aethelwold, Bishop of Winchester and Aelfhere, *Ealdorman* of Mercia. Initially Edward and his supporters were successful in occupying the throne but the resultant discontent among the losing party was enormous. The tensions between the factions continued to grow before ultimately exploding into violence in 978 with the murder of King Edward II the Martyr at Corfe Castle in Dorset. Aethelred then assumed the throne to usher in a new era of English history, one involving a recognisable English kingdom rather than an amalgamation of separate entities. The making of England was complete.[49]

It had not been a swift or painless process and it did not come about as the consequence of a single dramatic event or the vision of a single individual. It was instead the culmination of a series of historical trends and developments, many of them contradictory, spread over a period of almost 150 years. It did not happen with the collapse of Mercia under Viking assault in 877. It did not happen with the sealing of a formal alliance between Lord Aethelred and King Alfred in the 880s. It did not happen with the takeover of Mercia by King Edward the Elder in 918. It did not happen with the succession of King Athelstan to both kingdoms in 925 although this was a vital stage in the process. It might be said in retrospect to have reached its final stage with the succession of Edgar to both kingdoms in 959. All of these events were important parts of the process but ultimately that process was greater than all of these events in themselves. It was a process that could be seen to be complete with the succession of King Aethelred II in 978.

The making of England happened because of a long period of coexistence and co-operation involving the leaders and peoples of Mercia and Wessex. This began tentatively enough with the brief alliance between King Burgred of Mercia and King Aethelwulf of Wessex in 853. It widened and deepened to a significant extent during the defensive struggles of Lord Aethelred and King Alfred. This process continued during the successful offensive campaigns undertaken by their respective successors Lady Aethelflaed and King Edward the Elder. It moved to another level under King Athelstan, probably the first ruler of both Mercia and Wessex to be regarded as legitimate by the men of both kingdoms. It deepened again under Edmund and Eadred in the common pursuit of the defeat of the men of York. It reached its final fulfilment under King Edgar who in 975 could with justification be regarded as the first king of a truly united England.

CHAPTER 7

The Kingdom

INTRODUCTION

This chapter will consider the social background to the Mercian kingdom in its secular aspects. The wider background to English society in this period can be discovered by reading any of a number of books on the subject. What will be attempted here is a reconstruction of Mercian society based as much as possible on contemporary Mercian evidence only. This has the disadvantage of leaving us working with a rather limited number of sources but hopefully has the advantage of avoiding the introduction of anachronistic comparisons. A more general study of English society at this time can sometimes involve, where the evidence for a particular period or kingdom is thin, drawing on evidence from another time or another place and such evidence might actually be misleading. I have also avoided using information from literary sources for similar reasons. It is often difficult to establish the date or place of origin of such works, which are usually anonymous, during the Anglo-Saxon period. Even in cases where such information can be established, it remains difficult to be sure that examples of social behaviour they may contain are drawn from contemporary society rather than literary models from the past or from other, Biblical or foreign, societies.[1]

In the early medieval period in Western Europe, including England, existence depended almost entirely on the resources of the land. It was a largely agrarian society in which the land itself and its produce supported every man, woman and child in the English kingdoms. The crops and livestock supported on the land provided food for their tables and clothes for their bodies while the trees and minerals provided the raw materials for their houses and tools. The vast majority of people worked directly on the land cultivating crops, breeding livestock, hunting for game and fishing in the seas and rivers. It was their labour that supported the elite minority of rulers, warriors, traders, craftsmen and priests. This is the society recognised and portrayed in a simplified form by King Alfred in his contemporary translation of Boethius' *Consolation of Philosophy*, in which he describes society as consisting of three classes of men, 'praying men, fighting men and working men'.[2]

This basic agricultural economy appears to have functioned at a level, which usually produced enough to feed the working population and maintain an elite, while still allowing for a growth in the general level of population. In most years people probably thrived on a relatively healthy if basic diet while, less frequently, poor harvests or diseases of livestock pushed the population into famine. The indications of this can be found in the growth of the population and in the increase in trade which involves an exchange of surplus produce over and above that required to sustain the local population.

In the period covered by this book, international trade in a wide range of goods was becoming an increasingly important source of additional wealth for the nations of North West Europe including Mercia. The gradual coalescence of the large number of small warring units which had succeeded the Roman Empire into larger and more stable states brought in its wake increased peace and stability. In turn this made trade in a wide range of non-luxury items easier and more profitable not only for those directly involved but also for those rulers and nobles who were able to tap into this new source of wealth by levying tolls and customs on passing trade and by protecting and fostering markets for exchange in their own territories. It was this latter phenomenon which gave rise to major emporia or trading centres such as London in Mercia, *Hamwic* (near modern Southampton) in Wessex, York in Northumbria and, probably, Ipswich in East Anglia.

In terms of the Kingdom of Mercia, the main entry point for Continental trade seems to have been the settlement at London, which, prior to the mid-ninth century, was located upstream of the present City of London, around the Strand. It is here, in the area bounded by the Tyburn and the River Fleet, that archaeologists are beginning to discover traces of what was probably a very large and busy trading settlement of the eighth and ninth centuries. At its peak, it has been estimated to have extended for between 55 and 60 hectares with an estimated population of 5,000. This site has been dated by a range of contemporary artefacts, including two coin hoards found at Middle Temple and Waterloo Bridge and dated to 840 and 870 respectively. The memory of this settlement is preserved in the modern place-name Aldwych, the 'old trading settlement'. Modern building across much of this area means it is difficult to undertake more than occasional archaeological work and the picture of this settlement therefore remains fragmentary. The evidence to date suggests that it was similar to the better preserved and more accessible remains of its contemporary site at *Hamwic* near Southampton.[3]

The *Hamwic* site was a thriving urban trading centre consisting of a planned town with a regular grid pattern of streets running north-south and east-west. It was a fairly densely occupied site extending to around 40 hectares, with an estimated population of 2,500, and containing many timber houses and workshops. It was heavily involved in trade, especially cross-channel trade with the Franks but also with Scandinavia, Spain and even further afield. The workshops on the site housed a wide range of craftsmen including all sorts of metalworkers, glassworkers, boneworkers, textile workers, potters, leatherworkers and woodworkers. It was also a centre for minting the *sceatta* coinage. It was one of the largest urban centres in England and London appears to have been very similar.[4]

The Strand settlement itself has recently revealed evidence for a similar grid pattern of streets, metalled roads with associated drainage channels and possibly a defensive ditch. This site apparently went into decline in the second half of the eighth century for reasons that remain unclear but which may be related to a recession in long distance trade. The increase of Viking activity at this time almost certainly contributed to or accelerated this trend. There were attacks on London itself in 842 and 851, and Vikings spent the winter on Thanet in 853 and 866. In 871 the 'great army' entered the river Thames and in the following year occupied London itself for almost a year. In 879 another group of Vikings were based at Fulham over the winter. In 877 Vikings settled across Eastern Mercia and in 880 in nearby East Anglia. All of this must have made the Thames an undesirable if not unsafe destination for many traders.[5]

The future of London probably remained very uncertain until the occupation of the city by King Alfred and its handing over to Lord Aethelred as recorded by the Chronicle in 886. This occupation was probably initially a military project that was intended to secure this very exposed site by relocating it within the old Roman walls. This provided a defensible area that could be garrisoned as a deterrent if not always a barrier to Viking advance up the Thames. This immediate military purpose could be said to have been effectively achieved by 893 when, as already seen in Chapter 4, the garrison from London played an important part in countering the Vikings. In this sense, the initial restoration of London can be seen as part of the more general programme of *burh* construction initiated by Aethelred and Alfred at this time.

However, there was more to the restoration of London than this military purpose. The survival of two important documents from this period reveals that it encompassed the laying out of a trading town on the new site with house plots, streets, markets, a trading shore, tolls and mooring rights. The second of these documents, dated 898/9, records joint arrangements reached by King Alfred and Lord Aethelred about the restoration of London in the company of their respective senior clerical advisers, Archbishop Plegmund and Bishop Waerferth at Chelsea. Lord Aethelred's role in this process would be commemorated in the local name Aethelred's Hithe, which survived until the 1180s before being changed to Queenhithe. This economic restoration of London appears to have been a much slower process partly because the threat of Viking or Danish attack remained. The Danish settlement of

East Anglia and further Viking raids on Kent and Essex and up the Thames Valley continued to hinder the use of London as a trading port. It was probably only after King Edward's defeat of the Danes of East Anglia at Holme in 902 and his restoration of English control over Essex and East Anglia in 917 that more regular trade from London could resume.[6]

What sort of items were being traded from London either between the individual English kingdoms or beyond through these ports? Unfortunately, very little evidence survives today although the work of the archaeologists undoubtedly offers hope for the future. Few of the records of trade, which were inevitably of an ephemeral nature, have survived while many of the items involved were perishable and hence have left no trace in the archaeological record. There are a few significant exceptions to this general lack of contemporary documentary records and it is probably no coincidence that these relate to goods which were probably very important at the time.[7]

The first of these products is salt, which was essential in this period as a food flavouring and preservative and which was mined in great quantities at Droitwich and Nantwich in Mercia. The Mercian kings were fully aware of the vital importance of salt and as a result drew profit from taxation levied on this essential product. In 716 King Aethelbald granted land on the river Salwarp in Worcestershire to Worcester cathedral for the construction of a salt works in exchange for an existing salt works north of the same river. A charter of 900 reveals that Lord Aethelred was able to charge a toll of a shilling on every cartload and a penny on every packload of salt mined at Droitwich. There is also evidence in place names for traditional salt trading routes radiating out in all directions from Droitwich. This vital trade must have brought a significant income to the Mercian rulers.[8]

The second product is one about which we would be entirely ignorant except for the survival of a unique exchange of correspondence between two of the most important rulers of the period, Charlemagne, King of the Franks, and King Offa. These letters concern the trade dispute of the 790s between their kingdoms which involved an embargo on the export of woollen cloth from England to the Continent. The letters appear to indicate that this cloth represented a staple product in this cross-Channel trade. They discuss standard measures for this cloth, a form of regulation that clearly indicates the volume and significance of the trade. The significance of this woollen cloth can also be seen from the fact that during this dispute the Frankish ruler felt that it was a good target for his sanctions.[9]

The third product is lead, which was a by-product of silver mining that often played an important part in the construction of churches. It was mined in Mercia around Wirksworth in Derbyshire, and was extensively used during this period for protecting church roofs as well as in the production of pans for boiling salt. A charter of 835 survives in which Abbess Cynewaru of Repton grants land at Wirksworth to

Ealdorman Hunberht on condition that he supplies Archbishop Ceolnoth of Canterbury with 300 shillings worth of lead annually for the roof of his church. In addition, England was widely known on the Continent as a source of good quality lead and in 852 Abbot Lupus of Ferrieres in France wrote to King Aethelwulf seeking to secure supplies for the roof of his own church. The wealth derived from this activity made the nobles of Wirksworth rich, and allowed them to employ important artists to decorate their church and their tombs. This is revealed in the superb artistry and sophistication of the sarcophagus lid still to be found in Wirksworth church today.[10]

It is clear that tolls on trade provided kings with an important source of revenue. This is the reason for their high profile involvement in trade disputes and trade regulation. The charters of this period reveal the importance of such tolls through grants of rights to collection of tolls and of exemptions from tolls. King Aethelbald issued a number of charters granting the income from tolls to churches, including the toll due on two ships at London to Bishop Milred of Worcester. Kings Offa and Beorhtwulf confirmed the grants of the toll due on single ships at London to Abbess Sigeburga of Thanet and the Bishop of London respectively. A man named Ealdred, who is described as a toll-collector, is listed among the witnesses to a charter of King Beornwulf in 824.[11]

Detail from sarcophagus cover, St Mary's Church, Wirksworth, Derbyshire. (Photograph by W. Walker)

It was this expanding economy that produced a demand for a reliable medium of exchange in the form of a new silver coinage. As noted in Chapter 1, this coinage had probably originated under the kings of Kent, who introduced the silver penny based on contemporary Frankish designs for the new silver *denier* introduced in 755. The new coins were thus of the right weight and quality to make them readily acceptable in exchange for contemporary Frankish coins. They also provided a high silver content, which gave them an immense attraction as bullion in non-coinage economies like neighbouring Scandinavia or the Celtic countries. The attraction of these new silver coins for traders meant that those kings who controlled the minting process could levy a tax on the production of these coins. They did so by securing the surrender of more silver in exchange for these coins than contained in the coins themselves. In effect, they were making a profit on the sale of the coins. They were able to do so because the coins displayed their name and title, which provided a form of guarantee of quality to those receiving the coin. The new pennies easily replaced the smaller and much poorer quality *sceatta* coinage of the earlier period.[12]

The first mint of the kings of Kent at Canterbury subsequently fell under the control of King Offa when he conquered Kent in 785. Indeed, it may have played a major factor in inciting his interest in directly controlling Kent at this time. It was he who exploited this new source of revenue to the full with the appearance of large numbers of coins under his own name. This process of minting was carried on by succeeding rulers who continued to mint these coins as an important element in their efforts to promote trade. The evidence of the widely scattered pattern of single finds of this and later coins of the period indicates that these coins were actively used in trade and circulated throughout the English kingdoms. The location of the early mints in important trading centres such as London also indicates their role in trade. The same process explains the subsequent extension of minting to the new *burhs* as trade developed around these new focal points. The coins would also prove useful as a means of collecting or paying tributes and dues but this was probably a secondary function.

KINGS AND RULERS

When we come to consider King Alfred's three classes of men in more detail the sources provide us with a rather top-heavy view. The sources that survive record a great deal of information about the social elite, Alfred's 'praying men' and 'fighting men', but very little about the 'working men'. The rest of this chapter will focus on what the sources tell us about the two secular classes. The 'praying men' will be examined in Chapter 8.

The effective rulers of this largely agricultural society in Mercia as in the rest of England were called kings. It is important to note that these men were rulers of specific peoples rather than of territories, thus the most commonly used title of the Mercian king was the Latin *Rex Merciorum*, King of the Mercians, and not King of Mercia. The Mercian kings were descended from those men, who had been able to seize control during the confusion immediately following the Anglo-Saxon invasions and the subsequent struggle for power between various new groups. They were initially drawn from a royal dynasty established by the pagan King Penda in the opening years of the seventh century.[13]

It is perhaps worth saying something about the nature of the Mercian kingdom at this point. It has recently been suggested that Mercia was in fact a composite kingdom made up of a large number of small units in a sort of federal arrangement. This idea has been fuelled by the existence of the *Tribal Hidage*, an early tribute list that records the names of some twenty-nine independent units all apparently within the boundaries of the Mercia later ruled by King Offa. There can be no doubt that the origins of Mercia lay in the union of smaller units, this is evident from the early historical record from the writings of Bede through to the evidence of charters. However, this should not blind us to the evidence of later records which indicate that in spite of these very origins the later kingdom was actually a single solid entity.[14]

Fragment of sculpture showing a king, St Mary's Church, Wirksworth, Derbyshire. (Photograph by W. Walker)

The *Tribal Hidage* remains to be securely dated but would seem to be earlier rather than later and hence may reflect the circumstances in Mercia in an early period rather than under Offa and his successors. The fact that many of the names found in the document can no longer be identified may in itself imply that they were quickly subsumed in the wider kingdom. There is some evidence that, although the Mercian kingdom expanded by absorbing other units, it had already developed a more cohesive identity of its own. The process through which the former kingdom of the *Hwicce* was absorbed can be seen in the charters as it was gradually transformed from an independent kingdom into a province of Mercia. This shows that the idea of a kingdom formed from individual units is not necessarily antithetical to that of a single unified kingdom. The scant evidence that we have on this subject seems to indicate that some of the subdivisions of Mercia remained important as regions governed by *ealdormen*, but they show few signs of an ability to operate independently of the larger whole. They were probably in this respect much more like the shires of Wessex than some historians have recognised.

If the various subdivisions, like those of the *Hwicce*, *Magonsaete* etc., had been more independent it might have been expected that the dynastic disputes of the ninth century would have split the kingdom. In such circumstances, the rivalry of the competing dynasties with their own local bases and their own supporters might have been expected to result in their setting up their own rival kingdoms. Instead, it is clear that their interest lay in disputing control of the Mercian kingdom as a whole. There is no evidence at all to indicate that any candidate for the kingship ever sought to carve up the kingdom. In addition, the intervention of the Vikings might have been expected to result in the break-up of any sort of 'federal' Mercia into its component parts but instead, the unoccupied areas strained to retain their wider Mercian identity and remain unified. Its rulers retained their knowledge of the larger Mercia that had been lost and sought successfully to restore this during the tenth century. This evidence would seem to suggest that by the ninth century at least Mercia was much more a single entity than a loose federation of smaller units. The inhabitants of the kingdom appear to have considered themselves as Mercians regardless of their local allegiances.

The power of the kings who ruled over this kingdom was based on their exploitation of a number of rights over their subjects that they had accumulated in one way or another over the years. They had probably usurped some of these rights from their Romano-British predecessors just as they had usurped their lands and rule. They had probably brought others with them from their original Continental homes. They had adopted yet others in imitation or emulation of former Roman or neighbouring Continental or Welsh practice. In return for the exploitation of these various rights the kings were expected to perform a range of corresponding or related duties for their subjects. The origins of these duties were as diverse as those of the rights.

In the context of many national histories, there is a tendency to lose sight of the connections and influences linking English rulers with their contemporaries on the Continent. In reality, of course, the early English kings did not exist in a vacuum but were aware of the activities and powers not only of their immediate neighbours the Carolingians but also of more distant potentates like the Byzantine emperors whose rule provided a model for their own. As a result, many important ideas and innovations from the Continent provided models for English rulers, for example, coinage, *burhs*, military reforms, etc. This is not to imply that these rulers were mere copyists as even where innovations like the coinage clearly derived from the Continent they were usually adapted specifically to English circumstances.[15]

The key rights, subsequently known as the three necessities, claimed by the Mercian kings in this period all related to their main function of leadership in war. They were: the right to demand military service; the right to claim service for the building and upkeep of bridges; and the right to claim service for the construction and repair of fortifications. These rights allowed the kings to recruit armies to defend the kingdom, to transport these armies across their lands to oppose any invaders and to construct defences against any invasion. Equally, they allowed kings to recruit armies to attack other kingdoms, to transport such invading forces to other kingdoms and to construct fortifications against other kingdoms. These rights appear to have originated in Mercia, whose rulers are the first to record them in a charter of 749. The fundamental importance of these rights is demonstrated by the fact that they were always preserved even when exemptions were granted in charters from all other duties. In 792 King Offa imposed them for the first time outside Mercia on the Kentish monasteries in response to raids by 'pagan seamen'.[16]

If we are looking for some indication of the immense power wielded by these kings we should consider the results of their demands for *burhbot* or building of fortifications. As noted in Chapter 1, Offa's Dyke was almost certainly built by exploitation of this right. It is an immense achievement by any standards, covering 150 miles of frontier with extant stretches of dyke 80 miles in length. Another significant achievement of the Mercian rulers during this period is the construction of at least twenty-two *burhs* over a period of twenty years. This work was completed largely by Lord Aethelred and Lady Aethelflaed, as noted in Chapters 4 and 5. It is even more impressive when it is noted that as many as three of these fortresses were sometimes completed in a single year.[17]

It should not be thought that these rights were arbitrary or derived from some form of divine right but rather that they were customary or had arisen through practice over the years. In addition, the king normally wielded his powers not in an arbitrary way but rather with the advice and support of royal counsellors, usually the most prominent men in the land. Such men, usually working through the gathering of the *witan* or royal council, would advise the king on the customary extent of his powers and remind him of his compensating duties. This process ensured that the king would receive the full support of these key men in carrying out his policies while at the same time allowing these key supporters an influence in shaping royal policies. There is evidence for meetings of this council in the charters and the records of the church councils throughout this period.

Perhaps the most significant of the other royal rights was that of patronage. This included a wide range of rights to grant lands, goods, offices or privileges to their followers usually in return for services rendered in the past or in anticipation of services to be rendered in the future. They were expected by their subjects to use this mechanism to reward good service and dispense patronage whether in lands, goods, offices or privileges to those who deserved it. They also had the right to demand a wide range of dues and services from those settled on lands under their authority, including military service and various labour services. In return, they were expected to protect the land and property of their subjects by maintaining peace within the kingdom and, if necessary, defending it against attack by rival kingdoms.[18]

The kings also had the right to sit in judgement on their subjects and to impose suitable punishments on those so judged. This ranged from the making of new legislation, through arbitration of disputes between important individuals, to the judgement of cases brought before the royal court and the performance of summary justice on criminals. In return the kings were expected to uphold the law and dispense justice as fairly and impartially as possible. A significant number of surviving documents from this period relate to the resolution of such disputes at the royal court before the king and his *witan* or royal council. Unfortunately no law codes compiled by any Mercian king have survived. It is likely, however, that such laws did once exist as a reference in the introduction to the *Laws of King Alfred* states that he 'ordered to be written many of the ones [laws] that our forefathers observed . . . those which I found . . . in the days of . . . Offa, king of the Mercians . . . and which seemed to me most just, I collected herein'.[19]

There has been a great deal of speculation by noted experts about the possible content of these laws of King Offa. This speculation ranges from a maximalist view, which attempts to recover these laws using surviving traces of Mercian influence in much later law texts, to Wormald's more minimalist view, which relates Alfred's reference solely to a few surviving records of Mercian church councils. The real position was probably somewhere in between. It seems very unlikely that a king such as Offa, who demonstrated a powerful desire to emulate his great contemporary Charlemagne in a number of ways, would not have published a substantial body of laws in some form. On the other hand, Mercian legal terms discovered in later law texts may reflect the usage of Mercian scribes rather than the incorporation of specific Mercian laws. The solution may be that King Offa did issue a body of legislation, which has not survived, perhaps because Alfred chose to adopt only the Mercian church council resolutions for use in his own later code.[20]

Kings were also expected to protect native and foreign traders and their goods. The royal duty to maintain roads and bridges, though originally intended to speed the progress of royal armies, was increasingly also of direct benefit to trade and traders. In return, kings had the right to levy tolls and customs on this trade both within their territories and on their borders. As seen above, contemporary charters provide clear evidence for this practice. They had the right to mint coins for use in trade and commerce and to draw a profit from this process. In turn, it was in their interest to issue a sound and reliable coinage which would prove attractive to these traders.

In the earlier part of the period covered by this book, a number of *sub-reguli*, or sub-kings, still existed on the fringes of Mercia. They were clearly subordinate to the King of Mercia, but stood apart from the *ealdormen*. In origin, these men had been independent rulers or kings of small tribal kingdoms like those of the *Hwicce*, the South Saxons, etc. However, as part of the continuation of the same process which had produced the large Mercian kingdom itself, the more powerful Mercian kings had gradually reduced these once independent kings to tributary status. The *Tribal Hidage* provides an example of a tribute list recording the basis for assessment of tribute payments to an overlord from a long list of kingdoms. Thereafter, over a period of time, these tributary kings were eliminated or absorbed to be replaced by those appointed royal servants, the *ealdormen*, found elsewhere in Mercia. This process is considered in more detail in Chapter 1, with reference to the former kingdom of the *Hwicce*.[21]

This consideration of the status and role of Mercian kings must now lead us to consider the unique position of Lord Aethelred and his wife Lady Aethelflaed. They are usually addressed in the sources as *Ealdorman* and Lady and are therefore usually assumed to have carried only this status by modern historians. However, if the evidence of the original sources is examined more closely it becomes clear that there is rather more to it than this. It becomes evident that these individuals held a much higher status than that of an ordinary *ealdorman* and his wife and indeed there are some clear indications of royal status.[22]

It is clear from all the contemporary records, including, in particular, the charters of Aethelred and Aethelflaed, that they themselves did not use the royal title. It seems to be a clear implication from this that they were never actually consecrated. They also never issued a coinage bearing their names, barring any such coins appearing in the future which seems rather unlikely. The evidence that we have to date suggests that the coins minted at this time in Mercia, in Gloucester, Oxford and London, in fact bear the name of King Alfred. On the face of it these few facts would seem to build a conclusive case for accepting that Aethelred and his wife were not royal personages. Instead, they appear to be members of the Mercian nobility who are subordinate to King Alfred in the same way as any of his own West Saxon *ealdormen*. Indeed, this is how they have been viewed by most historians of this period.[23]

However, there is a great deal of evidence to indicate that Aethelred and Aethelflaed were much more than an ordinary *ealdorman* and his wife. In many ways they operated in the very same fashion as their predecessors the Mercian kings. They issued their own charters granting territory throughout Mercia with the consent and witness of bishops and other, clearly subordinate, *ealdormen*. They supervised the meetings of the Mercian *witan*, as mentioned in a number of these charters. They issued judgements intended to settle a number of long running disputes. They granted exemptions from royal rights including *feorm* or food rents and compensation rights. They recognised King Burgred as their predecessor. They also declare on a number of occasions that they act on behalf of 'the whole of Mercia'. These are all the actions of persons who wield the authority of kings rather than of nobles. There is also the point that this royal status is recognised by a number of contemporary and later writers. The contemporary compilers of the Irish and Welsh annals both record the death of Aethelflaed with the title *regina* under the year 918. The tenth-century historian *Ealdorman* Aethelweard bestows the title of *rex* on Aethelred of Mercia in his own version of the Chronicle. The status of the rulers of Mercia at this time was therefore not so clear cut.[24]

It is true that King Alfred often appears to support or endorse the actions set out in many of these Mercian charters but he does not invariably do so. In charters of 884, 888 and 915 Aethelred and Aethelflaed act independently of any other authority. The presence of King Alfred's name, like that of Mercian kings in earlier Kentish charters, signifies at most the endorsement of an outside overlord rather than the appearance of the native ruler. If King Alfred indeed considered himself as the direct ruler of Mercia or King of the Anglo-Saxons then why did he need the mediation of *Ealdorman* Aethelred at all? He could surely have simply issued charters for Mercia directly, with Aethelred appearing among the witnesses alongside all the other *ealdormen*. The answer to this lies in the peculiar circumstances noted in Chapter 4 which brought these two great individuals into close alliance.[25]

The special status of Lord Aethelred may also be recognised in King Alfred's will composed in 899. There Aethelred has the distinction of being singled out to receive a bequest of a sword worth 100 *mancuses*. He is the only *ealdorman* to be specifically named in the will although this may have been because he was related to the king. The king's other male relatives are also named. In contrast, although all three of his daughters, including Lady Aethelflaed, are left bequests none of them are named.[26]

EARLDORMEN

In the social strata below the kings were the major landowners, subsequently considered to be all those holding more than five hides of land. It was these men, the nobles, who made the rule of the kings effective by supporting it using their own local resources in terms of lands and men. It was a nobility of service in that these men provided services to the king in return for rewards in land or other benefits. It was these men who carried out royal instructions, including commanding armies, collecting taxes and enforcing justice. They were required to perform such services for the lands they already held but, in addition, if they wished to extend their holdings, they could do so by performing additional services.

The central importance of this system of service and reward can be seen in the evidence of the charters which provide a fragmentary but nevertheless revealing picture of it in operation. It is notable that the quality most admired in these nobles was *fidelitas* or faithfulness. It is mentioned in at least five surviving charters to laymen. It seems likely that the use of this term signifies that it had already been demonstrated by the particular nobleman concerned and that the grant concerned was a reward for this. However, it is not used in every grant and it is therefore possible that it involved an element of wishful thinking. If a man was awarded some land for his faithfulness perhaps he would feel more obliged to demonstrate this quality in the future.[27]

The greatest men in Mercia after the kings and the most senior of the nobles were the *ealdormen*. They were usually powerful men in their own right who owned large areas of land in a particular locality or region of the kingdom. They were made royal servants and appointed to the office of *ealdorman* by the king in order to exploit their local influence and support as a source of strength for the king himself. The role of these men was to represent the authority and power of the king in their local area. In this capacity, they performed a wide range of royal duties in the local region including leading the local contingent of the royal army, dispensing justice in local courts and supervising the local administration.[28]

The position of these *ealdormen* in the witness lists of contemporary Mercian charters, where they normally appear with the Latin title *dux* at the head of the lay witnesses, gives some idea of their key importance. In early charters, some of these men are addressed by other titles such as *præfectus*, *princeps*, *comes* or, less frequently, *patricius*. It would appear that such titles were sometimes used to indicate differences in status. In the charters of Offa, Ecgfrith and Cenwulf, the leading *ealdorman*, a man named Brorda, is sometimes singled out in this way. However, this practice was not consistently employed and in other cases these terms appear to be interchangeable with the term *dux*. In the later charters, the term *dux* becomes the standard form used.

One possibly more secure way of identifying those *ealdormen* in royal favour appears to be the use of the word *amicus*, or friend, in some charters. In a charter of 790 King Offa described *Ealdorman* Beorhtwald of Sussex as 'his friend and faithful *ealdorman*'.[29]

There is some evidence from entries in the Chronicle for the kind of duties undertaken by these *ealdormen*. An entry for the year 802 shows *Ealdorman* Aethelmund leading an army from the land of the *Hwicce* in an invasion of neighbouring Wessex. The Chronicle once again confirms their military importance by noting that no fewer than five *ealdormen* were among those who fell in battle in the army of King Ludeca in 827. The Welsh annals also mention *Ealdorman* Dudda leading a raid into South Wales in 866. The charters reveal further details of their duties. In 825 a charter of King Beornwulf shows *Ealdorman* Eadwulf acting as oathswearer on behalf of the Bishop of Worcester in a legal dispute over pasture. In another charter of 897 *Ealdorman* Aethelwulf is instructed to enforce the terms of a legal judgement on the churches of Worcester and Winchcombe.[30]

Unfortunately, it is impossible in the current state of our knowledge to work out exactly how many of these *ealdormen* there were at any time. Their numbers must have varied from time to time as new men were appointed and others died. They probably increased in number as those from subordinate kingdoms such as Kent or East Anglia were absorbed. They would certainly have been significantly reduced following the loss of large areas of the kingdom to Viking occupation after 877. The figure of five suggested by Finberg on the basis of the Chronicle entry for 827 is belied by the appearance of more than that in a number of surviving charters. The numbers listed as witnesses in the charters range from between six and twelve under Offa and Cenwulf, when they may include those from subject areas, to between five and ten for their successors. It is impossible to be more precise than this because of the small number of surviving charters, the lack of any consistency in witness lists and the fluctuations in the size and status of the kingdom itself. It seems probable that more *ealdormen* existed under King Offa when East Anglia, Sussex and Kent were subject to his authority. In contrast to this the numbers of *ealdormen* under Ceolwulf II and Aethelred were probably much reduced as a result of the loss of territory to the Vikings.[31]

We do not even have a clear picture of the spheres of influence or areas of authority ruled by these *ealdormen*. However, it seems likely that these was based either on old former kingdoms absorbed into Mercia, like that of the *Hwicce*, or on old divisions of Mercia itself, such as Middle Anglia. The few fragments of evidence that we have on this subject appear to confirm this impression. The Chronicle entry for 802 suggests that Aethelmund was *ealdorman* of the *Hwicce* and Asser refers to Aethelred Mucil, Alfred's Mercian father-in-law, as *ealdorman* of the *Gainas*. A charter of King Beorhtwulf, dated to 848, suggests that Hunberht may have been *ealdorman* of the *Tomsaete*, who occupied the valley of the river Tame. An *ealdorman* named Dudda who features as a charter witness also appears in an entry in the Welsh annals in 866 when he ravaged Glywysing in South Wales. He may therefore have been *ealdorman* of the *Magonsaete*, who occupied modern Herefordshire, which bordered on this area. A more unusual case is that of *Ealdorman* Aethelwulf, who appears to have been a Mercian, appointed to rule in Berkshire during the period of Mercian control over this province. He was certainly recorded as ruler of Berkshire under King Alfred but following his death in 871 he was buried at Derby in Mercia.[32]

What is certain is that these *ealdormen* did not originally supervise the later Mercian shires like their West Saxon counterparts since these particular administrative units only developed following the introduction of the *burhs*. This is clear from the close relationship between the principal *burhs* of Mercia and the new shires which were named after these same towns. Indeed, these new Mercian shires sometimes cut across earlier territorial divisions of Mercia. This is the case with the ancient kingdom of the *Hwicce* which was split between the later Gloucestershire and Worcestershire. The creation of these shires has often been attributed to the later West Saxon rulers

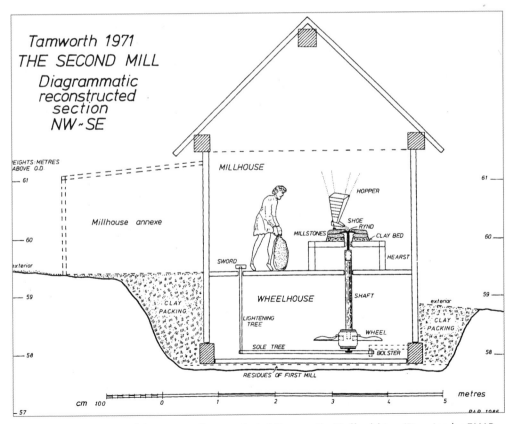

Drawn reconstruction of the watermill excavated at Tamworth, Staffordshire. (Drawing by F.W.B. Charles)

attempting to impose a familiar structure on their new kingdom. However, the possibility exists that this reform was, in fact, undertaken earlier than this by the Mercian rulers themselves. The construction and manning of these *burhs* necessitated the provision of strong bonds to their supporting hinterland whence they drew their garrison and supplies. We can see the intimate link between the call-up area for the garrison of the *burh* at Worcester, completed by 904, and the later shire, with both measured at 1,200 hides. This was obviously the most effective form for such links in terms of the shire and its central *burh*, and they were those eventually put in place. Indeed, in 914, the Chronicle strongly hints that such links were possibly already in place. In the entry for that year, it speaks of men from 'Hereford, Gloucester and the nearest *burhs*' rather than the men of the *Hwicce* defeating an attack by *Jarl* Harold. This does not prove that the Mercian shires were in existence at this early date. However, it does confirm that *burh*-based administrative units were beginning to take precedence over the old sub-kingdoms in some important contexts.[33]

In the period following the disappearance of a separate Mercian dynasty under King Edward of Wessex and his successors, the spheres of influence of the Mercian *ealdormen* began to increase considerably. Thus by the mid-tenth century a number of Mercian *ealdormen* were in control of wide areas of Mercia encompassing groups of the newly created shires. *Ealdorman* Athelstan controlled such a significant area of the former kingdom and all of East Anglia that he was nicknamed 'Half-King'. This process appears to have been the result of a requirement in the greatly expanded joint kingdom for local authority figures who nevertheless remained close to the king. In effect, as the size of the kingdom ruled by the king expanded so the size of the regions governed by his most senior nobles also expanded. This ensured that they remained as close to him as before in terms of status. More importantly, it provided them with a direct vested interest in his continued success which would thus be paralleled by their own. A similar process occurred in Wessex itself but on a much more limited scale.[34]

The fundamental status of these important officials as royal appointees rather than hereditary dynasties seems to be confirmed, at least in the earlier part of this period, by the absence of many clear examples of father to son succession. We need to be careful here as the evidence base for any conclusion on this is distinctly limited and we should beware of building an argument based on negative evidence. It would appear from a surviving document of 804 that *Ealdorman* Aethelmund of the *Hwicce* was not succeeded in this role by his son Aethelric who nevertheless inherited his other property. On the other hand, it seems likely from a number of records that the Mucel, and his father Esne, mentioned in a charter of King Wiglaf dated to 836, were the *ealdormen* of the same name who witnessed charters of the Mercian kings between Cenwulf and Beorhtwulf. There is slightly more evidence for what looks like dynasties of *ealdormen* towards the end of this period. For example, during the rule of

Aethelred and Aethelflaed we find *ealdormen* named Ealhhelm and Aethelfrith, who were subsequently succeeded by their descendants. Indeed, they went on to found powerful dynasties that flourished right through into the early eleventh century.[35]

It has often been assumed that *Ealdorman* Aethelfrith was a West Saxon intruded into Mercia by King Alfred but there is very little evidence for this. He does not appear as a witness in West Saxon charters. There is one interesting feature of this man's career in terms of his appearance in a number of charters issued by King Edward around 904. The charters involve grants of land at Risborough in Buckinghamshire and Wrington in Somerset and were intended to replace earlier documents apparently destroyed by fire, perhaps during the Viking attacks. These charters have sometimes been brought forward in attempts to prove that both Alfred and Edward controlled all of Mercia directly. The fact that *Ealdorman* Aethelred endorses the contents of these charters would seem to suggest otherwise. The explanation for these particular charters would appear to lie in the location of Aethelfrith's authority which was in south-eastern Mercia north of the Thames. This location made his situation of vital interest to the West Saxons as the first line of defence for their northern border. It was this very same area that Lady Aethelflaed would surrender to her brother in 911. This interest in itself would seem to be sufficient reason for King Edward's involvement in securing the rights of Aethelfrith. He was careful to do so, however, only with the involvement of Lord Aethelred of Mercia. It would not be surprising if there had originally existed identical charters for these lands in the name of Lord Aethelred.[36]

The frequent changes of *ealdormen* on the succession of kings from rival dynasties also suggests that these men were appointed to replace those loyal to their predecessors. This can clearly be seen from an examination of the witness lists of charters and the changes in these between reigns as recorded in Chapter 2. In contrast, there are very few changes in the names appearing on these lists or in the ranking of these names in the stable transition between Offa and his son Ecgfrith and their successor Cenwulf. This suggests a significant degree of continuity in administration and personnel between these reigns with the same key men in influential positions. In sharp contrast stand the often quite fundamental changes both in names and in positions in the lists to be seen between the reigns of rival kings like Ceolwulf I and Beornwulf, Beornwulf and Wiglaf and Wiglaf and Beorhtwulf. This clearly implies that the relative importance of such men at court depended directly on their relationship with the reigning king. One king's favourite was a potential opponent of his rival and successor and could therefore anticipate a rapid fall from grace. In this period the faithfulness of these men must have been severely tested.

In the period following the recovery of the Danish-occupied areas these English *ealdormen* were joined by their Danish equivalents the *jarls*. The latter appear to have occupied a similar position in terms of their own social hierarchy to that held by the English *ealdorman*. They are found in the Chronicle as military commanders subordinate to their kings but nevertheless in charge of major portions of their armies. They appear to have been closely linked to the Danish *burhs* each one of which appears to have contained a portion of their army and been commanded by a *jarl*. They appear as witnesses in later charters alongside their English counterparts under the same Latin title of *dux*. It seems clear that they were gradually absorbed into English society as part of the overall process of unifying the country after the recovery of the Danish areas.[37]

THEGNS

The next rank of people in Mercia were the middling nobles or *thegns*, who sat below the rank of *ealdorman* but above that of the ordinary freeman. Keynes has suggested that the charters provide 'little sense of the existence of a body of thegns serving the king'. This is an odd statement when nearly half of the extant charters recording grants by kings to laymen are grants to men described as *minister* or *thegn* and sometimes 'my *thegn*'. If these are not royal *thegns*, then what are they? There is certainly less evidence for these men than for the *ealdormen* but still enough not only to prove their existence but also to offer us some insights into their role. This may seem strange since these men were probably the key figures in supporting the royal administration in the localities. They provided the pivotal link in the mediation of power between the king and his most senior nobles and the more general population. It was these men who carried the commands and instructions of the king and the major lords to the ordinary population.[38]

They were very varied in status ranging from men like Wulfric Spott who held sufficient land to enable his descendants to become *ealdormen* to more minor royal servants with little more than the minimum of five hides. In a similar way some of these men based themselves close to the royal court with frequent appearances as charter witnesses but others remained more locally based appearing rarely at court or in the charter witness lists.

A significant number of charters granting lands to such men survive, and these demonstrate both the wide range of wealth they held and their commonality of status. They are all described as *ministri*, or *thegns*, regardless of the extent of their wealth. A charter of Offa dated to 775 records a whole family from this section of society, recording the grant of eight hides at Evenlode in Gloucestershire to the *thegn* Ridda and his family; his wife Bucga and his daughter Heahburh. In 883 a charter of *Ealdorman* Aethelred specifically grants twelve hides at Stoke Bishop to a man called Cynewulf, who was probably a *thegn*, because 'he has earned it from the lords of the Mercians'.[39]

The surviving sources occasionally provide evidence of some of the wide variety of duties undertaken by these men. In 915 the Mercian Register records the role played by these men in providing the officers to command the smaller units of the Mercian army. It describes how, at the storming of the Viking fortification at Derby in that year, a number of Lady Aethelflaed's *thegns* were killed. In 798 King Cenwulf's correspondence with the Papacy reveals that such men could be used as royal messengers. It was two *thegns* named Cildas and Ceolberht who carried his important diplomatic letters to Rome. The five men and three women who accompanied King Burgred and Queen Aethelswith to Rome and whose names are recorded in the *Liber Vitae* of Brescia were almost certainly from this section of society. Keynes' attempts to equate these particular individuals with the members of Aethelswith's own family are unconvincing as he fails to explain why Burgred's relations do not appear. After all King Burgred was the leader of this party and might be expected to be accompanied by his nearest and dearest. In contrast there seems little reason why his queen should be accompanied by her family.[40]

In the period following the recovery of the Danish-occupied areas these English *thegns* were joined by their Danish equivalents the *holds*. These men appear to have occupied a similar position in terms of their own social hierarchy to that held by the English *thegn*. In other words they stood in status below their *jarls* but above the ordinary freemen. They are found in the Chronicle in positions of military command subordinate to the *jarls* and appear as witnesses in later charters alongside their English counterparts under the same Latin title of *minister*.[41]

OTHERS

It is when we come to the range of people below the ranks of the middle nobility that we find ourselves largely starved of solid evidence. A wide range of men of different ranks existed at the lower levels of English society but we can only catch faint glimpses of them in our sources. This is perhaps not surprising since the main surviving sources from this period relate to the activities of the leaders of society rather than those of the minor players. Thus narrative sources like the Chronicle are largely concerned with important and newsworthy events. Such events most often involved important people, kings, bishops and *ealdormen*, while the deeds of minor figures were so much a part of everyday life that they were not considered worth reporting. In terms of charters and similar administrative documents an emphasis on the leaders of society arises from the chance survival of such documents. The charters that tend to survive were usually those considered most worthy of preservation and these were often those involving major grants by important people, again usually the kings, bishops and *ealdormen*.[42]

It is therefore very much a matter of chance that we find references to these lower members of society at all. A few appear in documentary records serving in various guises including *geneats*, reeves, grooms and swineherds while others can be inferred from these records. Thus Ecglaf was the *geneat* of a priest called Aethelwold, who was involved in the agreement of boundaries following the resolution of a property dispute with Bishop Waerferth of Worcester in 896. A man named Wulfsige was the reeve of Bishop Waerferth himself and featured in a number of his charters. A charter of King Beornwulf, dated to 825 and concerning a dispute over pasture, also refers to reeves, including one named Hama, and to swineherds. Another of 824 lists among its witnesses a man named Ealdred who is identified as a toll-collector. The references to tolls on ships and on cartloads and packs of salt remind us that there were sailors, carters and packmen.[43]

It is not certain but it seems likely that the moneyers whose names are recorded on the contemporary coinage derived from the more wealthy members of this group.

Fragment of sculpture showing a leadminer, St Mary's Church, Wirksworth, Derbyshire. (Photograph by W. Walker)

They were probably men who had made their fortunes through their skills but who yet owned little land. They were therefore effectively excluded from the nobility but nevertheless held considerable influence. The unnamed *faestingamen*, who appear in a number of charters granting exemption from the duty to provide hospitality for this particular category of official, were probably also members of this group.[44]

In one case we have a rare surviving monumental record of these minor figures. The church at Wirksworth in Derbyshire includes among its surviving fragments of sculpture the figure of a lead miner. He carries a hammer over his shoulder with which to mine the metal and a basket to transport it to the surface. This appears to be a rare representation, which may be of pre-Conquest date, of what might be termed an industrial worker. It is perhaps not surprising that such a miner should appear in this context. After all, the decorations of the church building itself and indeed the wealth of the whole Wirksworth area had been founded on the profits arising from the work of such men. If more such examples had survived might we have found representations of a salt-worker in Droitwich and a weaver in the Malvern Hills?

There is very little surviving information on the lowest ranks of society in Mercia during the period covered by this book and particularly on slaves. It is only towards the very end of this time that more records become available and a few fragments of evidence survive. The earliest surviving manumission of 925 records that King Athelstan freed a slave named Eadhelm and his children immediately after he became king. It does not record where the man came from, but it is just possible that he may have been a Mercian. More certainly, the will of Bishop Theodred of London, dated to sometime between 942 and 951, makes provision for the release of many of the slaves employed on his estates across Mercia.[45]

In spite of this, lack of evidence in the surviving sources it is clear that it was these supposedly lesser members of society who were of crucial importance. It was they who provided labour to till the soil, tend the flocks and herds and make the goods used by everyone. It was they who provided soldiers for the armies and priests for the churches.

THE ARMY

In this period the army was probably the most important public institution by far, certainly more important than the Church. It was the sole means of defence for a population against attack by hostile outsiders and its leadership in war represented the fundamental justification for the existence of kings and their *ealdormen*. It was also an important instrument of rule for these men who could also use it as a tool to enforce authority and impose justice on their own population. As a result, kings and their agents jealously preserved their right to summon men to serve in their armies. Thus military service was recognised in charters as an essential duty of the male population from which no exemption could be granted.

There has been a great deal of discussion about the structure and the basis of recruitment for armies during the Anglo-Saxon period. Unfortunately, the term 'peasant army', which is sometimes used to describe the military forces of this period is misleading. It suggests very strongly to modern readers a group of untrained farm labourers armed with little better than pitchforks when this was probably far from the case. In my own view it seems highly unlikely that there was ever at any point an army constructed on the basis of universal adult male service. This is simply because such an idea is simply impractical even in the present day and there will always be exceptions. An army recruited on such a basis at this time would involve too many men to be effectively controlled by its leaders. It would include too many unsuitable or ill-equipped recruits who would weaken the army rather than strengthen it. It would leave behind no one able to protect the women and children and defend the local area. It would similarly leave behind no one able to undertake the essential agricultural and craft activities many of which were essential in order to feed and equip the army itself. It should therefore be dismissed out of hand.[46]

It is almost certain that throughout the Anglo-Saxon period the army was recruited by some form of selective recruitment. This system allowed for the recruitment of suitable and well-equipped soldiers while not denuding the rest of the country of workers and potential reserves. The real question is whether the basis for this selection can be established. It is possible that the basis for recruitment may already have been that found in later practice, i.e. one man from every five hides of land. This is suggested by a contemporary reference in a charter of King Cenwulf dated to 801. This charter grants thirty hides of land in Middlesex free of burdens except the common burdens and specifically including among the latter the military service of 'only five men'. The use of the word 'only' here perhaps signifies that this represented a concession and under the later rule of one man from every five hides, six men would have been expected to serve for this land. If this was indeed the case, then the nature of this fairly restricted call up makes the men called up clearly quite select

The Repton Stone, the effigy of a Mercian warrior. (© Copyright, Martin Biddle)

individuals. Indeed, the fact that five hides of land also represented the admittedly later qualification necessary for a *ceorl* to achieve the status of *thegn* perhaps indicates that recruits were themselves expected to be equivalent to *thegns*. This sort of status for military recruits would not only match with the wider social status of *thegns* as warriors but also allow for the need to purchase expensive military equipment even if the latter excluded a sword and mailcoat.[47]

This is not to say that every soldier in the army would be a *thegn* but rather that the core of the army consisted of such men and their immediate followers. We know from the evidence provided by the contemporary text of the *Burghal Hidage* that many more fighting men than this minimum of one from every five hides were available for service. This text calls for an additional one man from each hide to be provided to garrison and maintain the new *burhs*. This makes perfect sense in the context of a selective summons for the main army since these additional troops could be supplied for garrison duty without necessarily diluting the strength of the main force. It makes no sense if we assume that all men served in the main army itself.[48]

In the period before the Viking attacks the Mercian army, like those of the other English kingdoms, had developed into an effective instrument for a specific purpose. It was designed for two main roles, one offensive and the other defensive. The first involved undertaking raids into the territory of neighbouring kingdoms either in retaliation for earlier attacks by these kingdoms or to induce these kingdoms to submit and pay tribute. The second entailed opposing the raiding army of a neighbouring kingdom either to minimise the resultant damage or if possible to defeat it altogether. It was the employment of these tactics that had brought about the Mercian supremacy under King Offa by successfully reducing the other kingdoms to tributary status. It was political divisions caused by rivalry for the throne that weakened Mercian armies under later kings rather than any military decline. They still remained effective against traditional enemies such as the Welsh even in the darkest periods of defeat.

Why did this apparently well-trained force find itself unable to cope with the threat presented by the Viking raids? As noted in Chapters 3 and 4, this can be explained partly by the political divisions in Mercia and partly by the new tactics employed by the Viking raiders. The new raiders arrived from the sea or up navigable rivers, routes that had previously been considered safe and were thus undefended. The Viking raids involved smaller more highly mobile forces which were able to move rapidly from place to place and so avoid contact with the much larger and less mobile English armies. If threatened they were able to rapidly construct effective defensive positions to shelter behind until an opposing force ran out of supplies. The English appear to have made limited use of fortifications in their own warfare and were therefore unfamiliar with the siege tactics necessary to reduce such defensive structures. Most importantly the custom of retaliatory raids on enemy territory was rendered completely useless by the fact that the Viking homelands were overseas and hence completely out of reach. A whole new series of problems therefore confronted English armies which they would need time to resolve. Unfortunately the 'great army' had no intention of allowing them any such luxury and hence East Anglia and Northumbria quickly collapsed and Mercia and Wessex almost followed suit.

It was left to those kingdoms which did survive the initial onslaught, namely Mercia and Wessex, to tackle these thorny problems. The fact that they managed to do so says a lot about their resilience and flexibility. A series of reforms was introduced to improve the effectiveness of their opposition. The first involved reducing the overall size of the traditional English army by reducing the numbers called up. In the words of the Chronicle, 'there was always half at home and half on active service, with the exception of those men whose duty it was to man the fortresses'. This allowed the English to have forces available for action to replace those returning home instead of having to end their campaigns prematurely. It also made the new armies smaller and better equipped but at the same time increased the speed of their mobilisation. This allowed the English to put their own smaller more mobile forces into the field against the Vikings in time to act against them. The consequences of this new arrangement can be seen in operation in the Chronicle entry for 917, when King Edward was able to replace one army with another and continue his campaign. The English used these new forces to pursue and harass Viking raiders and prevent them from devastating the countryside. They used them to intercept and trap them, most spectacularly perhaps at Tettenhall in 910. They also used them to besiege Viking camps closely, frequently forcing them to abandon their booty and retreat in disorder, as at Buttington in 894. On occasion, they even made a direct assault on such encampments destroying the Viking forces inside as at Benfleet in 894.[49]

The English leaders also constructed a series of fortified positions of their own in the shape of a network of *burhs* across Wessex and Mercia. These served a number of functions, providing safe refuges for the local people and their stores of food and effectively blocking many transit routes along roads, rivers and tracks to Viking armies. It has often been assumed that these *burhs* were a new and revolutionary development in Anglo-Saxon England and that they must have been modelled on Frankish fortifications. However, there is an increasing amount of evidence that such fortifications were not new in themselves. The duty of *burhbot* had existed for many years in Mercian charters and the construction of Offa's Dyke provides clear evidence that it was used in practice. More recently excavations have also revealed that important sites like Hereford and Tamworth already had fortifications in the eighth century before the Vikings arrived. What was new was the strategic defensive planning behind the location of the new *burhs* and their frequent association with towns and trade.

The Mercian Register shows clearly how these new fortifications were gradually, over a period of years, developed into a defensive network covering Mercian held territory and then extended into disputed or occupied lands as part of the process of reconquest. The *Burghal Hidage* provides evidence for the elaborate organisation behind their construction with its sophisticated allocations of manpower to garrison the ramparts. The Worcester charter dated to around 900 provides evidence for the way in which an individual *burh* was constructed. They provided safe refuge from Viking attack as at Towcester in 917. They also provided sources of troops to tackle Viking marauders as in 914 when men drawn from the garrisons of Hereford and Gloucester defeated *Jarl* Harold.[50]

These innovations finally allowed English armies to put up an effective defence against the Viking raiders. However, the real breakthrough in the warfare of this period came from the Viking decision to settle in East Anglia and Northumbria. This provided the English with the chance to resume their familiar tactics of retaliatory raiding against enemy territory which had proved so effective in the past. They could now hit back directly at their enemies and took full advantage of the fact. They commenced with raids into Northumbrian territory in Lindsey in 909. On these raids they were able to concentrate their own forces and exploit and strike at the weak points of their enemies. They pursued these raids with increasing ferocity until eventually they were able to turn these, after the decisive victories at Holme in 902 and Tettenhall in 910, into expeditions of conquest. Thereafter, they mounted almost annual expeditions into Viking-occupied territory which aimed at securing the complete submission of these regions to their rule.[51]

In this situation the Viking forces had lost their most important advantage, the virtual freedom from counter-attack. As a result, the military balance rapidly tilted back in favour of the English. Thereafter, the struggle became one of attrition and one more akin to previous English experience, the invasion and harrying of rival kingdoms to reduce them to submission. In contrast the Vikings, whose numbers

Fragment of sculpture showing a mythical beast, St Mary's Church, Wirksworth, Derbyshire. (Photograph by W. Walker)

were small and who were probably increasingly unable to rely on the local population for support, found themselves in difficulties. They attempted to defend themselves but their own lack of cohesion and their failure to win over the local population left them vulnerable to piecemeal conquest. In these circumstances they actually proved far less effective than had the defensive armies of the earlier English kingdoms.

The English armies of the start of this period were not in fact simply victims of obsolescence unable to cope with the Viking onslaught. They were well trained and effective forces designed to deal very effectively with rival English kingdoms. The reasons that they found themselves unable to cope with the Vikings were very similar to those which faced their Frankish contemporaries. They were not prepared for sudden assaults from the sea or along rivers, they were too large and cumbersome to tackle swift-moving mounted raiding parties, they were not trained to besiege fortifications and they were unable to counterattack this particular enemy on home soil. They sought to remedy these deficiencies by developing a system of *burhs*, by adopting a more selective method of recruitment, by developing effective siege tactics and by striking back at their opponents following the latter's settlement on English territory.

SUMMARY

The Mercian society of this period was similar to the society found in other English kingdoms and across north-western Europe at this time. It produced sufficient food in normal circumstances to sustain its population and a significant elite. It produced a range of products that supported significant and expanding trade with its neighbours. It maintained a position of political superiority over other English kingdoms for an extended period. It survived a long period of internal political tension and upheaval. It managed to stand up to some of the greatest upheavals in English history at the hands of the Vikings. It was eventually able to liberate much of its lost territory from occupation. In short it proved able not simply to sustain itself effectively but to expand both in political and economic terms.

CHAPTER 8

The Church

INTRODUCTION

It is difficult to provide a complete or well-rounded account of the Mercian Church in the period covered by this book as a result of two significant obstacles. The first is simply the overall scarcity of sources for such an account and the strongly regional focus of those few that do exist. This problem effects the wider history of Mercia in all its aspects and has already been mentioned elsewhere. The second is the essential nature of the Church that existed in England during the Anglo-Saxon period. The English Church had originally been envisaged and certainly subsequently developed as a Church for all the English peoples. It was not a series of churches for each of the individual peoples like the Northumbrians, Mercians and West Saxons but an English Church.

This English Church had its origins in the establishment of the two archbishoprics at Canterbury and York and in the recognition throughout this period of the seniority of the former. In England south of the Humber, Canterbury held authority over all the bishoprics, which meant that individual churchmen in Mercia and Wessex alike looked to Canterbury for spiritual leadership whatever their relationship to their own secular rulers. This effectively prevented the development of a fully independent Church in either Mercia or Wessex. There was an attempt by King Offa to establish a separate archbishopric for Mercia at Lichfield but this ultimately met with little success.

In order to try and overcome these difficulties this chapter will consist of two main elements. The first will be an account, as far as it is possible to reconstruct this, of the Church in Mercia as a whole during the period from 750 to 950. This account will draw on the surviving information about the Church in Mercia and, occasionally, from elsewhere in England. The second will focus on an individual figure, Bishop Waerferth of Worcester, as a representative of the wider Mercian Church during this period. This will allow us to take maximum advantage of the relative abundance of surviving sources from the diocese of Worcester during these years.

THE CHURCH IN MERCIA

In 750 the Church in Mercia was very much a part of the wider English Church as a whole. It had developed out of the complex interactions between the mission of St Augustine sent from Rome to Kent by Pope Gregory the Great in 597 and the mission of St Aidan brought from Iona to Lindisfarne by King Oswald in 634. This mixture left the English Church with a diocesan structure which was partly Roman, with its two archbishoprics at Canterbury and York based on the political structure of the former Roman province, and partly regional, with a series of bishoprics based on or contained within the boundaries of the various English peoples. As a result of the Mercian absorption of various smaller kingdoms, this had produced by 750 a total of six Mercian bishops in all, based in Lichfield, Worcester, Hereford, Leicester, Lincoln and London. The diocese of Lichfield was generally acknowledged as the original Mercian bishopric and hence the senior one.[1]

The effective result of this process was to leave the Kingdom of Mercia and neighbouring Wessex with no metropolitan of their own but with a number of bishops nominally under the authority of an archbishop based in the neighbouring and often rival Kingdom of Kent. In a period when bishops performed a vital role in supporting kings by providing divine sanction for their rule and trained staff to perform administrative duties in their government, this proved an unsatisfactory arrangement. Bishops and archbishops were largely nominated and appointed by the local ruler but the former were subject to ordination by the archbishop. This meant that the freedom of Mercian or West Saxon kings to appoint their own nominees to bishoprics within their own territories could be undermined by a hostile archbishop based in a kingdom controlled by a rival. In addition, as Mercian kings sought to extend their political control over neighbouring kingdoms they naturally sought to secure political control over appointments to bishoprics in these kingdoms. In this dual context control over the appointment of the Archbishopric of Canterbury could provide a useful means of controlling episcopal appointments whether at home or beyond one's borders.[2]

The most powerful kings of Mercia, like Aethelbald and Offa, actively sought to maintain effective political control over the Kingdom of Kent and hence over the appointment of the archbishop of Canterbury. In this way, their appointees once securely installed in Canterbury would be more likely to endorse their nominees to other bishoprics both within Mercia and beyond. In addition, effective control of the archbishopric allowed an active overlord the opportunity to interfere in the nomination of bishops and hence in the politics of other kingdoms. This policy was consistently pursued by Aethelbald's successor King Offa, who actually presided over the consecration of Archbishop Jaenberht at his own court on 25 February 765. However, Archbishop Jaenberht, a Kentishman, subsequently proved a big disappointment, turning out to be a staunch supporter of Kentish independence. In 776 he backed the revolt of Egbert against the Mercians and, free thereafter from Mercian control, pursued policies hostile to those of King Offa. It was not until 785 that King Offa recovered political control over Kent and hence some measure of influence over Archbishop Jaenberht. However, it seems that Offa was unable to persuade the archbishop to perform the important task of consecrating his son Ecgfrith as his successor. This ceremony was vital to Offa in securing the future of his dynasty and he could not rest until this issue was resolved even if it meant taking drastic measures.[3]

In 787, at the Synod of Chelsea, King Offa attempted to resolve this problem once and for all by the elevation of the Bishop of Lichfield in Mercia to metropolitan status. As recounted in Chapter 1, King Offa had finally succeeded in obtaining agreement to this from Pope Hadrian I after a great deal of persuasion. This arrangement effectively secured for King Offa the freedom to nominate his own candidates to bishoprics in Mercia. The newly upgraded Archbishop of Lichfield, Hygeberht, who was Offa's man, was made responsible not only for the six Mercian bishoprics but also for those of neighbouring East Anglia. More importantly, however, Archbishop Hygeberht also fulfilled what may have been his primary function by consecrating King Offa's son, Ecgfrith, as king and so his father's successor in the very same year.[4]

This politically inspired intrusion of an additional archbishop into the English Church was one that was apparently strongly resisted by many in the Church itself. They opposed it in some instances no doubt for political reasons but more often because it went against their traditions. The structure of the English Church, for all its faults, was one associated with some of its most important and respected figures, including St Augustine and Archbishop Theodore. It was therefore not something to tamper with without good reason and for many leading churchmen Offa's reasons were not sufficient. Therefore there seems to have been a campaign of resistance against the new structure from its inception. This campaign remained passive during the remainder of King Offa's reign but would emerge with more force under his successor, King Cenwulf.

In 792, meantime, the death of Archbishop Jaenberht provided Offa, who was once more in control of Kent, with an opportunity to replace this troublesome priest with someone more amenable in the shape of a Mercian churchman called Aethelheard. The new Archbishop's pro-Mercian views subsequently led to his expulsion from his see following the death of King Offa in 796. In that year he was forced to flee to Mercia when Kent recovered its independence under Eadberht *Praen*. It was probably this crisis that inspired King Cenwulf to make his vain attempt to have the existing archbishopric moved from Canterbury to London and hence under

A sarcophagus lid, St Mary's Church, Wirksworth, Derbyshire. (Photograph by W. Walker)

his protection and authority. In fact, King Cenwulf was only able to restore Archbishop Aethelheard to his see in 798, when he finally recovered direct control over Kent by deposing Eadberht *Praen*.[5]

In 798 King Cenwulf attempted to resolve the difficulties caused by the anomalous Mercian archbishopric through an elaborate compromise involving the abolition of the new archdiocese of Lichfield in exchange for the transfer of the southern archbishopric from Canterbury to London. This had been the site originally proposed by no less a person than Pope Gregory the Great. Cenwulf undoubtedly hoped in this way to achieve Mercian dominance of the archbishopric by the back door. An archbishop based directly on Mercian territory rather than in more independent Kent would need to pay due deference to his local ruler. In spite of this, very clever solution, which was intended to satisfy both the king and the Church, the idea would ultimately prove unacceptable. The proposal to move the archbishopric was rejected by Pope Leo, who nevertheless agreed to abolish the archdiocese of Lichfield. He was prepared to do no more than excommunicate Eadberht *Praen* and insist that Aethelheard be restored to his see in Canterbury. In 803 King Cenwulf was finally forced to concede the Mercian archdiocese. This was clearly a victory for the Church and one which demonstrated exactly what King Offa had sought to avoid, the capacity for independent thought and action of an English Church which was not entirely dependent on royal appointment.[6]

In 805, following the death of Archbishop Aethelheard, King Cenwulf, who remained in control of Kent, managed to secure the appointment of another Mercian to replace him in the person of Wulfred. This man was a keen reformer who revitalised the life of the cathedral clergy and reorganised the landholdings of the see. However, this reforming zeal also extended to attempting to eliminate secular influence from the churches of his see including the rich abbeys of eastern Kent. In 816 this brought him into direct conflict with his patron who had established his daughter Cwenthryth as abbess of Minster-in-Thanet. As a result, Cenwulf found himself in the invidious position of having to expel his own archbishop for a period between 817 and 821. The latter was only able to return to his see and resume his duties after the death of Cenwulf in the latter year.[7]

It was not until after the succession of King Beornwulf in 823, that the new king and Archbishop Wulfred were able to resolve the outstanding issues. As a new king from a rival dynasty, Beornwulf was probably anxious to secure the support of the archbishop for his kingship and, in particular, consecration at his hands. As a result, in 825 the two men were able to resolve matters substantially in favour of the archbishop by recognising his authority over the Kentish monasteries. In turn this decision left Abbess Cwenthryth isolated in her opposition to Wulfred's claims. As a sister of the deceased King Cenwulf, she could no longer count on royal support from his successful rival and probably found herself increasingly isolated. She held out as long as possible but in 826 finally made peace with Archbishop Wulfred who recognised her right to retain the abbacy.

In 832 the death of Archbishop Wulfred caused considerable difficulties for King Wiglaf, who was no longer in direct control of Kent following his recent defeat at the hands of Egbert of Wessex. As a result, there appears to have been a dispute over the see involving rival candidates, Ceolnoth and Swithred, each probably backed by one of these rival monarchs. It was not until the following year that Ceolnoth, who has been seen as the West Saxon candidate, won this contest emerging as archbishop in 833. However, there is no direct evidence to prove who backed Ceolnoth in this contest and the fact that he attended a synod held under the auspices of King Wiglaf at Croft in Mercia in 836 may perhaps suggest otherwise. Indeed, charter evidence suggests that King Wiglaf had regained control over Middlesex in 831 and it is possible that within another two years he had gained sufficient influence in Kent to secure Ceolnoth's appointment.[8]

Whatever the actual origins of Ceolnoth, there can be no doubt that he was compelled in time to acknowledge the gradual shift of power from Mercia to Wessex that occurred during his period of office. The increasing absorption of the Mercian rulers in their own domestic disputes saw secular control over Kent fall to the West Saxon rulers. As a corollary to this they also secured increased influence over the archbishopric. In 838 King Egbert of Wessex and his son Aethelwulf, who had been appointed to rule over Kent under his father, made a number of important grants to Archbishop Ceolnoth, which recognised his authority over the Kentish minsters of Reculver and Thanet and guaranteed free elections in Canterbury itself in return for his allegiance.[9]

When Ceolnoth died in 870, he was succeeded by a man named Aethelred whose origins are unclear but who was almost certainly not Mercian. At this point King Burgred of Mercia was not in a position to influence events in Kent but was completely absorbed in a struggle to retain control of his own kingdom in the face of Viking attack. The events of the next decade and particularly the disintegration of Mercia under Viking assault must have appeared to spell the final demise of Mercian involvement with the archbishopric. However, this was not in fact to be the case and the very next incumbent of the post in 890, a man named Plegmund, would preside over a final flowering of Mercian involvement.[10]

The origins of this dramatic restoration of Mercian influence at the head of the English Church probably lay with King Alfred and his close alliance with Aethelred of Mercia. In the decade 880 to 890 this alliance was flourishing, with co-operation in the restoration of London, in plans for a common defence against the Viking threat and in arrangements for reviving the battered English Church. It was in this atmosphere that King Alfred chose the Mercian Plegmund to lead the English Church. The sources describe the choice as a case of the best man for the job and there can be little doubt about this. However, it is perhaps possible that it signified more than this and that it was another way to draw Mercia and Wessex closer together. The installation of a Mercian at the head of the English Church could not but help to reinforce Mercian allegiance to this Church and hence reconcile them to the secular superiority of King Alfred who had made the appointment. The sensitivity and astuteness already shown by Alfred in his dealings with Mercia, including his respectful treatment of Lord Aethelred and his careful handling of London, perhaps suggest as much. It is surely not unlikely that part of his motive in appointing Plegmund may have been to show similar sensitivity to the Mercian Church. The appointment was therefore not only beneficial to the Church but helped to cement the alliance between Mercia and Wessex.[11]

In addition to their attempts to control appointments to the Archbishopric of Canterbury itself, the kings of Mercia sought to enforce their control over the wider English Church much as they enforced control over the other English kingdoms. The main means of doing so was through a series of regular meetings or synods involving the wider English Church. These normally took place under the authority of the King of Mercia and the Archbishop of Canterbury. In the main period of Mercian supremacy between about 785 and 816 we have clear evidence from associated diplomas and letters to show that these synods had become in effect annual events. They were frequently held at the same traditional sites, most notably, Chelsea, *Clofesho* and *Acleah*. Unfortunately, a number of these sites can no longer be identified, probably because they were open-air venues that have since fallen into disuse. The few that can be identified are almost always located in Mercia, in the London diocese and near the River Thames. This allowed the synods to take place under the supervision of Mercian overlords, while still being accessible to bishops and churchmen from throughout the southern archdiocese, including outside Mercia.[12]

The recorded presence of King Offa and later King Cenwulf at these synods, often accompanied by their leading *ealdormen*, clearly demonstrates their concern to supervise the proceedings. The gatherings provided an opportunity for the Church to decide matters relating to dogma, worship and administration but this was always done under the eyes of the king. The king could also use these occasions to secure the agreement of the Church as a whole to important royal initiatives like the initial creation of the diocese of Lichfield in 787 and its subsequent abolition in 803. The importance of these synods as ways of influencing the Church is demonstrated by the fact that King Offa, even after the appointment of his own Mercian archbishop, continued to hold joint synods involving the archbishops of Lichfield and Canterbury. In normal circumstances the new archbishop would have been expected to hold his own separate synod but this arrangement might have prevented Offa from continuing to monitor and influence events in the archbishopric of Canterbury. The regular synods also presented opportunities to conduct secular business including dealings with neighbouring kingdoms and sub-kingdoms under Mercian influence or overlordship.

It seems likely that the Mercian rulers viewed these councils as one means of influencing the wider English Church. In turn, the clergy may have viewed these occasions as opportunities to seek the favour of powerful secular rulers. The pattern of meeting of these synods reflects this close relationship between secular rulers and the Church. They become a regular feature of the later reign of Offa following his recovery of Kent and the submission of Archbishop Jaenberht. They become most prevalent during the early reign of King Cenwulf and the period of office of the co-operative Archbishop Aethelheard. They start to founder after the election of the more independent Archbishop Wulfred and decline sharply after the latter's breach with Cenwulf in 816. There are no synods recorded between 816 and 824 when a combination of Cenwulf's dispute with Wulfred and rapid changes in the kingship itself made such occasions difficult to arrange. Thereafter, Mercian internal dynastic struggles and the associated decline in royal authority made them less likely than ever.

Cross head, St Michael's Church, Cropthorne, Worcestershire. (Photograph by W. Walker)

The Mercian bishops who regularly attended these synods were appointed by the kings and were presumably usually fairly amenable to their control. Unfortunately there is very little surviving information about the origins or connections of the majority of these bishops. There is therefore no way to examine the links that probably existed between many of them and the kings or between many of them and the secular nobility. It is, for example, possible that the ninth-century bishops of Lindsey called Beorhtred and Burgheard may have been linked to the 'B' dynasty of kings. Similarly, Bishop Cynefrith of Lichfield and Bishop Ceolred of Leicester may have been related to the 'C' dynasy of kings. The career of Bishop Waerferth which will be examined later in this chapter will need to stand for all these largely unknown men.[13]

At the level below that of the diocesan structure there were in existence a number of important monasteries under abbots or abbesses. Many of these abbeys were in the hands of powerful local families and were used by them as useful sources of patronage and religious sanction. The abbots or abbesses who ruled these houses were often drawn from the families of their patrons as will become clear below. In addition to ruling their own monasteries, the abbots appear to have functioned also as useful literate royal servants. In the 790s Abbot Wada acted as an ambassador of King Cenwulf to Pope Leo in Rome, apparently with disappointing results. When he was killed in Wales in 916, Abbot Egbert had probably been fulfilling a similar task for Lady Aethelflaed. The potential reward for performing such tasks was the possibility of elevation to a bishopric. This was the case with men such as Abbot Utel, who became Bishop of Hereford, Abbot Hrethun, who became Bishop of Leicester and perhaps Abbot Aethelhun of Berkeley, who may have been appointed Bishop of Worcester in succession to Waerferth in 915.[14]

The most notable of these monasteries were those in Kent, including Reculver and Minster-in-Thanet, which became the object of a bitter dispute between the kings of Mercia and the archbishops of Canterbury. There were also many such monastic churches in Mercia itself which represented sources of ecclesiastical and family power. The church at Repton, which had been founded around 675, subsequently became the burial place of King Aethelbald and thereafter a favoured church of many Mercian rulers. It also became the mausoleum for King Wiglaf and a shrine for his grandson St Wigstan both members of the 'W' dynasty. Similarly, in 811, King Cenwulf founded Winchcombe in Gloucestershire, which became a home for his unmarried daughter Cwenthryth before she took control of the Kent monasteries. It went on to become a shrine for St Cynehelm the family saint and martyr and Cenwulf was later buried there in 821. The abbey of Berkeley in Gloucestershire provided a convenient retirement home for members of the family of the *ealdormen* of the *Hwicce*, including Ceolburh, the widow of *Ealdorman* Aethelmund. The abbey of Breedon in Leicestershire was governed by an abbot called Eanmund in 848 when it received a grant from King Beorhtwulf.[15]

At this time, there were no parish churches to fulfil the role of pastoral care at the level below the bishoprics. Instead, there existed a number of important churches or minsters which had often been founded by important individuals, either kings or *ealdormen*, with the dual purpose of serving them, their families and descendants and undertaking the pastoral care of those living on their surrounding estates. The best preserved example is that at Deerhurst in Gloucestershire. It was probably founded by *Ealdorman* Aethelmund at the start of the ninth century as a family church fitted to his new status as ruler of the *Hwicce*. He was subsequently buried there and his son Aethelric made grants of land to the church in 804. These churches were usually run by priests appointed by and sometimes drawn from within the founding family and were sometimes dedicated to a family saint. It was these churches that served the mass of the population during this period. They provided a focus for Christian worship that also sought to reinforce the bond between landowners and their tenants.[16]

The priests, who officiated at the local minster churches and who provided the staffing for the cathedral churches, appear much less frequently than their superiors in the surviving records. In spite of this, they provided the backbone of the Church rather like their equivalent, the *thegns*, did for secular society. They were regularly to be found in the entourage of kings and bishops, to minister to their spiritual needs or to assist them in their offices respectively. This much is indicated by their appearance in the witness lists to a number of charters. Although their abilities probably varied considerably, they generally appear to represent a more literate body of men than their secular counterparts. They were therefore extremely useful in a whole host of administrative capacities. It was undoubtedly such men who wrote charters, letters, memoranda and other documents for their masters. They also composed the chronicles and historical records of the period. A few of these men were particularly erudite including Athelstan and Werwulf, who were asked to participate in King Alfred's translation programme according to Asser. In 798 a priest called Byrne was employed by King Cenwulf to ensure that his letter concerning the Mercian archbishopric reached the Pope.

They were rewarded for these skills both in terms of grants of land and of preferment to more senior church offices. The Mercian priest Plegmund achieved the ultimate in terms of the latter by his appointment as Archbishop of Canterbury in 890. A charter of 899 reveals that a priest called Werwulf, perhaps the very scholar that assisted Alfred, received a grant of five *manentes* of land in Gloucestershire from Bishop Waerferth. Another priest called Aethelwold was involved in a dispute with Bishop Waerferth concerning land at Woodchester in Gloucestershire, which was settled by Lord Aethelred in 896. Aethelwold appears to have been a married priest, at least judging from the reference to a son called Ealhmund in the record of this settlement. This was by no means unusual at this time.[17]

A great deal of building work was lavished on many monasteries and minster churches during this period as their patrons sought to enhance their own status in the eyes of their tenants and their neighbours as well as increasing their own chances of salvation by erecting elaborate stone structures. The churches at Deerhurst in Gloucestershire, Repton in Derbyshire and Breedon-on-the-Hill in Leicestershire all preserve evidence of such work. The minster at Deerhurst was probably built by *Ealdorman* Aethelmund and his son Aethelric who owned the land in the early ninth century and who were probably buried there. The church at Repton was already in existence by the middle of the eighth century but was subsequently redesigned and rebuilt at various times well into the ninth century, notably by King Wiglaf and his successors. The church at Breedon had a number of important patrons, including Offa, Beorhtwulf and *Ealdorman* Hunberht, all of whom may have contributed to its elaborate decoration. It is one of the accidents of history that it is often these local churches that subsequently lost their significance and were forgotten that best preserve fragments of their original structures. In contrast many of the more famous and important buildings, including all the main cathedrals and many other major churches, were subject to significant reconstruction at a later date with consequent loss of most of their early or original features.[18]

The patrons of these individual churches quite naturally also sought to foster and increase the landholdings of their own particular establishment. There is evidence from the surviving charters that they were sometimes less than scrupulous about how they did so. In particular, they were not averse to obtaining lands or rights for their chosen church from other churches often those of less successful rivals. This should not necessarily be condemned since in contemporary eyes it may simply have been viewed as common sense. If someone wished to glorify God and support the Church it was only natural to seek to do so without doing anything detrimental to their own interests. This behaviour is most evident where the Mercian kings are involved, largely as a result of the pattern of charter survival, but it was probably not confined to them. They sought to appropriate the lands and churches of their predecessors and subordinates for the benefit of their own. Kings Offa and Cenwulf took control of the patronage of the Kentish coastal monasteries from the Kentish kings. Kings Aethelbald and Offa similarly gradually assumed control of patronage towards the bishopric of Worcester from their sub-kings of the *Hwicce*.

As a result of dynastic rivalry within Mercia itself, the kings also sought to increase the wealth and power of their own churches and weaken those of their rivals. King Aethelbald had granted the monastery at Cookham in Berkshire to Canterbury, but King Offa took control of this church and left it to his widow Queen Cynethryth although he later made restitution to Canterbury for this seizure. King Offa also left Glastonbury to his widow but his successor King Cenwulf wrested control of it from her for the benefit of his own son Cynehelm. Although there is less evidence for such activity under the later Mercian kings it seems likely that were not immune to this process. Indeed, the open dynastic conflict in ninth-century Mercia would seem to offer fertile ground for such work. This must have produced great insecurity for many churches just as it brought insecurity for individual *ealdormen*.[19]

An important aspect of the Church in the early part of this period, and one which related to the strong influence of local noble families over churches, was the prominent role of women. A significant number of the religious foundations, more specifically the abbeys, of this period were ruled by women. There had been an early tradition in the English Church of joint houses of monks and nuns being governed by an abbess. This arrangement had been designed to provide the unmarried or widowed daughters of important royal or noble families with an appropriate situation. They could live in relative safety and security in this protected accommodation surrounded by their own court of monks and nuns and live in the style to which they were accustomed while devoting their lives to the service of God.

This original tradition had already begun to decline as pressure from within the increasingly male dominated Church sought to marginalise the role of women. However, it was still possible for some prominent individual women with strong support from their male relatives to buck this trend. Thus Queen Cynethryth, widow of King Offa, ended her days as Abbess of Bedford, and Ceolburh, widow of *Ealdorman* Aethelmund, did so as Abbess of Berkeley. The most prominent of these women was Cwenthryth, the daughter of King Cenwulf, who was able to assume control of the three abbeys of Winchcombe, Minster-in-Thanet and Reculver with the active support of her father. This significant degree of influence brought her into direct conflict with Wulfred, Archbishop of Canterbury, who was promoting reform including the removal of secular influence from monasteries. In 816 the two commenced a ten-year dispute concerning the abbacy of Minster-in-Thanet which was only resolved by a compromise in 826.[20]

One of the reasons for disputes about the ownership or control of churches and their lands was the wealth invested in them. The Church, through its ownership of land and livestock and its position as a receiver of donations from the faithful, was also very rich. It therefore attracted the attentions of many who were anxious for a share in that wealth. The Church also had surplus wealth to invest in the economy and in trade. It took full advantage of its opportunities in this sphere and sought to increase these, wherever possible, by seeking exemptions from tolls. In 743 or 745 Bishop Milred of Worcester secured exemption from tolls for two ships at London from King Aethelbald. The Church also recognised the importance of London, as a centre of trade with the Continent and consequently many churches had a presence there. In charters of 889 and 898 the Archbishop of Canterbury and the Bishop of Worcester were both granted a presence in the heart of the trading centre of the newly reconstructed London. They were given control of prime waterfront properties by King Alfred and Lord Aethelred from which they could export their goods direct to the Continent.[21]

Another symbol of the power and wealth of the Church in this period was the fact that the archbishops had the right to issue coins. There are surviving coins engraved with the names of the following archbishops of Canterbury; Ceolnoth, Wulfred, Aethelred and Plegmund. In some cases these coins acknowledged the superiority of a king but in other cases they did not. In the latter case they were surely symbolic of the independent economic status of these great landowners. They were in control of sufficient landed wealth to permit them to mint their own coins to encourage trade.[22]

In the period covered by this book, a great deal of attention has been focussed on an alleged decline in learning in the English Church. This has occurred partly as a result of the complaints set out by King Alfred in his writings and partly by way of a contrast to the comparative glory of the surrounding eras of the age of Bede and the tenth-century reform. In the foreword to his translation of Gregory the Great's *Pastoral Care*, King Alfred laments that 'there were very few [men] this side of the Humber who could comprehend their services in English or even translate a letter from Latin into English' and similarly that '[Men] could not understand anything of them [Latin books], since they were not written in their own language'.[23]

We need, however, to be careful about how much reliance we invest in these statements. King Alfred, quite naturally, wished to highlight the importance of his own reforming activities by exaggerating the contrast between the state of the Church before and after this as much as possible. In addition, it seems very likely that he is really talking about the position in his own native Wessex and neighbouring Kent. He would certainly have been more familiar with the detailed picture in these areas. We also know from surviving examples that the skills of scribes employed in drafting charters in Kent declined sharply in the latter half of the ninth century. However, we should beware of the assumption that this necessarily reflects the position in the other English kingdoms, including Mercia. Indeed, the very fact that Alfred drew a significant number of the scholars involved in his reforms, notably Plegmund, Waerferth and two otherwise unknown priests, called Athelstan and Werwulf, from Mercia itself strongly suggests that this was not the case.[24]

It should be remembered that the second half of the eighth century saw the completion of a remarkable process of evangelisation in Germany undertaken largely by English missionaries. This enterprise involved many men and women drawn from Wessex, Northumbria and probably Mercia, including major figures such as St Boniface, Lull, etc. These great figures could certainly not be accused of being deficient in any way in terms of their scholarship. They used their knowledge and learning to benefit their new converts on the Continent and proved an inspiration to the Frankish Church itself. The role of Mercia in this venture is not highlighted in the surviving sources which largely focus on Northumbria and Wessex. However, a letter sent by Bishop Milred of Worcester to Archbishop Lull of Mainz in 754 or 755 does indicate close links between the Mercian Church and that in Germany. In it Bishop Milred describes St Boniface and Lull as his 'close friends' and speaks of a recent visit and the exchange of books and gifts. This suggests that at the very least Mercian churchmen contributed to this venture by offering it their support and assistance.[25]

This huge emigration of talent to Germany may, perhaps, have contributed to a relative decline in learning in England itself as the best scholars went abroad. However, we have sufficient evidence to show that the Mercian Church, particularly but not solely in West Mercia, remained healthy and vibrant during the second half

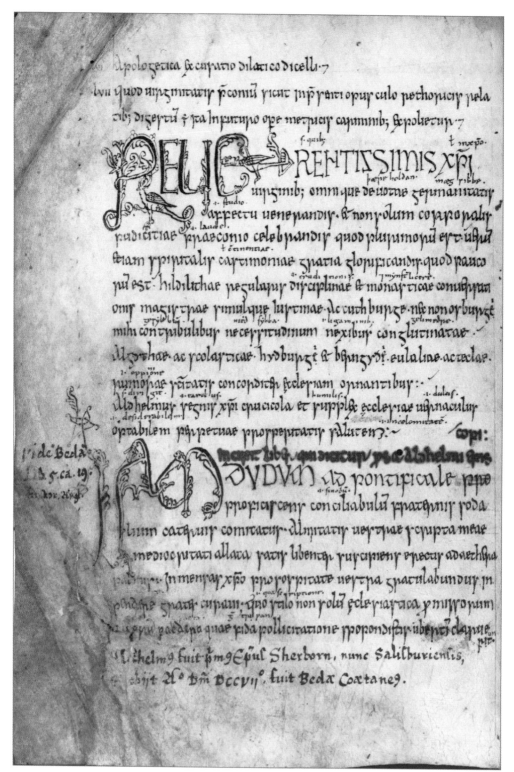

A ninth-century Mercian manuscript of the *De Virginitate* of St Aldhelm. (BL Royal 5 F iii, f. 2v)

of the eighth century and on through the ninth. Bishop Milred of Worcester, as noted above, was a great scholar who had studied the classical authors and who produced some notable surviving poetry. A number of very capable archbishops of Canterbury were drawn from Mercia during this period. The scholarship of Archbishop Plegmund and Bishop Waerferth of Worcester and other Mercians attracted the attention of King Alfred and caused him to invite them to assist in his plans for the restoration of learning in his native Wessex.[26]

There is even some admittedly limited evidence about the state of learning among Mercian laymen during this period. In the 790s Alcuin wrote to King Offa acknowledging his keenness to encourage reading. In 904 *Ealdorman* Aethelfrith sought to secure the renewal of his charters from King Edward and Lord Aethelred, the previous charters having been destroyed by fire. This provides evidence for the value of written records to such men but does not in itself imply that Aethelfrith could read such documents himself. A more positive sign of literacy among the lay nobility is provided by the existence of a number of surviving private prayerbooks from ninth-century Mercia. These will be discussed in more detail later, but it will suffice to note here that their use in private devotions strongly suggests that their lay owners, including women, were literate.[27]

The period between the so-called Golden Age of Northumbria and the reforms introduced by King Alfred has also often been viewed as a period of decline in culture. However, the evidence which survives is sufficient to suggest that this was far from being the case. Specifically, the active patronage of art under the auspices of the Mercian kings during the later eighth and ninth centuries belies this. In this particular sphere, the period was, in fact, one of vibrant activity, especially in the fields of church building, religious sculpture and manuscript production. A number of great works of art were produced and although relatively few survive to this day, those that do exist reveal the high standards of the time.

In terms of church building, although the structures of the main churches, the cathedrals and many of the abbeys, have been lost, replaced by later structures, there remain sufficient survivals among smaller churches to offer a glimpse of what once existed. The common themes of Mercian church building that do survive indicate relatively small, intimate stone churches decorated with intricate and sometimes lavish carving on the building itself and in associated sculpture. The best surviving examples of building work can be found at Deerhurst in Gloucestershire, Repton in Derbyshire and Breedon-on-the-Hill in Leicestershire. The now small parish church at Deerhurst preserves many portions of its original structure including walls, doors and windows and a number of fragments of sculpture including a magnificent font. The later churches at Breedon and at Wirksworth in Derbyshire incorporate many remarkable fragments of their original architectural decoration including both abstract designs and figures. The elaborate friezes to be seen at Breedon are particularly stunning and provide a strong impression of the overall decorative scheme of the now lost original church. The later church at Repton stands over an elaborate original crypt which is preserved in its entirety and once contained the shrine of St Wigstan. A visit to any of these churches will convince anyone of the skill of the Mercian architects and sculptors.[28]

In terms of religious sculpture, once again there are sufficient fragments remaining to allow for a partial appreciation of the skill of Mercian and other artists and craftsmen and the tastes of Mercian patrons. An intricate carved cross, the head of which is now preserved in the parish church at Cropthorne in Worcestershire, is unrivalled in the precision and delicacy of its carving. A charter of King Beorhtwulf dated 840 or 841 was granted at Cropthorne, suggesting that at that time it was an important site, certainly important enough to warrant and support a visit by the royal court. The remarkable sarcophagus lid preserved at Wirksworth in Derbyshire with its scenes from the life of Christ is an exceptional example of Mercian stonecarving which can stand comparison with any from this period or later. The elaborate Headda shrine preserved at Peterborough Abbey is another excellent tribute to the Mercian sculptors of this period. The beautiful free-standing crosses from

The font, St Mary's Church, Deerhurst, Gloucestershire. (Photograph by W. Walker)

Sandbach in Cheshire and Bakewell in Derbyshire provide further evidence of the skills of Mercian craftsmen. There are many fragments demonstrating similar excellent workmanship remaining at sites throughout Mercia, including; Caistor and Peterborough in Northamptonshire, Edenham in Lincolnshire, Elstow in Bedfordshire, Fletton in Huntingdonshire, Acton Beauchamp in Herefordshire and St Oswald's in Gloucester. The last of these is associated with the building of the minster there by Aethelred and Aethelflaed.[29]

In terms of religious and secular manuscript texts there are also enough survivals to show that Mercia was far from being the literary desert portrayed by King Alfred. Manuscript survival rates are patchy and there are more texts of Mercian origin from the middle of the period covered by this book than from either the beginning or the end. Nevertheless, these survivals do represent a fairly wide range of different kinds of text. The Lichfield Gospels were not produced in Mercia themselves but represent instead perhaps the attempts by the bishops to restock their libraries after the losses suffered during the Viking invasions. They were probably produced in Ireland or Iona and were certainly in Wales at one point. It is not until the end of the tenth century in the time of Bishop Wynsige that they are first recorded as being at Lichfield. There remain however sufficient manuscripts to indicate the kinds of work produced by Mercian scribes and illustrators during this period. They encompass Bibles, Gospels, Mass texts and Prayerbooks. The illuminated works range in scope from the simple beauty of the Hereford Gospels to the glorious marvels of the Book of Cerne.[30]

The most notable feature of this range of manuscripts is perhaps a series of ninth-century private prayerbooks. They include the Harley Prayerbook, the Royal Prayerbook, the Book of Nunnaminster and the Book of Cerne. They represent a unique investment in personal piety among a literate elite within Mercia. They compliment in a sense the personal investment in piety demonstrated by the family churches. These prayerbooks were designed to be used in their private devotions by wealthy and literate individual members of Mercian society. Unfortunately, it is not possible to identify the individuals for whom these books were commissioned although the Book of Nunnaminster may possibly have belonged to Queen Ealhswith, the Mercian wife of King Alfred. It contains an Old English prayer in the feminine form, showing that it was intended for use by a woman, and the record of a grant of property to Nunnaminster, which was a foundation of Ealhswith. It is notable that three out of the four prayerbooks were composed in the feminine form and hence were intended for women.[31]

The contents of these private prayerbooks reflect the individual personalities and interests of their patrons as no other contemporary texts can. They usually consist of a number of texts built around a common theme presumably one of central interest to their owner. Thus, the Royal Prayerbook features Christ as the healer of mankind and

Page from the Book of Cerne, a Mercian prayerbook. (By permission of the Syndics of Cambridge University Library, Ms. L1.1.10, f. 21v)

so includes prayers, hymns, miracle stories, remedies and charms, including some possibly pagan inspired ones, on healing. The Book of Nunnaminster revolves around meditations on the life of Christ and incorporates various sources on this theme including some of Irish origin. The latter is interesting in view of the possible association of this work with Queen Ealhswith and in light of the interest shown by her husband Alfred in Irish holy men. The Book of Cerne, the most elaborate of these prayerbooks, is built around participation in the Communion of the Saints. It may once have belonged to Bishop Aethelwold of Lichfield since his name appears in an acrostic poem included in the text.

The charters produced in Mercia, mainly at Worcester, during this era, including those from the worst period of Viking activity, provide a sharp contrast to those from contemporary Canterbury. The Worcester scribes demonstrate a clear and legible style while those from Canterbury show evidence not only of poor style but poor grammar also. It is generally accepted that a series of Kentish charters; two of 860 and 862 issued for King Aethelberht of Wessex, one of 873 issued for Archbishop Aethelred and one of 889 issued for the Bishop of Rochester, provide evidence of how the Viking depredations affected Canterbury. The loss of the best scribes whether to death, slavery or flight meant that those that remained however unqualified had to carry on as best they could. In contrast places in West Mercia which had been relatively unaffected by the Viking raids were able to protect and preserve their best men. As a result, the standards of charter production in places like Worcester remained consistent throughout this period. The charter granted by Bishop Waerferth of Worcester to Wulfsige his reeve in 904 demonstrates this perfectly. It recorded a small local transaction for a fairly minor local official but it was well written in good Latin by a competent scribe.[32]

It is also significant that the Mercian Church continued to produce saints during this period. The appearance of new saints is usually a sign of an active spirituality. The Mercians entered this period with a number of existing saints such as St Chad, St Guthlac of Crowland, St Rumwold, St Mildburh and St Werburh. They added to these a number of new saints during this period including St Aethelheard, St Plegmund, St Aethelberht, St Ealhmund, St Eardwulf, St Cynehelm, St Wigstan and St Beorhthelm. It is clear that some of these saints represented political martyrs rather than what might be considered true saints. This was the case with the likes of St Cynehelm, St Wigstan and St Beorhthelm whose cults were probably fostered by their relatives as a way of promoting their dynastic claims to the throne among the public. A similar case can be made for St Aethelberht of East Anglia, who was a political victim of King Offa and whose subsequent cult probably represents an expression of wider discontent with the latter's rule. St Ealhmund and St Eardwulf were also victims of political assassination but their fate was part of the politics of

Panel showing saints, possibly from a sarcophagus, St Hardulph's Church, Breedon-on-the-Hill, Leicestershire. (Photograph by W. Walker)

neighbouring Northumbria rather than Mercia itself. In contrast however there are more traditional saints like St Aethelheard and St Plegmund who sought to reform the Church and were surely worthy holders of the title.[33]

The impact of the pagan Vikings on the Christian community of the Mercian Church was even more devastating than that on the kingdom as a whole. The comparative lack of records for Viking activities in Mercia itself should not blind us to the fact that the Church must have suffered terribly at their hands. We know from contemporary English, Continental and Irish records that these pagans specifically targeted the Christian Church. In these circumstances it was inevitable that church buildings were plundered and destroyed, clergy were kidnapped or killed and church treasures were looted and carried off. The famous *Codex Aureus* manuscript contains a marginal note recording how it was ransomed from the hands of Viking looters by *Ealdorman* Alfred of Surrey and his wife Werburh. The famous Lichfield Gospels may have been rescued in a similar fashion. This could certainly explain how this manuscript originally housed at Llandeillo Fawr in Wales arrived in its current home. In 914 Bishop Cyfeiliog of Ergyng in South Wales was kidnapped by Viking raiders and had to be ransomed by King Edward. A number of later charters record cases of the loss of earlier landbooks or charters as a result of Viking depredations. The latter presumably burned down the dwellings of the owners with these papers inside, rather than simply burning the papers themselves which would have been meaningless to the illiterate Vikings. This picture of losses among communities of scholars and in the contents of their libraries is hardly one that is conducive to church learning.[34]

In the wake of the passage of the 'great army' in the 860s and 870s, the churches of Mercia were undoubtedly plundered and burned, their treasures looted and their clergy slaughtered or sold into slavery, like those elsewhere. We know that Repton suffered considerably from occupation by the army in 874, although parts of the stone church itself clearly survived, perhaps by dint of its use as shelter. Thereafter, the permanent settlement of Vikings in the eastern half of the kingdom from 874 onwards led to the effective eclipse of the Mercian Church in that area. Thus we have no record of any known bishops of London, Lincoln or Leicester from that date but have evidence of the subsequent need to re-establish these sees. The eastern abbeys appear to have suffered a similar fate with a number, for example Crowland, being re-founded in the tenth century.[35]

However, it should not be imagined that the entire Mercian Church simply collapsed in the face of this ruthless pagan onslaught. It fought back, much like its lay counterparts, led by its remaining bishops including those of Lichfield, Hereford and particularly Worcester. It made major contributions to the defence of the kingdom both through prayer and spiritual renewal and through more practical action. It should be remembered that the Viking attacks were viewed as a scourge sent by God to punish the Mercians for their sins. In this context prayer and moral reform were just as important to the English survival and recovery as other more practical activities.

Already in 872 a charter of Bishop Waerferth of Worcester reveals that Mercian bishops were raising finance for payments of tribute as part of attempts to buy protection from Viking attacks. In 875 they initiated daily prayers for the remission of sins under King Ceolwulf II. They subsequently played an active role in the construction of the system of *burhs* by assisting in the process of fortifying their own cathedral towns. The sort of arrangements which must have been made are fortuitously revealed by the survival of an agreement drawn up around 900 between Bishop Waerferth and Lord Aethelred and Lady Aethelflaed. Under the terms of this agreement, the Bishop received concessions in rights and dues within the new *burh* from these rulers in return for a substantial contribution towards the construction of the new fortification. This *burh* effectively preserved Waerferth's church and hence allowed his clergy to make a vital contribution to the subsequent restoration of Christianity and learning throughout Mercia and beyond.[36]

In the aftermath of the attacks, the Mercian Church was revitalised internally by the foundation of new churches and the re-establishment of existing churches throughout

Mercia. This was part of a process arising from a natural desire to give thanks to God for the survival of their Christian community. It was made physically possible by the profits of increasingly successful warfare against the pagan Danes. In the period around 900, Lord Aethelred and Lady Aethelflaed founded a new minster in their capital of Gloucester which was subsequently dedicated to St Oswald after the transfer of his relics there from Bardney in 909. In 901 they donated land to the religious community at Much Wenlock in Shropshire and presented it with a gold chalice worth 30 *mancuses* in honour of St Mildburh. At some date after the reconstruction of the *burh* at Chester in 907, they built a new church there to house the relics of St Werburh. On the basis of archaeological work, it seems likely that they also constructed or restored the church of St Frideswide in Oxford sometime before 911. At around this same time, the lost see of Leicester must have been re-established at Dorchester-on-Thames to provide spiritual supervision for the area of Mercia along the middle Thames. It also seems likely that the rebuilding of the late Saxon church at Leicester was begun under the auspices of Lady Aethelflaed after her recovery of the town in 918. Subsequently, many lesser nobles followed the example of their superiors by engaging in church building activity. In the later tenth century, Lady Wulfrun, who had been taken captive by the men of York in 944, founded a new church at Wolverhampton. All of these actions contributed to the revitalisation of the Mercian Church and in many respects paved the way for the tenth-century reform movement.[37]

The process of renewal also extended beyond Mercia with figures such as Archbishop Plegmund of Canterbury and Bishop Waerferth of Worcester playing a key role in the wider reforms of King Alfred. It was Archbishop Plegmund who supervised and directed the reform of the Church initiated under King Alfred. Bishop Waerferth played a more hands-on role by playing a significant part in the king's ambitious project to extend literacy by translating key Latin texts into English. He personally translated *The Dialogues* of Pope Gregory the Great into English and, although his competence for this task has recently been called into question, he completed it alone and unaided. This was in contrast to other examples of King Alfred's translations which appear to have been completed by teams, for example, Pope Gregory's *Pastoral Care* itself. He may have been involved in the translation of Bede's *Ecclesiastical History*, which shows clear Mercian influence. He also played a part in the process of the dissemination of these works and other works of this period across England. He was the recipient of a surviving original copy of the *Pastoral Care*, sent to him by Alfred along with an *aestel*, or bookmark, which may have taken the form of the famous Alfred jewel. It is also known from some of the language used in the text that Mercian scholars took part in the compilation of King Alfred's law code. The appearance of a number of items of traditional Mercian legal terminology not found in West Saxon texts suggests that this was the case.[38]

In the meantime, what happened to the Mercian Church in the Danish-occupied areas of eastern England? It is usually assumed that the Church simply disappeared from these areas altogether following the death or expulsion of its priests and the destruction of its churches. This may not perhaps be the full picture. There are one or two scraps of information to suggest that some form of Christian activity may have survived in the occupied areas. The position in contemporary York is perhaps instructive in this context. The Archbishop of York managed to maintain a Christian presence in this city almost right through the occupation. It provided a focal point for the conquered Christian population and a centre for the gradual process of conversion of the pagan Danes. It is possible that the Mercian bishops of Lichfield and Dorchester were given a roving commission to engage in similar activities in the occupied territories of Mercia. The subsequent elevation of Bishop Osketel of Dorchester to the position of Archbishop of York in 955 perhaps suggests this possibility. A man who had been closely involved in the active process of conversion and subjugation of Danish-occupied territory would obviously make a very useful archbishop of newly recovered York. Another possible indication of some form of church activity in Danish territory is the record of Lord Aethelred's retrieval of the relics of St Oswald from Bardney in Lindsey in 909. This suggests the possibility that some sort of clerical presence had been maintained at this church in order to preserve these relics through the period of Viking raids and settlements. Otherwise they could surely not have survived intact to be recovered by Aethelred.[39]

In the period of English recovery when the leaders of Mercia and Wessex were undertaking the reconquest of Danish-occupied territory, the Mercian Church again played an important role in both the spiritual and the more practical areas of church activity. The Church was vital in the conversion of those pagan Danes who had settled in England. This was initially pursued through the introduction of baptism into the process of making agreements and treaties with the pagan Danes. In this context Danish leaders were often encouraged if not compelled to accept baptism as part of the terms of any treaty between the English and the Danes as with Guthrum of East Anglia at Wedmore in 878. Lord Aethelred himself had stood sponsor alongside King Alfred to the Viking Haesten's sons at some time before 893. In the Mercian context the conversion of the Danes of York was listed as one of the concessions they offered during their proposed submission to Lady Aethelflaed in 918.[40]

In the wake of the successful recovery of the Danish-occupied areas the Mercian Church made a vital contribution to the eventual unification of England. In contrast to their lay counterparts, Mercian churchmen had long been accustomed to working in the context of a wider English Church. They had been ordained by the Archbishop of Canterbury and had met and consulted with bishops from other kingdoms in regular synods during the Mercian hegemony. This had already accustomed them to working closely with colleagues from other kingdoms and made the possibility of a politically unified England a more natural prospect for them. The subsequent close co-operation of Mercian and other churchmen in King Alfred's educational reforms can only have enhanced this feeling. In addition, the presence of the Mercian, Plegmund, in the post of archbishop of Canterbury during the crucial years from 890 to 923 must have further eased the process of integration.

The new English Church that began to emerge from this process, often in advance of an English state itself, would shortly burst into the frenzy of what has been called the tenth-century reform. This movement grew from the situation in which the English found themselves at the end of the process of unification in 954. The Scandinavian threat had been brought to an end in that year with what proved to be the final reduction of the independent kingdom of York. The English, whose entire society had been geared up to meet the costs of incessant warfare for the past eighty years, suddenly found themselves faced with a problem. They had increasingly directed their resources in money and land towards military purposes but the sudden advent of peace in that year had made most of these resources surplus to requirements. As a result, they found themselves with resources in money and land which could be put to other uses. At the same time, this long period of intermittent warfare had brought an immense amount of devastation and destruction in its wake. Certainly a great deal of this damage had been repaired, especially where that proved vital to military activities, but some of it had not, particularly the damage inflicted on the Church.

In this circumstance, the English naturally directed a large portion of their newly surplus resources into reconstruction and in particular the reconstruction of the Church. This process developed in a number of ways; the building or restoration of churches, the commissioning of manuscripts and the endowment of new or existing churches with land. It was accompanied by a renewal of the intellectual and spiritual life of the Church, which thrived in the peace created with the fall of York. This process brought about a spectacular renewal of church life throughout England but particularly in Mercia. However, that story lies beyond the scope of this work.[41]

A MERCIAN BISHOP, WAERFERTH OF WORCESTER

Waerferth was ordained bishop of Worcester on 7 June 873 by Archbishop Aethelred of Canterbury during the reign of King Burgred. He lived through the greatest crisis in Mercian history and conscientiously performed his duties in the face of the most difficult circumstances. He died at some point during the year 915 in the reign of the Lady Aethelflaed when a new Mercia was emerging from the wreck of the old. During this crucial period, he had successfully steered his own diocese through the troubles that confronted it. At the same time he managed to fulfil a vital role in the survival of the wider kingdom and the English lands beyond. In some ways he seems an extraordinary individual but in others he represents the wider tradition of Mercian churchmen.[42]

It seems almost certain that Waerferth was a native of the land of the *Hwicce*. He was raised in the monastic community at Worcester and a number of his relatives lived locally, including Cynehelm and Cyneswith both of whom would later receive grants of land from their kinsman. He appears to have received a good education and was later described as a 'most learned' man. He certainly possessed a good knowledge of Latin and was the first scholar to translate *The Dialogues* of Pope Gregory the Great into English. He was undoubtedly one of those few men able to render Latin into English referred to by King Alfred in his prologue to the translation of Pope Gregory's *Pastoral Care*. It was his scholarly abilities that attracted the attention of King Alfred and brought about his involvement in Alfred's pioneering work of translating important works into English. He appears to have provided this support from a distance, perhaps by correspondence, as he is not named among those who personally advised the king on his translation of Pope Gregory's *Pastoral Care*. He also appears to have developed good administrative and advocacy skills which would stand him in good stead in later life.[43]

The Worcester copy of King Alfred's translation of Pope Gregory the Great's *Pastoral Care*. (The Bodleian Library, Oxford, Ms. Hatton 20, f. 1r)

It was through his scholarly activities that Waerferth became a close friend and advisor of King Alfred of Wessex. He was presented with a copy of Alfred's translation of *Pastoral Care* for his cathedral church which still survives to this day. In 899 Waerferth was one of only three bishops to be singled out and specifically named in the great king's will in which he received a bequest of 100 *mancuses* of gold. However, he did not neglect his contacts with the leaders of Mercia either and he was in regular attendance at their *witan* or royal council as well as being a consistent charter witness. In a charter dated between 889 and 899 Waerferth was described by Lord Aethelred and Lady Aethelflaed as their 'friend'. In return, the bishop was able to call on their aid in a number of disputes with others concerning lands lost by Worcester.[44]

Waerferth was also a devout Christian, who ministered to the spiritual needs of both his diocese and his kingdom. In 875 he instituted regular daily prayers for the remission of the sins of King Ceolwulf II in the period of national disaster following the loss of part of the kingdom to the Vikings. This important activity directly addressed what contemporaries believed were the principal cause of the Viking success. The Vikings were a scourge sent by God to punish sin and could best be dealt with by way of moral reform within the kingdom. At some point between 889-899, he similarly agreed to institute daily prayers for the souls of the new Mercian rulers, Lord Aethelred and Lady Aethelflaed.[45]

Waerferth was also a very able administrator, and one who did not neglect the more practical needs of his diocese or the wider kingdom. In 872 he was involved in raising cash from his diocese to assist in making payments in an attempt to buy off the Vikings. He played a prominent role in the construction of the *burh* at Worcester. He also diligently pursued a number of long-standing Worcester claims to lost lands, for example, those at Woodchester and Sodbury in Gloucestershire. He managed to achieve some success in this difficult process by exploiting to the full his close relationship with the new Mercian rulers. In 896 he managed to reduce the outright seizure of some woodland at Woodchester to a lease for three lives with reversion to Worcester. In 903 he was able to extract a payment of 40 *mancuses* of gold in exchange for surrendering his claim to the land at Sodbury. In both of these disputes he made good use of the written charters of his church in his efforts to establish the Worcester claim. He also sought to obtain the benefits of trade for his church and in 889 received a grant of land from Lord Aethelred at *Hwaetmundes Stane* in recently recovered London. This placed him in an excellent position to participate in the Continental trade of this great port. In 898/9 he was one member of an important group, which included King Alfred, Lord Aethelred, Lady Aethelflaed and Archbishop Plegmund of Canterbury, that met to discuss arrangements for the restoration of the *burh* at London. On this occasion he also received the grant of a plot of land at a place subsequently known as Aethelred's Hithe and later still Queenhithe.[46]

He was assisted in all these activities by a close-knit group of relatives, friends and supporters who formed a diocesan court which acted in his support. Most of them appear regularly as witnesses in the charters that he issued as bishop. One such is Abbot Cynehelm of Evesham who was a regular witness and who may have supported the work of his bishop by deputising for him in a religious capacity. The Mercian priest, Werwulf, who according to Asser played a prominent role in support of King Alfred's programme of translation, may have been another of his following. Certainly, in 899 Waerferth granted five *manentes* of land at Ablington on Coln in Gloucestershire to a priest of this same name. They also included his reeve, Wulfsige, who deputised for him in an administrative capacity with 'loyal efficiency and humble

Charter of Bishop Waerferth of Worcester to his reeve Wulfsige, 904. (BL Add. Charter 19791)

obedience' and was duly rewarded in 904 with a hide of land at Aston Magna in Gloucestershire.[47]

In some respects, Waerferth also appears to have acted as the leading bishop of Mercia during the rule of Lord Aethelred and Lady Aethelflaed. He certainly features more often in surviving documents than any other bishop. This may simply be the result of the comparatively more successful survival of Worcester sources. It seems more likely however that it was a genuine reflection of those immense personal abilities that had also attracted the attention of King Alfred. As a result, he effectively outshone his contemporaries in Hereford and Lichfield. He certainly had a long and successful career in both Church and public service during one of the most difficult and traumatic periods of the entire history of the Church in England.[48]

In return for his many services, Bishop Waerferth received a significant number of rewards both for himself and for his church and its community. In 875 he was granted some 60 *mancuses* of gold and freedom for his diocese from the obligation to feed royal horses and their grooms. In 899 he received 100 *mancuses* of gold as a bequest in the will of King Alfred of Wessex. In 903 he received a one-off payment of 40 *mancuses* of gold and 15 shillings per annum thereafter in compensation for the loss of land at Sodbury. In 904 the church of Worcester was granted a half share of all royal rights in Worcester with the exception of tolls on salt in return for its prayers for the souls of Lord Aethelred and his wife both during their lifetime and after their death.[49]

SUMMARY

It is clear from the consideration both of the Church as a whole and of the career of Bishop Waerferth in particular that the Church in Mercia was far from moribund during this period. It had already played its part in the conversion of England, it had contributed to the conversion of Germany and it had played a full role in the first flowering of Christian learning in England. In the face of the onslaught of the pagan Vikings it struggled to maintain its priceless spiritual, intellectual and physical heritage. It is arguable that it succeeded in this process rather more successfully than its Northumbrian or West Saxon neighbours. Thereafter, it played a key role in the revival and subsequent unification of Christian England. It placed its spiritual support firmly behind the military recovery of England and its leaders, the new Mercian rulers Aethelred and Aethelflaed and their West Saxon successors. It threw its intellectual weight behind the restoration of English Christian culture through active participation in the wider educational revival initiated by King Alfred and continued by his successors. It invested its great wealth in the restoration and rebuilding of an English Christian society in all its spiritual and secular aspects. It became fully involved in many reconstruction projects ranging from the restoration of the trading city of London to the building of many local *burhs*, and from the establishment of the new see of Dorchester and the revival of the archbishopric of Canterbury to the rebuilding of individual churches throughout Mercia.

In the newly united kingdom it would go on to participate in the great reform of the English Church initiated by King Edgar. Indeed, in this process prominent Mercians would once again play a central role. The reforms were carried out under such major figures as Archbishop Dunstan and Bishop Oswald of Worcester, both of whom governed the same great diocese that had been the base for Bishop Waerferth and the centre from which the Mercian Church had directed its efforts to restore the larger English Church after the Viking invasions. The reform was supported by the funds and grants provided by key secular figures including a number of important *ealdormen*. These included Aelfhere of Mercia and Aethelwine of East Anglia, the latter known as *Amicus Dei*, or 'Friend of God', who were members of important Mercian families and who continued to hold authority in Mercia. It is clear that the Mercian Church and its congregation continued to play an important role in the wider history of England.

Conclusion

This book has sought to reveal the important role played by the Kingdom of Mercia, its rulers and its people in the making of the wider Kingdom of England. This has been a difficult task because of the dearth of sources for the period itself but also because of the West Saxon bias of most of those that do survive. This bias has all too often been unrecognised or ignored when it should be recognised and addressed. Keynes has stated recently that there is nothing in the text of the Chronicle that could offend a Mercian. However, it seems likely that few Mercians would have been content with its complete lack of acknowledgement of their role in events during the reigns of Alfred and Edward. The Chronicle singularly fails to highlight the significance of their role in a number of crucial events including the Battle of Tettenhall in 910. The surviving sources for this period and the events they portray stand in need of significant re-evaluation in order to allow us to achieve a balanced assessment of the respective contributions of Mercia and Wessex during these important years. Only in this way can a more objective view of the process that ultimately resulted in the birth of a unified England be achieved.[1]

In the eighth and ninth centuries, each of the individual English kingdoms sought to dominate the others and if possible to subdue them. In this contest Mercia for long periods achieved a position of dominance under powerful kings like Aethelbald and Offa. These kings undertook largely successful military campaigns, which aimed at the complete absorption of the many minor kingdoms, like those of the *Hwicce*, Essex, Surrey and Sussex. It proved more difficult for Mercia or its main rivals to digest larger kingdoms like Kent and East Anglia in this way. The latter were often subsumed for a time but rarely for long periods and not on a permanent basis. Instead, these kingdoms drifted in and out of subject status as the power of individual Mercian or West Saxon overlords waxed and waned. It proved virtually impossible for Mercia to overcome its major rivals, the kingdoms of Wessex and Northumbria. Even the most powerful rulers, like Offa of Mercia and Egbert of Wessex, could only manage to dominate these rival kingdoms for relatively short periods. They were never able to transform this ephemeral dominance into any sort of direct control.

This was the case partly because such eighth- and ninth-century rulers lacked the administrative structures required to enforce the direct subjugation of such large kingdoms. Equally they were not able to win the necessary consent for such direct rule from the nobles of these kingdoms. This was the only alternative in circumstances where no effective administrative solution was available. It was almost always a case of such rulers imposing their authority as overlords by conquest on unwilling subjects. As a result, this process ultimately proved to be counter-productive. It may have been the way to achieve a temporary Mercian or West Saxon hegemony but it could never be the route to a unified kingdom of the English.

The latter could only be achieved through a process of co-operation and consent involving rival kingdoms. This would probably have been impossible without the intervention of the Viking invasions. It was the reality of piecemeal conquest by these formidable pagan enemies that focussed the minds of the rulers and peoples of England on the notion of joining forces, initially simply for protection. The fate of East Anglia and Northumbria graphically illustrated the bleak prospect facing Wessex and Mercia, if they had to face the Vikings alone. It was this powerful catalyst that drove these former bitter rivals into active co-operation for the first time.

In practice, their initial attempt at an alliance proved too fragile in the face of the Viking menace. The tentative military co-operation embarked on at the siege of Nottingham in 868 quickly crumbled in an atmosphere of mutual suspicion and was not repeated. It would need the further demonstration of Viking power in the 870s that brought both Mercia and Wessex to the very brink of conquest to ram home the urgent need for an alliance. This was once again based on a royal marriage but, on this occasion, it is usually portrayed in the sources as the extension of West Saxon overlordship over Mercia on the earlier pattern. In many ways, the relative strength of the two powers involved and their previous history makes this a natural assumption. However, this is very much a West Saxon interpretation of events which is in need of reassessment. It should, where necessary, be discarded and the underlying process should be exposed.

A closer consideration of events reveals that the relationship between Aethelred of Mercia and King Alfred was a much more complex one than simply that of an overlord and his subject. There was inevitably an element of this in the formal arrangements with Aethelred adopting a more subordinate role. However, in practice it seems to have functioned more like an alliance of close co-operation between two men who respected each other than one of straight-forward dominance. It is clear that, in contrast to their predecessors, both men worked hard to make this alliance work. They each made concessions to ensure that it held together during the most critical years. King Alfred recognised Aethelred's authority over Mercia and, in token of this, surrendered control of newly occupied London to him. In turn Lord Aethelred forbore his entitlement to the use of the royal title and the issue of coins. They also worked jointly in a number of ways to further cement their alliance. They participated in a series of joint campaigns against the Vikings where West Saxon and Mercian troops fought side by side. They worked together on the detailed plans for the reconstruction of London. They undertook a major joint effort in the building of their *burhs*.

It was this new kind of alliance between genuine partners, even if unequal partners, which sowed the seeds that would bear fruit in the later unification of England. It gradually brought about an atmosphere of co-operation and trust that had not previously existed between these rival kingdoms and which was a necessary ingredient for any future process of unification. It was this that would slowly overcome earlier suspicions about domination of one kingdom by another. This co-operation continued under the siblings Aethelflaed and Edward. The eminently successful pattern established by Aethelred and Alfred provided them with a clear example to follow. They worked in parallel to restore English control over those areas under Danish occupation. They no longer carried out joint campaigns, largely as a result of the different directions taken by their offensive strikes, Edward against East Anglia and Aethelflaed against Northumbria. Nevertheless, they continued to pursue broadly similar objectives and share similar strategies and techniques to achieve them.

The new spirit of co-operation and trust instigated by these rulers slowly bridged the gap between the nobles within the two kingdoms. This was a vital element in establishing the sort of links that made the eventual unification of England possible. In 918 when King Edward deposed Aelfwynn and assumed direct rule over Mercia he seems to have done so with the consent of an important section of Mercian society. He probably secured this support on the basis of an undertaking to make provision for a separate succession in Mercia after his death. The evidence of the succession arrangements at Edward's death in 924 appear to confirm this. The very idea of a West Saxon king being accepted, however temporarily, as ruler of Mercia would previously have been unthinkable. The fact that this was no longer the case is stark testimony to how the situation had changed.

This significant shift in the relationship between Mercia and Wessex, from rivals to close allies, did not complete the making of England by itself. The increased co-operation between these two kingdoms and even their rule by a single king did not mean that union would inevitably follow. Indeed, there is evidence that important forces continued to work towards the preservation of Mercian independence. The concern expressed by Mercian sources at the time of Aelfwynn's deposition, and the subsequent arrangements for a separate succession in Mercia and Wessex, prove that Mercians remained very conscious of their own separate traditions and status.

As we examine the sources closely, it becomes increasingly obvious that the actual making of England was not the result of any plan or scheme. It was in fact the result of a number of dynastic accidents. First, the lack of a male heir to succeed Lord Aethelred, eventually and in spite of Aethelflaed's period of rule, made West Saxon rule in Mercia, however temporary, a necessity in the face of the continued threat from the Danes.

It was clearly intended that this be a temporary arrangement under Edward with careful plans being laid for a separate succession in Mercia and Wessex. Second, the sudden and unexpected death of Aelfweard of Wessex only 16 days after his father provided his half-brother Athelstan with an opportunity to succeed to both kingdoms. In spite of Athelstan's long period of joint rule the two kingdoms remained distinct entities. It was probably only the relative youth of his two immediate successors that prevented the restoration of separate rule in the face of the continuing threat from the kingdom of York. The priority shown towards dealing with this threat was rewarded by the completion of the map of modern England with the conquest of York in 954.

The reign of Eadwig saw the two increasingly close kingdoms divided once more with Eadwig ruling Wessex and Edgar Mercia. However, this division perhaps demonstrates how far they had come after twenty-five years of unity under a single dynasty. The tensions that produced this split were probably more political than regional and both rulers relied on support that was more family-based than purely territorial. The division was based on the rival family and political associations of these two princes although it did find an echo in the division of the kingdom. The distinctions between the nobles of Mercia and Wessex had clearly become less important as their political and family connections extended across the wider English scene. The subsequent early and unexpected death of Eadwig once again produced a situation in 959 that resulted in the final unification of the kingdoms under a single ruler.

This event marked the end of independent Mercia but it took longer for the unified England to develop. It was perhaps only in 975 after the long reign of Edgar and more than half a century of almost uninterrupted joint rule that the two kingdoms finally began to view themselves as a single whole. It naturally took longer for more recently acquired York to fuse with the existing joint kingdom of Mercia and Wessex into one new unitary kingdom. This was probably finally completed by 1066 when a largely united kingdom faced a double foreign invasion. This is not to say that the individual segments that made up this new state did not retain distinct identities which were sometimes revived, for example, in temporary divisions of the kingdom or in the earldoms of the eleventh century. Men could still call themselves West Saxons, Mercians or Northumbrians but they knew that when it came to the crunch they were all English.

This book has tried to show that the making of England was not in fact the result of a rapid conquest of Mercia achieved by Alfred and his son Edward followed by a more protracted conquest of Northumbria. It was a much longer process involving a long period of increasingly close co-operation and the gradual coalescence of two kingdoms into one. The subsequent tempering of this united kingdom under a second wave of Viking attacks followed by the Danish conquest in the late tenth century and early eleventh century produced a new England. It was far from being the product of a West

Saxon conquest. It was a new kingdom, a *Rex Anglorum*, rather than a greater Wessex. It drew on the traditions of both its major predecessors and of the wider English Church of Pope Gregory, Archbishop Theodore, Bede and the series of Church synods.

The West Saxon dynasty ruled the new kingdom largely as a result of its fortunate survival through the worst days of the Viking crisis. In comparison the only other survivor among Anglo-Saxon leaders, Aethelred of Mercia, was handicapped in a number of ways. He was not, as far as we can tell, a member of a well established existing dynasty and he held a smaller and weaker power base during the crucial period between the 870s and 890s. He was also unfortunate in leaving no male descendants or close relatives to succeed him and possibly contest the rule of a wider kingdom with those of his ally King Alfred.

If the Mercians had not been their active partners, it is difficult to imagine that the West Saxons alone would have been able to conquer all of the other English kingdoms even after the disaster of the Viking conquest. It had already proved beyond the abilities of some of the most powerful rulers of Mercia and Wessex, including King Offa and King Egbert. The advantage the later West Saxon kings derived from the secure co-operation of the Mercians brought them uncontested control of more than half of the former kingdom of Mercia. It was possession of this vantage point that allowed them to pursue the rapid recovery of the areas conquered by the Danes. Even so, it took the combined resources of Mercia and Wessex over twenty years to recover East Anglia and the East Midlands, and a further thirty-five years to subdue York. In this context, it is difficult to imagine how the West Saxons alone could have pursued such ambitious aims and the subjugation of Western Mercia all from a base restricted to south of the Thames.

This book has sought to lay the foundations for believing that the making of England was a product of the combined efforts of the Mercians and West Saxons, assisted from time to time by the intervention of chance or fate. It seems likely that this picture will be clarified and augmented further in the future. In terms of the sources further study of the Chronicle and the Mercian Register will provide a balance for each. The identification of many currently unidentified place-names will clarify the geography of some key events including the pattern of Mercian *burhs* and the location of *Brunanburh*. Closer study of Mercian charters will add to our knowledge of the kingdom and its role in this crucial period. Excavations of important established Mercian sites, including Offa's Dyke, important religious centres and the *burhs*, will add to our knowledge not only of these particular sites but of the wider kingdom. In addition, the chance discovery of other artefacts and structures in the former kingdom can only add to the meagre sum of our existing knowledge. The picture is therefore a hopeful one for the future of Mercian history in this crucial period of English history.

TABLE 1

THE MERCIAN 'C' AND 'W' DYNASTIES

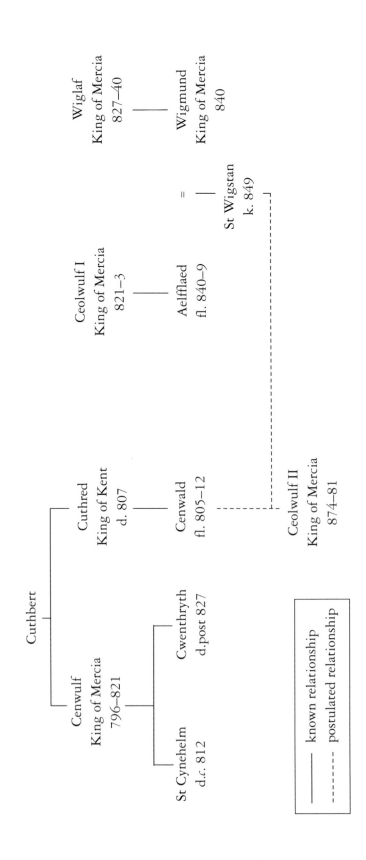

Cuthbert

Cenwulf
King of Mercia
796–821

Cuthred
King of Kent
d. 807

Wiglaf
King of Mercia
827–40

St Cynehelm
d.c. 812

Cwenthryth
d.post 827

Cenwald
fl. 805–12

Ceolwulf I
King of Mercia
821–3

Aelfflaed
fl. 840–9

=

St Wigstan
k. 849

Wigmund
King of Mercia
840

Ceolwulf II
King of Mercia
874–81

——— known relationship

------- postulated relationship

TABLE 2

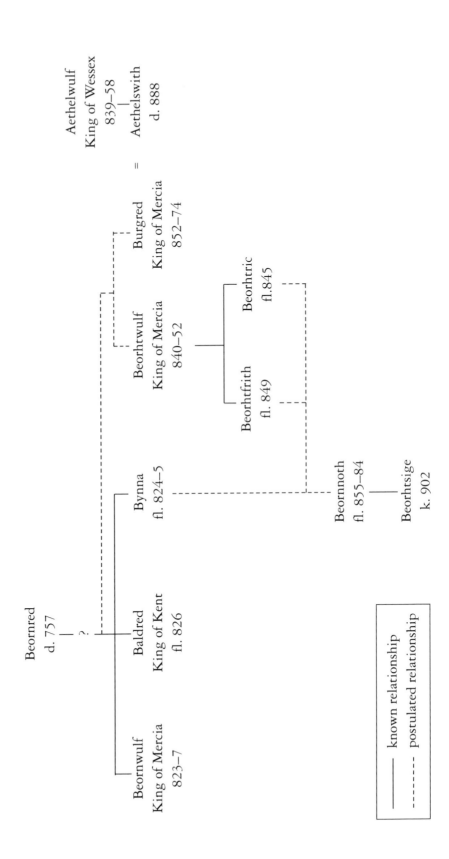

THE MERCIAN 'B' DYNASTY

Beornred
d. 757

Beornwulf
King of Mercia
823–7

Baldred
King of Kent
fl. 826

Bynna
fl. 824–5

Beorhtwulf
King of Mercia
840–52

Burgred
King of Mercia
852–74

=

Aethelwulf
King of Wessex
839–58

Aethelswith
d. 888

Beorhtric
fl.845

Beorhtfrith
fl. 849

Beornnoth
fl. 855–84

Beorhtsige
k. 902

known relationship
postulated relationship

TABLE 3

MERCIAN AND WEST SAXON RULERS AND CONNECTIONS

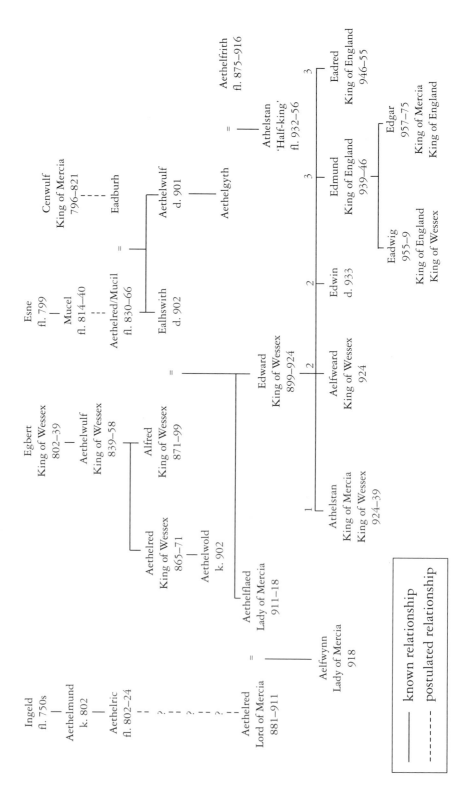

Glossary

atheling a throne-worthy man, usually the son of a king but occasionally the grandson of a king

burh originally any fortified place but during the late ninth and tenth centuries it came to be applied to the fortified town sites built by Lord Aethelred, King Alfred and their successors

ceorl a freeman in possession of less than the 5 hides of land required to achieve noble status

ealdorman a royal official usually appointed by the king from among his more prominent nobles to govern a region on his behalf within the larger kingdom. In Latin this official usually appears as *dux* but sometimes as *præfectus*, *princeps*, *comes* or *patricius*

faestingaman a freeman with duties in respect of the sustenance of the king and court

geneat a freeman with duties in respect of mounted escort and patrol

hide a measure of land developed for the purposes of assessment for tribute or taxation. It originally represented sufficient land to support a single extended family

hold a Scandinavian rank considered broadly equivalent to the English *thegn*

jarl a Scandinavian rank considered broadly equivalent to the English *ealdorman*

mancus in English use a unit of account equivalent to thirty silver pennies but also a gold coin used in diplomatic gifts

manentes   a measure of land of unknown size

sceatt   name given to the smaller silver coins in use in the English kingdoms before the introduction of the silver penny under Offa

thegn   a nobleman holding more than 5 hides of land and therefore liable for military or other service under the king. In Latin this official usually appears as *minister*

witan   a royal council, usually consisting of nobles, both *ealdormen* and *thegns*, and clergy close to the king

Notes

Introduction

1. F.M. Stenton, *Anglo-Saxon England* (2nd edn, Oxford, 1971), A. Williams, *Kingship and Government in Pre-Conquest England* (London, 1999), P. Stafford, *Unification and Conquest* (London, 1989), J. Campbell (ed.), *The Anglo-Saxons* (Harmondsworth, 1982) and S. Keynes, 'England 700–900' in R. McKitterick (ed.), *The New Cambridge Medieval History*, Vol. II (Cambridge, 1995). E. Johns, *Re-assessing Anglo-Saxon England* (Manchester, 1996) and S. Keynes, 'England c. 900–1016' in T. Reuter (ed.), *The New Cambridge Medieval History*, Vol. III (Cambridge, 1999) show more awareness of Mercia in the reigns of Alfred and Edward.

2. On the origins and early history of Mercia see N. Brooks, 'The Formation of the Mercian Kingdom' in S. Bassett (ed.), *The Origins of the Anglo-Saxon Kingdoms* (Leicester, 1989), pp. 159–70 and W. Davies, 'Annals and the Origin of Mercia' in A. Dornier (ed.), *Mercian Studies* (Leicester, 1977), pp. 17–29.

3. On the conversion of Mercia see *Bede: A History of the English Church and People*, tr. L. Sherley-Price (Harmondsworth, 1955), pp. 177 and 184.

4. P. Wormald, 'The Age of Bede and Aethelbald' in Campbell (ed.), *The Anglo-Saxons*. There are three main translations of the Anglo-Saxon Chronicle (ASC): D. Whitelock (ed.) with D.C. Douglas and S.I. Tucker, *The Anglo-Saxon Chronicle* (London, rev. edn, 1961); M. Swanton (ed.), *The Anglo-Saxon Chronicle* (London, 1996); and G.N. Garmonsway (ed.), *The Anglo-Saxon Chronicle* (London, 1953). I have chosen to use the Whitelock translation, which has easily the most user-friendly format.

5. The text of the Mercian Register (MR) can be found in any of the main translations of the ASC. I have used that found in the edition by Whitelock *et al.*, which is the most readily accessible.

6. Asser can be found most conveniently in translation in S. Keynes and M. Lapidge (eds), *Alfred the Great* (Harmondsworth, 1983), pp. 67–110.

7. A. Campbell (ed.), *Chronicle of Aethelweard* (CA) (Edinburgh, 1962).

8. The main Celtic sources are S. MacAirt (ed.),*The Annals of Ulster to AD 1134* (AU) (Dublin, 1955/77), The Welsh Annals (AC) in J. Morris (ed.), *Nennius: British History and The Welsh Annals* (Chichester, 1980) and T. Jones (ed.), *Brut Y Tywysogion:Peniarth Ms. 20* (BYT) (Cardiff, 1952). There are only occasional references to events in England in similar Continental sources and these are identified in the appropriate places.

9. The editions of these later twelfth- and thirteenth-century historians which have been used will be identified in the appropriate references.

10. P.H. Sawyer (ed.), *Anglo-Saxon Charters* (ASCh.) (London, 1968). An updated version of this volume with full editions (although not translations as yet) of many of the individual charters can be found on the internet at http://www.trin.ca.ac.uk/users/sdk13/chartwww. Translations of a selection of the more interesting charters and other documents can be found in D. Whitelock (ed.), *English Historical Documents Volume I c. 500–1042* (EHD) (London, 2nd edn, 1979). An important summary of those listed as witnesses in the various charters can be found in S. Keynes, *An Atlas of Attestations in Anglo-Saxon Charters* (Cambridge, 1998). The letters of Alcuin can be found in S. Allott (ed.), *Alcuin of York (Alcuin)* (York, 1974). See E. Mason, *St Wulfstan of Worcester* (Oxford, 1990) for the subsequent preservation of the Anglo-Saxon legacy at Worcester.

11. There are three key works on the coinage during this period: R.H.M. Dolley (ed.), *Anglo-Saxon Coins* (London, 1961); M.A.S. Blackburn (ed.), *Anglo-Saxon Monetary History* (Leicester, 1986); and M.A.S. Blackburn and D.N. Dumville (eds), *Kings, Currency and Alliances* (Oxford, 1998).

12. C. Fox, *Offa's Dyke* (London, 1955), F. Noble, *Offa's Dyke Reviewed* (Oxford, 1983).

13. H.M. Taylor and J. Taylor, *Anglo-Saxon Architecture*, 3 vols (Cambridge, 1965–78).

14. M.P. Brown, *Anglo-Saxon Manuscripts* (London, 1991) and L. Webster and J. Backhouse (eds), *The Making of England* (London, 1991).

Chapter 1

1. ASC 757, EHD No. 177, ASCh. S 1782. A. Williams, A.P. Smyth and D.P. Kirby (eds), *A Biographical Dictionary of Dark-Age Britain* (BDDAB) (London, 1991), pp. 17–18 and M. Lapidge, J. Blair, S. Keynes and D. Scragg (eds), *The Blackwell Encyclopedia of Anglo-Saxon England* (BEASE) (Oxford, 1999), pp. 11–13 for Aethelbald.

2. ASC 757, Stenton, *Anglo-Saxon England*, chapter 7, B. Yorke, *Kings and Kingdoms of Early Anglo-Saxon England* (London, 1990), pp. 111–17, D.P. Kirby, *The Earliest English Kings* (London, 1991), chapter 8 and L. Dutton, *The Anglo-Saxon Kingdoms* (Lampeter, 1993), pp. 241–58 for Offa.

3. D. Hill, *An Atlas of Anglo-Saxon England* (Oxford, 1981), Map Nos 42 and 145, BEASE, Map 10.

4. R. Collins, *Charlemagne* (London, 1998) for the contemporary Frankish background.

5. AC 760, BYT 760.

6. ASCh. S 105, 34, 111, EHD No. 80 or ASCh. S 155, ASCh. S 1264.

7. ASCh. S 49 and 108, *Simeon of Durham: A History of the Kings of England* (SD), tr. J. Stephenson (repr., Lampeter, 1987), the annal for 771.

8. ASCh. S 58, 59 and 60.

9. ASC 776, ASCh. S 38.

10. AC 778.

11. ASC 779, ASCh. S 108, EHD No. 79 and ASCh. S 1258.

12. The Royal Frankish Annals (RFA) 774, 788 in *Carolingian Chronicles*, tr. B. Scholz (Ann Arbor, 1970). See Collins, *Charlemagne* for the Franks.

13. ASCh. S 58–59, 113, 148, ASC 802.

14. AC 783, Keynes and Lapidge, *Alfred the Great*, p. 71.

15. Fox, *Offa's Dyke*, Part III, pp. 277–93.

16. ASCh. S 92.

17. D. Hill, 'Offa's and Wat's Dykes: Some Aspects of Recent Work' in *Transactions of the Lancashire and Cheshire Antiquarian Society*, 79, 1977, pp. 21–33.

18. RFA 793, J. Haywood, *Dark Age Naval Power* (London, 1991), pp. 104–9.

19. P. Rahtz and R. Meeson, *An Anglo-Saxon Watermill at Tamworth* (London, 1992).

20. R. Shoesmith, *Hereford City Excavations I and II* (London, 1980 and 1982).

21. ASCh. S 123.

22. D.M. Metcalf, 'Monetary Affairs in Mercia in the Time of Aethelbald' in Dornier, *Mercian Studies*, pp. 87–106.

23. B. Hobley, 'Lundenwic and Lundenburh: two cities rediscovered' in R. Hodges and B. Hobley (eds), *The Rebirth of Towns in the West* (London, 1988), pp. 69–82, and Bede, p. 204.

24. C.E. Blunt, 'The Coinage of King Offa' in Dolley, *Anglo-Saxon Coins*, pp. 36–62 for the new penny coinage.

25. C. Cubitt, *Anglo-Saxon Church Councils* (Leicester, 1995), chapters 6 and 8.

26. *Alcuin*, No. 35.

27. RFA 768.

28. Cubitt, *Church Councils*, chapter 6 and EHD No. 191.

29. EHD No. 205, 204. Blunt, 'Coinage of King Offa', pp. 36–62.

30. H.R. Loyn and J. Percival (eds), *The Reign of Charlemagne* (London, 1975), No. 39.

31. ASC 786. ASC 757 for the saga account of this bloodbath in 786. ASC 839 for the exile.

32. ASC 789 for the marriage.

33. ASC 787. Blunt, 'Coinage of King Offa', pp. 36–62.

34. EHD No. 192, *Charlemagne: Translated Sources*, tr. P.D. King (Kendal, 1987), p. 334, EHD No. 20, *Two Lives of Charlemagne: Einhard and Notker the Stammerer*, tr. L. Thorpe (Harmondsworth, 1969), p. 75.

35. EHD No. 196 and 197.

36. ASCh. S 133, EHD No. 197 and 196, *Alcuin*, No. 41, King (tr.), *Charlemagne: Sources*, p. 334.

37. RFA 791.

38. ASC 792. SD 792.

39. ASC 794, S.J. Ridyard, *The Royal Saints of Anglo-Saxon England* (Cambridge, 1988), pp. 243–4, R.R. Darlington and P.J.

McGurk (eds), *The Chronicle of John of Worcester, Volume II* (JW) (Oxford, 1995), the annal for 794.

40. ASC 796, *Roger of Wendover: Flowers of History* (RW), tr. J.A. Giles (repr. Lampeter, 1993), the annal for 796.

41. *Alcuin*, No. 38, EHD No. 195.

Chapter 2

1. ASC 796, *Alcuin*, No. 46.

2. Stenton, *Anglo-Saxon England*, pp. 225–38, Yorke, *Kings and Kingdoms*, chapter 6, Kirby, *Earliest English Kings*, chapter 9 and Dutton, *AS Kingdoms*, pp. 262–74 for this period.

3. Keynes, *Atlas*, Tables X and XVII, ASCh. S 124. BDDAB, p. 83 and BEASE, pp. 111–13 for Cenwulf.

4. Cubitt, *Church Councils*, chapter 8 for the synods.

5. *Alcuin*, No. 49, EHD No. 204.

6. EHD No. 205 and 210.

7. ASC 798, *Alcuin*, Nos 49 and 50, Yorke, *Kings and Kingdoms*, p. 64, AC 798.

8. SD 801, ASC 802, 784 and 839.

9. ASC 802.

10. EHD No. 210.

11. BDDAB, p. 24 for Aethelmund.

12. ASCh. S 59.

13. ASCh. S 139 and 148, P. Wormald, *How Do We Know So Much About Anglo-Saxon Deerhurst?* (Deerhurst, 1993), ASCh. S 1187, 1433, Keynes, *Atlas*, Tables X and XVII.

14. N. Brooks, *The Early History of the Church at Canterbury* (Leicester, 1984), chapter 7(b), BDDAB, pp. 240–1 and BEASE, pp. 491–2 for Wulfred.

15. A.W. Haddan and W. Stubbs, *Councils and Ecclesiastical Documents Relating to Great Britain and Ireland*, Vol. III (3 vols, 1869–71), p. 563, ASC 814, 815, Cubitt, *Church Councils*, chapter 7 for the synod of Chelsea and chapter 8 for the wider dispute.

16. AC 816, 818, ASC 815.

17. ASC 821, AU 821, Keynes, *Atlas*, Table XVII, R.C. Love (ed.), *Three Eleventh Century Anglo-Latin Saints Lives* (Oxford, 1996), pp. 50–89, BDDAB, p. 98, BEASE, p. 269 for Cynehelm.

18. Keynes, *Atlas*, Table XVII, EHD No. 83 and ASCh. S 186, AC 822, ASC 823, BDDAB, pp. 77–8 for Ceolwulf I.

19. ASCh. S 1435.

20. ASCh. S 187, Keynes, *Atlas*, Table XVII and Yorke, *Kings and Kingdoms*, pp. 118–20.

21. B. Colgrave (ed.), *The Life of Bishop Wilfred by Eddius Stephanus* (Cambridge, 1927), chapter 40, ASC 757.

22. Keynes, *Atlas*, Table XVII, BDDAB, p. 60 for Beornwulf.

23. ASC 824.

24. Cubitt, *Church Councils*, pp. 220–2, Brooks, *Canterbury*, p. 136.

25. ASC 825, 826, D. Greenway (ed.), *Henry, Archdeacon of Huntingdon, Historia Anglorum – The History of the English People* (HH) (Oxford, 1996), p. 263.

26. Yorke, *Kings and Kingdoms*, pp. 119–20.

27. Keynes, *Atlas*, Table XVII, ASC 827, BDDAB, pp. 235–6 for Ludeca.

28. ASC 829, Yorke, *Kings and Kingdoms*, p. 191.

29. ASC 830, ASCh. S 188, Cubitt, *Church Councils*, p. 287. ASC 838, 842 for the Vikings.

30. Keynes, *Atlas*, Table XVII, BDDAB, pp. 59-60 for Beorhtwulf.

31. Keynes, *Atlas*, Table XVII, ASCh. S 197.

32. ASC 842, AC 849.

33. J. Booth, 'Monetary Alliance or Technical Co-operation?: The Coinage of King Berhtwulf of Mercia (840–852)' in Blackburn and Dumville, *Kings, Currency and Alliances*, pp. 63–103. See S. Keynes, 'King Alfred and the Mercians' in Blackburn and Dumville, *Kings, Currency and Alliances*, p. 6 n. 21, which may provide some support for a lack of central control on minting with an example of a coin showing obverses of both Beorhtwulf and Alfred.

34. ASCh. S 1271, Keynes and Lapidge, *Alfred the Great*, p. 67, Keynes, *Atlas*, Tables XVII and XXI.

35. A.T. Thacker, 'Kings, Saints and Monasteries in Pre-Viking Mercia' in *Midland History*, 10, 1985, pp. 1–25, BDDAB, p. 236 for Wigstan.

36. Thacker, 'Kings, Saints and Monasteries', pp. 1–25.

37. ASC 851, ASB 850 in J.L. Nelson (ed.), *Annals of St Bertin* (Manchester, 1991).

38. ASC 852, Keynes, *Atlas*, Table XVII.

39. Keynes, 'Alfred and the Mercians', p. 5 n. 17 for a rather different interpretation of Mercia during this period.

Chapter 3

1. ASCh. S 134, RFA 809, ASC 838, 842, 851, EHD No. 90 or ASCh. S 206, BDDAB, pp. 68–9, Keynes, 'Alfred and the Mercians', pp. 1–45 for Burgred.

2. ASC 793, A.C. Evans, *The Sutton Hoo Ship Burial* (London, 1986), pp. 113–15, N. Lund and C.E. Fell (eds), *Ohthere and Wulfstan: Two Voyagers at the Court of King Alfred* (York, 1984), pp. 18–22, ASC 789.

3. EHD No. 193.

4. P.H. Sawyer, *The Age of the Vikings* (London, 2nd edn, 1971), A.P. Smyth, *Scandinavian Kings of the British Isles* (Oxford, 1988), H.R. Loyn, *The Vikings in Britain* (Oxford, 1994), P.H. Sawyer, 'The Age of the Vikings and Before' and S. Keynes, 'The Vikings in England' in P.H. Sawyer (ed.), *The Oxford Illustrated Encyclopaedia of the Vikings* (Oxford, 1997), pp. 1–47 and 48–82 respectively.

5. K. Leyser, 'Early Medieval Warfare' in J. Cooper (ed.), The Battle of Maldon (London, 1993), pp. 87–108.

6. Haywood, *Naval Power*, pp. 118–21.

7. ASC 851.

8. ASC 853.

9. Keynes, 'Alfred and the Mercians', pp. 8–9.

10. EHD No. 90 or ASCh. S 206, ASC 855, AC 853, 854, AU 856.

11. ASC 865.

12. ASC 866.

13. ASC 867, RW 867, SD 867.

14. ASC 868, 869.

15. JW 868, Keynes and Lapidge, *Alfred the Great*, p. 88.

16. ASC 870.

17. Smyth, *Scandinavian Kings*, chapter 16 for this royal martyr.

18. ASC 871, CA 871.

19. ASC 872, EHD No. 94.

20. RW 872.

21. ASC 873, RW 873, SD 873.

22. ASC 874, S. Keynes, 'Anglo-Saxon Entries in the *Liber Vitae* of Brescia' in J. Roberts, J.L. Nelson and M.R. Godden (eds), *Alfred the Wise* (Woodbridge, 1997), pp. 99–119, EHD No. 220. ASC 888 for Aethelswith.

23. ASC 874, EHD No. 95, ASCh. S 216, Yorke, *Kings and Kingdoms*, p. 123, BDDAB, p. 78 for Ceolwulf II.

24. Keynes, 'Alfred and the Mercians', pp. 14–19.

25. ASC 874.

26. ASC 875, M. Biddle and B. Kjolbye-Biddle, 'Repton and the Vikings' in *Antiquity*, 66, 1992, pp. 36–51, ASC 865, 871.

27. ASC 876, 877.

28. ASC 877.

29. Sawyer, *Age of Vikings*, chapter 6, A.P. Smyth, 'The Effect of Scandinavian Raiders on the English and Irish Churches: A Preliminary Reassessment' in B. Smith (ed.), *Britain and Ireland 900–1300* (Cambridge, 1999), pp. 1–38, J. Haywood, *The Penguin Historical Atlas of the Vikings* (Harmondsworth, 1995), pp. 48–50 and N. Brooks, 'England in the Ninth Century: The Crucible of Defeat' in

TRHS, 5th Series, 29, 1979, pp. 1–20.

30. Biddle and Kjolbye-Biddle, 'Repton and the Vikings', pp. 36–51.

31. P. Griffith, *The Viking Art of War* (London, 1995), ASC 865, 892 and 867.

32. E. Moltke, *Runes and their Origins: Denmark and Elsewhere* (Copenhagen, 1985), pp. 197 and 294, ASB 860.

33. ASC 892, 871, 875, 876 and 896.

34. R. Abels, *Lordship and Military Obligation in Anglo-Saxon England* (London, 1988) and C.W. Hollister, *Anglo-Saxon Military Institutions on the Eve of The Norman Conquest* (Oxford, 1962) for the background.

35. ASC 868, 867 and 871.

Chapter 4

1. A.P. Smyth, *King Alfred the Great* (Oxford, 1996), R. Abels, *Alfred the Great* (London, 1999), D. Sturdy, *Alfred the Great* (London, 1995) and J. Peddie, *Alfred: Warrior King* (Stroud, 1999) are prominent among recent publications.

2. BDDAB, p. 27, BEASE, p. 14, Keynes, 'Alfred and the Mercians', pp. 19–34 for Aethelred. Keynes offers a rather different interpretation of the evidence for relations between Alfred and Aethelred. ASCh. S 1702, Keynes, *Atlas*, Table XVII.

3. See chapter 2 above, EHD No. 81, ASCh. S 1187 and 218.

4. ASC 877, CA 877.

5. ASC 865, 866, 868, 872, 873, EHD No. 94, ASCh. S 1278.

6. AU 877, EHD No. 25.

7. ASC 866, 869, 871, 872, CA 877.

8. ASC 878.

9. Keynes and Lapidge, *Alfred the Great*, pp. 84–5.

10. ASC 879, 880,

11. AC 878, AU 878.

12. AC 881. BL Ms. Cotton Tiberius A. xiii, fol. 14v for the Mercian king list.

13. ASCh. S 218.

14. ASCh. S 219.

15. ASC 886.

16. Keynes, 'Alfred and the Mercians', pp. 27–30, Keynes, *Atlas*, Tables XVII and XXI.

17. Keynes, 'Alfred and the Mercians', pp. 29–30.

18. Keynes and Lapidge, *Alfred the Great*, p. 96, AC 894, MR 915.

19. BDDAB, pp. 21–2, Keynes and Lapidge, *Alfred the Great*, p. 90.

20. Keynes and Lapidge, *Alfred the Great*, pp. 171–2 or EHD No. 34 for the text of this treaty. R.H.C. Davis, 'Alfred and Guthrum's Frontier' in Davis, *From Alfred the Great to Stephen* (London, 1991), pp. 47–55, D. Dumville, 'The Treaty of Alfred and Guthrum' in Dumville, *Wessex and England: From Alfred to Edgar* (Woodbridge, 1992), pp. 1–23 for commentary.

21. D. Hill and A.R. Rumble (eds), *The Defence of Wessex: The Burghal Hidage and Anglo-Saxon Fortifications* (Manchester, 1996) for the West Saxon burhs and pp. 226–7 for the burh at Worcester.

22. EHD No. 99 or ASCh. S 223, ASCh. S 1280.

23. ASC 890, 885, 892.

24. ASC 893. CA 893.

25. T.M. Owen, 'The Battle of Buttington: with a Brief Sketch of the Affairs of Powys and Mercia' in *Montgomeryshire Collections*, 7, p. 260.

26. AU 893, ASC 893.

27. CA 894.

28. ASC 894, 895.

29. J. Nelson, *Charles the Bald* (London, 1992), p. 263 and Haywood, *Atlas of the Vikings*, p. 60 for the Frankish bridge.

30. ASC 895, 896, AC 895.

31. ASC 900, Smyth, *Alfred*, pp. 435–7.

32. ASC 902, ASC 900. BEASE, pp. 505, 509 and E.B. Fryde, D.E. Greenway, S. Porter and I. Roy (eds), *The Handbook of British Chronology* (London, 3rd edn, 1986), p. 7 for Aethelwold as ruler of Northumbria and East Anglia.

33. Keynes, *Atlas*, Table XVII for Beornnoth.

34. AU 902, AC 902, . J. Radner (ed.), *Fragmentary Annals of Ireland* (Dublin, 1978), p. 169, F.T. Wainwright, 'Ingimund's Invasion' in Wainwright, *Scandinavian England* (Chichester, 1975), pp. 131–61, BDDAB, p. 160.

35. ASC 903, ASC 901 for Aethelwulf and ASC 897 for Aethelhelm.

36. ASC 903, MR 902, C.R. Hart, 'The Battles of Holme, Brunnanburh and Ringmere' in Hart, *The Danelaw* (London, 1992), pp. 511–15, F.T. Wainwright, 'The Chronology of the Mercian Register' in *EHR*, LX, 1945, pp. 385–92 for the date of this battle.

37. ASC 906.

38. MR 907. Wainwright, 'Ingimund's Invasion', pp. 131–61.

39. ASCh. S 396.

40. ASC 909, MR 909, C. Stancliffe and E. Cambridge (eds), *Oswald: Northumbrian King to European Saint* (Stamford, 1999), pp. 119–22.

41. ASC 910, MR 910.

42. MR 910, Radner, *Fragmentary Annals*, p. 169.

43. ASC 911, MR 911, CA 911, M. Hare, *The Two Anglo-Saxon Minsters of Gloucester* (Deerhurst, 1993).

Chapter 5

1. F.T. Wainwright, 'Aethelflaed, Lady of the Mercians' in Wainwright, *Scandinavian England*, pp. 305–24 and D. Stansbury, *The Lady who Fought the Vikings* (South Brent, 1993), BDDAB, pp. 21–2 and BEASE, p. 14 for LadyAethelflaed. (It is surprising that the last of these has no separate entry for Aethelflaed given her unique position in the Anglo-Saxon period. The fact that its account of her was

written by a man perhaps speaks volumes.) The ASC 672 does record a one-year rule for Seaxburh, wife of Cenwealh of Wessex, after her husband's death but Bede refutes this, recording the succession of four sub-kings instead (Bede, p. 225). Since Bede is the more contemporary source we should regard Seaxburh's 'rule' as at best unproven.

2. Keynes and Lapidge, *Alfred the Great*, p. 77.

3. Keynes, *Atlas*, Tables XVII, XXI and XXXV, ASCh. S 221, 223, 367, 367a, 371, MR 910, Radner, *Fragmentary Annals*, p. 169.

4. J. Crick, 'Men, Women and Widows: Widowhood in Pre-conquest England' in S. Cavallo and L. Warner (eds), *Widowhood in Medieval and Early Modern Europe* (London, 1999).

5. ASC 911, ASCh. S 367, 367a and 371.

6. MR 912.

7. ASC 912.

8. ASC 913.

9. MR 913.

10. MR 914.

11. A.P. Smyth, *Scandinavian York and Dublin* (Dublin, 1987), Vol. I, chapter 6 for the contemporary situation in York.

12. ASC 914.

13. MR 914.

14. ASC 914.

15. MR 915.

16. MR 915, R. Coates, 'Aethelflaed's Fortification of Weardburh' in *Notes and Queries*, 243, 1988, pp. 8–12.

17. ASCh. S 225.

18. MR 915.

19. ASC 915.

20. ASC 918.

21. MR 916.

22. ASCh. S 425.

23. ASC 916.

24. ASC 917.

25. MR 917.

26. ASC 917.

27. MR 918.

28. Smyth, *York and Dublin*, chapter 6 for the background, MR 918.

29. MR 918, ASC 918, AC 918, AU 918, ASCh. S 223.

30. ASCh. S 1280, 225, 367.

31. ASC 918, MR 918.

32. Keynes and Lapidge, *Alfred the Great*, p. 105.

33. C. Fell, *Women in Anglo-Saxon England* (London, 1984), Chap. 5, P. Stafford, *Queens, Concubines and Dowagers* (London, 1983), P. Stafford, *Queen Emma and Queen Edith* (Oxford, 1997), Part II but especially pp. 93–4, P. Stafford, 'The Portrayal of Royal Women in England: Mid-Tenth to Mid-Twelfth Centuries' in J.C. Parsons (ed.), *Medieval Queenship* (Stroud, 1994), pp. 143–67, BEASE, pp. 383–4.

34. Keynes, *Atlas*, Tables X and XVII, Blunt, 'Coinage of King Offa', pp. 36–62.

35. *Alcuin*, No. 46.

36. There is currently no published edition of the Mercian Register. The best summary on it can be found in P.E. Szarmach, 'Aethelflaed of Mercia: *Mise en page*' in P.S. Baker and N. Howe (eds), *Words and Works* (Toronto, 1998), pp. 105–26. See also Wainwright, 'The Chronology of the Mercian Register', pp. 385–92, ASC p. xiv, JW, p. 358 n. 1 and HH, pp. 304–9.

37. BDDAB, p. 22, C.R. Hart, 'Athelstan Half-King and his Family', in The Danelaw, pp. 569–604, R. Fleming, *Kings and Lords in Conquest England* (Cambridge, 1991), Figure 2.1 and index, D. Whitelock (ed.), *Anglo-Saxon Wills* (Cambridge, 1930), No. 3 for Aethelflaed's namesakes. E. Van Houts, *Memory and Gender in Medieval Europe* (London, 1999), pp. 100–4 for the role of women in preserving history.

38. MR 910–918.

39. JW 919, *William of Malmesbury, The Kings Before the Norman Conquest* (WM-GR), tr. J. Stephenson (Lampeter, 1989), p. 109, HH, p. 309.

Chapter 6

1. Stafford, *Unification*, Part I, chapters 2 and 3, Stenton, *Anglo-Saxon England*, chapter X and E. John, 'The Age of Edgar' in *The Anglo-Saxons* for this period.
2. ASC 918, MR 918.
3. WM-GR, p. 116, MR 924.
4. ASCh. S 226. BDDAB, pp. 127–8 and BEASE, pp. 162–3 for Edward.
5. ASC 918, 920.
6. ASC 919.
7. ASC 920.
8. MR 921.
9. ASC 924, MR 924, B. Yorke, 'Aethelwold and the Politics of the Tenth Century' in B. Yorke (ed.), *Bishop Aethelwold* (Woodbridge, 1988), pp. 69–73.
10. ASC 924, MR 924, M. Wood, *In Search of the Dark Ages* (London, 1981), chapter 6, M. Wood, 'The Making of Aethelstan's Empire: an English Charlemagne?' in P. Wormald (ed.) with D. Bullough and R. Collins, *Ideal and Reality in Frankish and Anglo-Saxon Society* (Oxford, 1983), BDDAB, pp. 50–1 and BEASE, pp. 16–17 for Athelstan.
11. ASC 933 for *Atheling* Edwin.
12. ASC 937, Keynes, *Atlas*, Tables XXXVI to XXXIX and Hill, *Atlas*, Maps 146, 147, 154 and 155.
13. ASC 926.
14. Smyth, *York and Dublin*, Vol. II, chapters 1 and 2 for the background.
15. ASC 927, SD 927.
16. Hart, 'Athelstan "Half-King"' in *The Danelaw*, pp. 569–604, BDDAB, p. 51, Keynes, *Atlas*, Table XXXVIII.
17. ASC 927.
18. BDDAB, p. 51, R. McKitterick, *The Frankish Kingdoms under the Carolingians* (London, 1983), pp. 313–14, EHD No. 24, T. Reuter, *Germany in the Early Middle Ages* (London, 1991), p. 145 for these links.
19. ASC 933, EHD No. 26, ASCh. S 420.
20. ASC 934, ASCh. S 425, 407, 426, 427, 1792, SD 934.
21. EHD Nos 25 and 24, N. Price, 'The Vikings in Brittany' in *The Saga-Book of The Viking Society*, XXII, 1989, pp. 42–51.
22. EHD No. 24, McKitterick, *Frankish Kingdoms*, pp. 313–19.
23. ASC 885, Keynes and Lapidge, *Alfred the Great*, p. 87.
24. WM-GR, p. 118, *Snorri Sturlusson: Heimskringla*, tr. S. Laing (London, rev. edn, 1961), pp. 84–111, G. Jones, *A History of the Vikings* (Oxford, rev. edn, 1984), pp. 94–5.
25. Smyth, *York and Dublin*, Vol. II, chapters 3 and 4, I. Williams (ed.), *Armes Prydain* (Dublin, 1972).
26. JW 937.
27. ASC 937, AC 937, AU 937.
28. EHD No. 24, McKitterick, *Frankish Kingdoms*, p. 313.
29. ASC 939, AU 939. BDDAB, p. 126 for Edmund.
30. ASC 943, SD 940, RW 940.
31. ASC 943, SD 941, RW 940 and 941.
32. Keynes, *Atlas*, Tables XXXVIII, XLV and L for Orm.
33. SD 941, RW 941.
34. ASC 943, SD 942, RW 942, Keynes, *Atlas*, Table XLV.
35. ASC 943, SD 943, RW 943.
36. ASC 944, CA 944, Keynes, *Atlas*, Tables XLII and XLV, BDDAB, p. 117, A. Williams, '*Princeps Merciorum Gentis*: the Family, Career and Connections of Aelfhere, *Ealdorman* of Mercia 956–983' in *ASE*, 10, 1982, pp. 143–72, RW 946.
37. ASC 945, RW 945.
38. ASC 946. BDDAB, p. 113.
39. ASC 947.

40. ASC 948.

41. ASC 949, BDDAB, pp. 131–2 for Eric Bloodaxe.

42. ASC 952.

43. AU 952, Smyth, *York and Dublin*, Vol. II, chapter 8 for a different interpretation.

44. ASC 954, RW 950. Keynes, *Atlas*, Table XLV for Oswulf.

45. ASC 956. BDDAB, p. 191 for Olaf.

46. BDDAB, p. 193 for Oscetel.

47. ASC 955, 957, Stafford, *Unification*, pp. 47–50, Yorke, 'Aethelwold and Politics', pp. 74–9, Keynes, *Atlas*, Table LII for a graphic illustration of this division.

48. ASC 959.

49. ASC 975, Stafford, *Unification*, pp. 57–9, Yorke, 'Aethelwold and Politics', pp. 81–5, S. Keynes, *The Diplomas of King Aethelred 'the Unready' 978–1016* (Cambridge, 1990), pp. 163–74.

Chapter 7

1. Williams, *Kingship and Government*, chapters 4, 5, 6 and 7, H.R. Loyn, *The Governance of Anglo-Saxon England* (London, 1984), H.R. Loyn, *Anglo-Saxon England and the Norman Conquest* (London, 2nd edn, 1991) for the wider background to contemporary society. Keynes, 'Alfred and the Mercians', p. 5 n. 17 for a rather different view of Mercian society.

2. Keynes and Lapidge, *Alfred the Great*, p. 132.

3. A. Vince, *Saxon London* (London, 1990), chapters 2 and 3, Hobley, 'Lundenwic and Lundenburh', pp. 62–89, R. Hodges, *Towns and Trade in the Age of Charlemagne* (London, 2000), pp. 112–17.

4. *Excavations at* Hamwic, Vol. I, ed. A. Morton (London, 1992) and Vol. II, ed. P. Andrews (York, 1997).

5. ASC 886, 893.

6. Vince, *Saxon London*, pp. 21–2, Hodges, *Towns and Trade*, pp. 112–17, and T. Dyson, 'King Alfred and the Restoration of London' in *London Journal*, 15, 1990, pp. 99–110.

7. Loyn, *Anglo-Saxon England*, chapters 2 and 3.

8. ASCh. S 102 and 223.

9. EHD No. 197.

10. ASCh. S 1624, EHD No. 218.

11. ASCh. S 86-88, 91, 98, 143, and S88. EHD No. 80 or ASCh. S 1433.

12. Blunt, 'Coinage of King Offa', pp. 36–62 and chapter 1 above.

13. Williams, *Kingship and Government*, chapters 4 and 5, Loyn, *Governance*, chapters 1 and 4.

14. Keynes, 'England 700–900' in McKitterick, *New Cambridge Medieval History*, Vol. II, p. 27 and Keynes, 'Alfred and the Mercians', p. 5 n. 17 for this view and Loyn, *Governance*, p. 35 for the Tribal Hidage.

15. W. Levison, *England and the Continent in the Eighth Century* (Oxford, 1946).

16. Loyn, *Governance*, pp. 33–4, BEASE, pp. 456–7, ASCh. S 134.

17. See chapters 1, 4 and 5 above.

18. Loyn, *Governance*, pp. 100–6, Williams, *Kingship and Government*, p. 50 and Cubitt, *Church Councils*, chapter 8.

19. Keynes and Lapidge, *Alfred the Great*, p. 164.

20. P. Wormald, 'In Search of King Offa's "Law-code"' in I. Wood and N. Lund (eds), *Peoples and Places in North Western Europe 500–1600* (Woodbridge, 1991), pp. 25–45.

21. Loyn, *Governance*, p. 35 and C. Hart, 'The Kingdom of Mercia' in Dornier, *Mercian Studies*, pp. 43-61 for the Tribal Hidage and chapter 1 above.

22. Chapter 4 above.

23. ASCh. S 217-225, Keynes, 'Alfred and the Mercians', pp. 29-31.

24. ASCh. S 222, AC 918, AU 918, CA 893.

25. ASCh. S 291, 220 and 225.

26. Keynes and Lapidge, *Alfred the Great*, p. 177.

27. ASCh. S 114, 133, 139, 148 and 163.

28. Loyn, *Governance*, pp. 47–50, Williams, *Kingship and Government*, pp. 52–6, Keynes, 'Alfred and the Mercians, p. 5 n. 17 for a different view of Mercian *ealdormen*.

29. Keynes, *Atlas*, Tables X and XVII, ASCh. S 133.

30. ASC 802, 827, AC 866, ASCh. S 1437 and 1442.

31. H.P.R. Finberg, *Early Charters of the West Midlands* (Leicester, 2nd edn, 1972), p. 86.

32. ASC 802, Keynes and Lapidge, *Alfred the Great*, p. 77, ASCh. S 147, AC 866, CA 871.

33. Loyn, *Governance*, pp. 133–40, BEASE, pp. 420–1, ASCh. S 223 and 1280, ASC 914.

34. Hart, 'Athelstan "Half-King"', pp. 569–604, Fleming, *Kings and Lords*, Figure 2.1, A. Williams, *'Princeps Merciorum Gentis'*, pp. 143–72.

35. ASCh. S 1187 and 190, Keynes, *Atlas*, Tables XVII, XXXVIII, XLII, XLV, L and LVI.

36. ASCh. S 367, 367a and 371, Keynes, *Atlas*, Tables XVII, XXXI and XXXV.

37. ASC 871 and 910.

38. Loyn, *Governance*, pp. 47–50, Keynes, 'Alfred and the Mercians', p. 5 n. 17 for a supposed lack of *thegns* in the charters.

39. ASCh. S 109, 218.

40. MR 915, EHD No. 204 and 205, Keynes, 'Liber Vitae' of Brescia' in Roberts *et al.*, *Alfred the Wise*, pp. 99–119.

41. ASC 903 and 910.

42. Loyn, *Governance*, pp. 50–3.

43. ASCh. S 1441, 1437, EHD No. 84 or ASCh. S 1433.

44. Lord Stewartby, 'Moneyers in the Written Records' and Paul Bibire, 'Moneyers Names in Ninth-Century Southumbrian Coins' in Blackburn and Dumville, *Kings, Currency and Alliances*, pp. 151–3 and 159–61.

45. EHD No. 140, 106.

46. Loyn, *Governance*, pp. 31–6, Williams, *Kingship and Government*, pp. 67–8, Abels, *Lordship and Military Obligation*, chapter 3.

47. EHD No. 73 or ASCh. S 106

48. Hill and Rumble, *The Defence of Wessex*, p. 34.

49. ASC 893 and 917.

50. MR 911 to 920, Hill and Rumble, *The Defence of Wessex*, pp. 226–7, ASCh. S 223, ASC 920, 914.

51. MR 909, ASC 902, MR 910.

Chapter 8

1. H. Mayr-Harting, *The Coming of Christianity to Anglo-Saxon England* (London, 3rd edn, 1991), Part I.

2. Brooks, *Canterbury*, chapters 4, 6, 7 and 9, Cubitt, *Church Councils*, chapter 8, Kirby, *Earliest English Kings*, chapter 8, Yorke, *Kings and Kingdoms*, chapter 6, and chapters 1 and 2 above for relations between the archbishops and Mercian rulers.

3. Brooks, *Canterbury*, chapter 6 (a) and (b), ASC 765, ASCh. S 107, ASC 776, ASCh. S 123 and chapter 1 above.

4. ASC 787, Cubitt, *Church Councils*, chapter 8, Brooks, *Canterbury*, chapter 6 (c) and (d).

5. ASC 796, 798, Brooks, *Canterbury*, chapter 6 (e) and chapter 2 above.

6. EHD No. 204, 205 and 210, Brooks, *Canterbury*, chapter 6 (f) and (g) and chapter 2 above.

7. ASC 805, Brooks, *Canterbury*, chapter 7 (b), Cubitt, *Church Councils*, chapter 7 and chapter 2 above.

8. ASC 832 and 833, Brooks, *Canterbury*, chapter 7 (c) and (d), ASCh. S 190 and 188.

9. ASCh. S 286.

10. Brooks, *Canterbury*, chapter 7 (e).

11. ASC 890, Brooks, *Canterbury*, chapter 7 (f) and chapter 4 above.

12. Cubitt, *Church Councils*, chapter 8 and

Part 1 for the general background to these councils or synods.

13. Hill, *Atlas*, No. 259 and Keynes, *Atlas*, Tables VIII, XIII and XIV for the bishops.

14. Keynes, *Atlas*, Tables IX, XV and XVI, EHD No. 204, MR 916, Cubitt, *Church Councils*, pp. 216–17, JW 915.

15. H.M. Taylor, *St Wystan's Church, Repton* (Derby, 1989), BEASE, pp. 390–2 and ASCh. S 167, BEASE, p. 480, ASCh. S 1187, 193 and 197, B.C.J. Williams, *The Story of St Mary and St Hardulph's Church* (Nottingham, 1996), BEASE, pp. 73–4.

16. J. Blair (ed.), *Pastoral Care Before the Parish* (Leicester, 1992), Wormald, *Anglo-Saxon Deerhurst*, ASCh. S 1187.

17. Keynes and Lapidge, *Alfred the Great*, p. 93, ASCh. S 1279 and 1441.

18. Taylor, *Repton*, BEASE, pp. 390–2, A. Porter, *The Priory Church of St Mary at Deerhurst* (Much Wenlock, 1996), BEASE, pp. 138–9, Williams, *St Mary and St Hardulph*, BEASE, pp. 73–4.

19. Cubitt, *Church Councils*, pp. 224–6 and 227.

20. ASCh. S 1258 and 1187, Brooks, *Canterbury*, chapter 9 (b).

21. ASCh. S 98, 346 and 1628.

22. C. Keary, *English Coins in the British Museum: Anglo-Saxon*, Vol. I (London, 1887).

23. Keynes and Lapidge, *Alfred the Great*, p. 125.

24. Anglo-Saxons, p. 159, Webster and Backhouse, *Making of England*, p. 261, ASCh. S 327, 331, 344 and 1276, Keynes and Lapidge, *Alfred the Great*, pp. 92–3.

25. T. Reuter (ed.), *The Greatest Englishman* (Exeter, 1980), C.H. Talbot (ed.), *The Anglo-Saxon Missionaries in Germany* (London, 1954), No. 48.

26. BEASE, pp. 314–15, Brooks, *Canterbury*, chapter 6 (b), Keynes and Lapidge, *Alfred the Great*, pp 92–3.

27. ASCh. S 367, 367a and 371. See also ASCh. S 222 and 225 for other lost landbooks and note 31 below for the prayerbooks.

28. Taylor, *Repton*, Wormald, *Anglo-Saxon Deerhurst*, Williams, *St Mary and St Hardulph*, M.R. Handley, *St Mary the Virgin, Wirksworth* (undated), A. Dornier, 'The Anglo-Saxon Monastery at Breedon-on-the-Hill, Leicestershire' in Dornier, *Mercian Studies*, pp. 155–68, BEASE, pp. 390–2, 138–9 and 73–4.

29. Webster and Backhouse, *Making of England*, pp. 239–47, ASCh. S 196, EHD No. 98, Handley, *St Mary, Wirksworth*, R. Cramp, 'Schools of Mercian Sculpture' in Dornier, *Mercian Studies*, pp. 191–233.

30. Webster and Backhouse, *Making of England*, pp. 127–8 and 195–220, Brown, *Manuscripts*.

31. Webster and Backhouse, *Making of England*, pp. 209–11 and Brown, *Manuscripts*, pp. 40–1, H. Wheeler, 'Aspects of Mercian Art: the Book of Cerne' in Dornier, *Mercian Studies*, pp. 235–44.

32. Webater and Backhouse, *Making of England*, pp. 261–2 and ASCh. S 1281.

33. Thacker, 'Kings, Saints and Monasteries', pp. 1–25, Love, *Three Saints Lives*, pp. 50–89, Ridyard, *Royal Saints*, pp. 243–4.

34. Webster and Backhouse, *Making of England*, pp. 199–201 and 127, ASC 914, ASCh. S 222, 367, 367a and 371.

35. ASC 874, Biddle and Kjolbye-Biddle, 'Repton and the Vikings' pp. 36–51, Keynes, *Atlas*, Table XIV, Hill, *Atlas*, No. 259.

36. ASCh. S 1278, 215 and 223.

37. Hare, *Two Minsters*, A.T. Thacker, 'Chester and Gloucester: early Ecclesiastical Organisation in Two Mercian Burghs' in *Northern History*, 18, 1982, pp. 199–211, MR 909, ASCh. S 221, N. Higham, *The Origins of Cheshire* (Manchester, 1993), p. 130, J. Blair, *Anglo-Saxon Oxfordshire*

(Stroud, 1994), pp. 111–13, ASC 944, BDDAB, p. 241.

38. Brooks, *Canterbury*, chapter 7 (f), BDDAB, p. 204, M. Godden, 'Waerferth and King Alfred: the Fate of the Old English *Dialogues*' in Roberts *et al.*, *Alfred the Wise*, pp. 35–51, Keynes and Lapidge, *Alfred the Great*, pp. 124–7, Wormald, 'King Offa's "Law-code"' in Wood and Lund, *Peoples and Places*, pp. 25–45.

39. Smyth, *Scandinavian York*, Part II, chapter 3, ASC 955, MR 909

40. ASC 878, 893, MR 918.

41. H.R. Loyn, *The English Church 940–1154* (London, 2000) for the monastic reform.

42. BDDAB, p. 235 and BEASE, p. 469.

43. ASCh. S 1282 and 1283, Keynes and Lapidge, *Alfred the Great*, pp. 92–3 and 126, Godden, 'Waerferth and Alfred?' in Roberts *et al.*, *Alfred the Wise*, pp. 35–51.

44. The Anglo-Saxons, p. 158, Keynes and Lapidge, *Alfred the Great*, p. 177, Keynes, *Atlas*, Table XIV, ASCh. S 223.

45. ASCh. S 215, 223.

46. ASCh. S 1278, 1441, 1446, 346 and 1628.

47. ASCh. S 1278–1283, Keynes and Lapidge, *Alfred the Great*, p. 93, ASCh. S 1279.

48. Keynes, *Atlas*, Table XIV.

49. ASCh. S 215, Keynes and Lapidge, *Alfred the Great*, p. 177, ASCh. S 1446 and 1280.

Conclusion

1. Keynes, 'Alfred and the Mercians', p. 41.

Bibliography

PRIMARY SOURCES

Alcuin of York, ed. S. Allott, York, 1974

Alfred the Great, ed. S. Keynes and M. Lapidge, Harmondsworth, 1983

Anglo-Saxon Charters (ASCh.), ed. P.H. Sawyer, London, 1968

The Anglo-Saxon Chronicle, ed. G.N. Garmonsway, London, 1953

The Anglo-Saxon Chronicle, ed. M. Swanton, London, 1996

The Anglo-Saxon Chronicle (ASC), ed. D. Whitelock with D.C. Douglas S.I. and Tucker, London, rev. edn, 1961

Anglo-Saxon Prose, ed. M. Swanton, London, 1993

Anglo-Saxon Wills, ed. D. Whitelock, Cambridge, 1930

The Annals of St Bertin (ASB), ed. J.L. Nelson, Manchester, 1991

The Annals of Ulster to AD 1134 (AU), ed. S. MacAirt, Dublin, 1955–77

Armes Prydain, ed. I. Williams, Dublin, 1972

Bede: A History of the English Church and People, tr. L. Sherley-Price, Harmondsworth, 1955

Brut Y Tywysogion: Peniarth Ms. 20 (BYT), ed. T. Jones, Cardiff, 1952

Carolingian Chronicles, tr. B. Scholz, Ann Arbor, 1970

Charlemagne: Translated Sources, tr. P.D. King, Kendal, 1987

Chronicle of Aethelweard (CA), ed. A. Campbell, Edinburgh, 1962

The Chronicle of John of Worcester (JW), Vol. II, ed. R.R. Darlington and P.J. McGurk, Oxford, 1995

English Historical Documents Volume I c. 500–1042 (EHD), ed. D. Whitelock, London, 2nd edn, 1979

Fragmentary Annals of Ireland, ed. J. Radner, Dublin, 1978

Henry, Archdeacon of Huntingdon, Historia Anglorum – The History of the English People (HH), ed. D. Greenway, Oxford, 1996

The Life of Bishop Wilfred by Eddius Stephanus, ed. B. Colgrave, Cambridge, 1927

Nennius: British History and The Welsh Annals, ed. J. Morris, Chichester, 1980

The Reign of Charlemagne, ed. M.R. Loyn and J. Percival, London, 1975

Roger of Wendover: Flowers of History (RW), tr. J.A. Giles, repr., Lampeter, 1993

Simeon of Durham: A History of the Kings of England (SD), tr. J. Stephenson, repr., Lampeter, 1987

Snorri Sturlusson: Heimskringla, tr. S. Laing, London, rev. edn, 1961

Three Eleventh-Century Anglo-Latin Saints Lives, ed. R.C. Love, Oxford, 1996

Two Lives of Charlemagne: Einhard and Notker the Stammerer, tr. L. Thorpe, Harmondsworth, 1969

William of Malmesbury, The Kings Before the Norman Conquest (WM-GR) tr. J. Stephenson, Lampeter, 1989

Secondary Sources

Printed Books

Abels, R. *Alfred the Great*, London, 1999

——. *Lordship and Military Obligation in Anglo-Saxon England*, London, 1988

Bassett, S. (ed.). *The Origins of the Anglo-Saxon Kingdoms*, Leicester, 1989

Blackburn, M.A.S. (ed.). *Anglo-Saxon Monetary History*, Leicester, 1986

—— and Dumville, D.N. (eds). *Kings, Currency and Alliances*, Oxford, 1998

Blair, J. *Anglo-Saxon Oxfordshire*, Stroud, 1994

—— (ed.). *Pastoral Care Before the Parish*, Leicester, 1992

Brooks, N. *The Early History of the Church at Canterbury*, Leicester, 1984

Brown, M.P. *Anglo-Saxon Manuscripts*, London, 1991

Campbell, J. (ed.). *The Anglo-Saxons*, Harmondsworth, 1982

Cavallo, S., and Warner, L. (eds). *Widowhood in Medieval and Early Modern Europe*, London, 1999

Collins, R. *Charlemagne*, London, 1998

Cooper J. (ed.). *The Battle of Maldon*, London 1993

Cubitt, C. *Anglo-Saxon Church Councils*, Leicester, 1995

Davis, R.H.C. *From Alfred the Great to Stephen*, London, 1991

Dolley, R.H.M. (ed.). *Anglo-Saxon Coins*, London, 1961

Dornier, A. (ed.). *Mercian Studies*, Leicester, 1977

Dumville, D. *Wessex and England: From Alfred to Edgar*, Woodbridge, 1992

Dutton, L. *The Anglo-Saxon Kingdoms*, Lampeter, 1993

Evans, A.C. *The Sutton Hoo Ship Burial*, London, 1986

Excavations at Hamwic, Vol. I, ed. A. Morton, London, 1992 and Vol. II, ed. P. Andrews, York, 1997

Fell, C. *Women in Anglo-Saxon England*, London, 1984

Finberg, H.P.R. *Early Charters of the West Midlands*, Leicester, 2nd edn, 1972

Fleming, R. *Kings and Lords in Conquest England*, Cambridge, 1991

Fox, C. *Offa's Dyke*, London, 1955

Fryde, E.B., Greenway, D.E., Porter, S., and Roy, I. (eds). *The Handbook of British Chronology*, London, 3rd edn, 1986

Gelling, M. *The West Midlands in the Early Middle Ages*, Leicester, 1992

Griffith, P. *The Viking Art of War*, London, 1995

Haddan, A.W., and Stubbs, W. *Councils and Ecclesiastical Documents Relating to Great Britain and Ireland*, 3 vols, 1869–71

Handley, M.R. *St Mary the Virgin, Wirksworth*, undated

Hare, M. *The Two Anglo-Saxon Minsters of Gloucester*, Deerhurst, 1993

Hart, C.R. *The Danelaw*, London, 1992

Haywood, J. *Dark Age Naval Power*, London, 1991

——. *The Penguin Historical Atlas of the Vikings*, Harmondsworth, 1995

Heighway, C. *Anglo-Saxon Gloucestershire*, Stroud, 1987

Higham, N. *The Origins of Cheshire*, Manchester, 1993

Hill, D. *An Atlas of Anglo-Saxon England*, Oxford, 1981

—— and Rumble, A.R. (eds). *The Defence of Wessex: The Burghal Hidage and Anglo-Saxon Fortifications*, Manchester, 1996

Hodges, R. *Towns and Trade in the Age of Charlemagne*, London, 2000

—— and Hobley, B. (eds). *The Rebirth of Towns in the West*, London, 1988

Hollister, C.W. *Anglo-Saxon Military Institutions on the Eve of The Norman Conquest*, Oxford, 1962

Hooke, D. *The Anglo-Saxon Landscape: The Kingdom of the Hwicce*, Manchester, 1985

John, E. *Re-assessing Anglo-Saxon England*, Manchester, 1996

Jones, G. *A History of the Vikings*, Oxford, rev. edn, 1984

Keary, C. *English Coins in the British Museum: Anglo-Saxon*, Vol. I, London, 1887

Keynes, S. *An Atlas of Attestations in Anglo-Saxon Charters*, Cambridge, 1998

——. *The Diplomas of King Aethelred 'the Unready' 978–1016*, Cambridge, 1990

Kirby, D.P. *The Earliest English Kings*, London, 1991

Lapidge, M., Blair, J., Keynes, S., and Scragg, D. (eds). *The Blackwell Encyclopedia of Anglo-Saxon England* (BEASE), Oxford, 1999

Levison, W. *England and the Continent in the Eighth Century*, Oxford, 1946

Loyn, H.R. *Anglo-Saxon England and the Norman Conquest*, London, 2nd edn, 1991

——. *The English Church 940–1154*, London, 2000

——. *The Governance of Anglo-Saxon England*, London, 1984

——. *The Vikings in Britain*, Oxford, 1994

Lund, N., and Fell, C.E. (eds). *Ohthere and Wulfstan: Two Voyagers at the Court of King Alfred*, York, 1984

Mason, E. *St Wulfstan of Worcester*, Oxford, 1990

Mayr-Harting, H. *The Coming of Christianity to Anglo-Saxon England*, London, 3rd edn, 1991

McKitterick, R. *The Frankish Kingdoms under the Carolingians*, London, 1983

Moltke, E. *Runes and their Origins: Denmark and Elsewhere*, Copenhagen, 1985

Nelson, J. *Charles the Bald*, London, 1992

The New Cambridge Medieval History, Vol. II, ed. R. McKitterick, Cambridge, 1995 and Vol. III, ed. T. Reuter, Cambridge, 1999

Noble, F. *Offa's Dyke Reviewed*, Oxford, 1983

Parsons J.C. (ed.). *Medieval Queenship*, Stroud, 1994

Peddie, J. *Alfred: Warrior King*, Stroud, 1999

Porter, A. *The Priory Church of St Mary at Deerhurst*, Much Wenlock, 1996

Rahtz, P., and Meeson, R. *An Anglo-Saxon Watermill at Tamworth*, London 1992

Reuter, T. *Germany in the Early Middle Ages*, London, 1991

—— (ed.). *The Greatest Englishman*, Exeter, 1980

Richter, M. (ed.). *Canterbury Professions*, Canterbury, 1973

Ridyard, S.J. *The Royal Saints of Anglo-Saxon England*, Cambridge, 1988

Roberts, J., Nelson, J.L., and Godden, M.R. (eds). *Alfred the Wise*, Woodbridge, 1997

Sawyer, P.H. *The Age of the Vikings*, London, 2nd edn, 1971

——. *Anglo-Saxon Lincolnshire*, London, 1998

—— (ed.). *The Oxford Illustrated Encyclopaedia of the Vikings*, Oxford, 1997

Shoesmith, R. *Hereford City Excavations I and II*, London, 1980 and 1982

Smith, B. (ed.). *Britain and Ireland 900–1300*, Cambridge, 1999

Smyth, A.P. *King Alfred the Great*, Oxford, 1996

——. *Scandinavian Kings of the British Isles*, Oxford, 1988

——. *Scandinavian York and Dublin*, Dublin, 1987

Stafford, P. *The East Midlands in the Early Middle Ages*, Leicester, 1985

Stafford, P. *Queen Emma and Queen Edith*, Oxford, 1997

——. *Queens, Concubines and Dowagers*, London, 1983

——. *Unification and Conquest*, London, 1989

Stancliffe, C., and Cambridge, E. (eds). *Oswald: Northumbrian King to European Saint*, Stamford, 1999

Stansbury, D. *The Lady who Fought the Vikings*, South Brent, 1993

Stenton, F.M. *Anglo-Saxon England*, Oxford, 2nd edn, 1971

Sturdy, D. *Alfred the Great*, London, 1995

Talbot, C.H. (ed.). *The Anglo-Saxon Missionaries in Germany*, London, 1954

Taylor, H.M. *St Wystan's Church, Repton*, Derby, 1989

—— and Taylor, J. *Anglo-Saxon Architecture*, 3 vols, Cambridge, 1965–78

Van Houts, E. *Memory and Gender in Medieval Europe*, London, 1999

Vince, A. *Saxon London*, London, 1990

Wainwright, F.T. (ed.). *Scandinavian England*, Chichester, 1975

Webster, L., and Backhouse, J. (eds). *The Making of England*, London, 1991

Williams, A. *Kingship and Government in Pre-Conquest England*, London, 1999

——, Smyth, A.P., and Kirby, D.P. (eds). *A Biographical Dictionary of Dark-Age Britain* (BDDAB), London, 1991

Williams, B.C.J. *The Story of St Mary and St Hardulph's Church*, Nottingham, 1996

Wood, I., and Lund, N. (eds), *Peoples and Places in North Western Europe 500–1600*, Woodbridge, 1991

Wood, M. *In Search of the Dark Ages*, London, 1981

Wormald, P. *How Do We Know So Much About Anglo-Saxon Deerhurst?*, Deerhurst, 1993

—— (ed.) with Bullough, D., and Collins, R. *Ideal and Reality in Frankish and Anglo-Saxon Society*, Oxford, 1983

Yorke, B. *Bishop Aethelwold*, Woodbridge, 1988

——. *Kings and Kingdoms of Early Anglo-Saxon England*, London, 1990

Articles

Bibire, Paul. 'Moneyers' Names in Ninth-Century Southumbrian Coins' in Blackburn and Dumville (eds), *Kings, Currency and Alliances*, pp. 159–61

Biddle, M., and Kjolbye-Biddle, B. 'Repton and the Vikings' in *Antiquity*, 66, 1992, pp. 36–51

Blunt, C.E. 'The Coinage of King Offa' in Dolley (ed.), *Anglo-Saxon Coins*, pp. 36–62

Booth, J. 'Monetary Alliance or Technical Co-operation?: The Coinage of King Berhtwulf of Mercia (840–852)' in Blackburn and Dumville, *Kings, Currency and Alliances*, pp. 63–103

Brooks, N. 'England in the Ninth Century: The Crucible of Defeat' in *TRHS*, 5th Series, 29, 1979, pp. 1–20

——. 'The Formation of the Mercian Kingdom' in Bassett (ed.), *The Origins of the Anglo-Saxon Kingdoms*, pp. 159–70

Coates, R. 'Aethelflaed's Fortification of Weardburh' in *Notes and Queries*, 243, 1988, pp. 8–12

Cramp, R. 'Schools of Mercian Sculpture' in Dornier (ed.), *Mercian Studies*, pp. 191–233

Crick, J. 'Men, Women and Widows: Widowhood in Pre-conquest England' in Cavallo and Warner (eds), *Widowhood in Medieval and Early Modern Europe*, pp. 24–36

Davies, W. 'Annals and the Origin of Mercia' in Dornier (ed.), *Mercian Studies*, pp. 17–29

Davis, R.H.C. 'Alfred and Guthrum's Frontier' in Davis, *From Alfred the Great to Stephen*, pp. 47–55

Dornier, A. 'The Anglo-Saxon Monastery at Breedon-on-the-Hill, Leicestershire' in Dornier, *Mercian Studies*, pp. 155–68

Dumville, D. 'The Treaty of Alfred and Guthrum' in Dumville, *Wessex and England: From Alfred to Edgar*, pp. 1–23

Dyson, T. 'King Alfred and the Restoration of London' in *London Journal*, 15, 1990, pp. 99–10

Godden, M. 'Waerferth and King Alfred: the Fate of the Old English *Dialogues*' in Roberts *et al.*, *Alfred the Wise*, pp. 35–51

Hart, C.R. 'Athelstan Half-King and his Family', in Hart, The Danelaw, pp. 569–604

——. 'The Battles of Holme, Brunnanburh and Ringmere', in Hart, The Danelaw, pp. 511-15

——. 'The Kingdom of Mercia' in Dornier, *Mercian Studies*, pp. 43–61

Hill, D. 'Offa's and Wat's Dykes: Some Aspects of Recent Work' in *TLCAS*, 79, 1977, pp. 21–33

Hobley, B. 'Lundenwic and Lundenburh: two cities rediscovered' in Hodges and Hobley (eds), *The Rebirth of Towns in the West*, pp. 69–82

John, E. 'The Age of Edgar' in Campbell (ed.), *The Anglo-Saxons*, pp. 160–89

Keynes, S. 'Anglo-Saxon Entries in the *Liber Vitae* of Brescia' in Roberts *et al.*, *Alfred the Wise*, pp. 99–119

——. 'England 700–900' in McKitterick (ed.), *The New Cambridge Medieval History*, Vol. II, pp. 18–42

——. 'England c. 900–1016' in Reuter (ed.), *The New Cambridge Medieval History*, Vol. III, pp. 456–84

——. 'King Alfred and the Mercians' in *Kings, Currency and Alliances*, pp. 1–45

——. 'The Vikings in England' in Sawyer (ed.), *The Oxford Illustrated Encyclopaedia of the Vikings*, pp. 1–47

Leyser, K. 'Early Medieval Warfare' in Cooper (ed.), *The Battle of Maldon*, pp. 87–108

Metcalf, D.M. 'Monetary Affairs in Mercia in the Time of Aethelbald' in Dornier, *Mercian Studies*, pp. 87–106

Nelson, J. 'A King Across the Sea' in *TRHS*, 5th Series, 36, 1986, pp. 45–68

Owen, T.M. 'The Battle of Buttington: with a Brief Sketch of the Affairs of Powys and Mercia' in *Montgomeryshire Collections*, 7, p. 260

Price, N. 'The Vikings in Brittany' in *The Saga-Book of The Viking Society*, 22, 1989, pp. 42–51

Sawyer, P.H. 'The Age of the Vikings and Before' in Sawyer, *The Oxford Illustrated Encyclopaedia of the Vikings*, pp. 48-82

Smyth, A.P. 'The Effect of Scandinavian Raiders on the English and Irish Churches: A Preliminary Reassessment' in Smith, *Britain and Ireland 900–1300*, pp. 1–38

Stafford, P. 'The Portrayal of Royal Women in England: Mid-Tenth to Mid-Twelfth Centuries' in Parsons, *Medieval Queenship*, pp. 143–67

Stewartby, Lord. 'Moneyers in the Written Records' in Blackburn and Dumville, Kings, Currency and Alliances, pp. 151–3

Szarmach, P. 'Aethelflaed of Mercia: *Mise en Page*' in Baker and Howe (eds), *Words and Works*, pp. 105–26

Thacker, A.T. 'Chester and Gloucester: Early Ecclesiastical Organisation in Two Mercian Burghs' in *Northern History*, 18, 1982, pp. 199–211

Thacker, A.T. 'Kings, Saints and Monasteries in Pre-Viking Mercia' in *Midland History*, 10, 1985, pp. 1–25

Wainwright, F.T. 'The Chronology of the Mercian Register' in *EHR*, LX, 1945, pp. 385–92

——. 'Ingimund's Invasion' in Wainwright, *Scandinavian England*, pp. 131–61

——. 'Aethelflaed, Lady of the Mercians' in Wainwright, *Scandinavian England*, pp. 305–24

Wheeler, H. 'Aspects of Mercian Art: the Book of Cerne' in Dornier, *Mercian Studies*, pp. 235–44

Williams, A. '*Princeps Merciorum Gentis*: the Family, Career and Connections of Aelfhere, *Ealdorman* of Mercia 956–983' in *ASE*, 10, 1982, pp. 143–72

Wood, M. 'The Making of Aethelstan's Empire: an English Charlemagne?' in Wormald *et al.*, *Ideal and Reality in Frankish and Anglo-Saxon Society*, pp. 250–72

Wormald, P. 'The Age of Bede and Aethelbald' in Campbell, *The Anglo-Saxons*, pp. 70–100

——. 'In Search of King Offa's "Law-code"' in Wood and Lund (eds), *Peoples and Places in North Western Europe 500–1600*, pp. 25–45

Yorke, B. 'Aethelwold and the Politics of the Tenth Century' in Yorke, *Bishop Aethelwold*, pp. 69–73

Index